SHIPS

SHIPS

THE HISTORY AND SPECIFICATIONS OF 300 WORLD-FAMOUS SHIPS

CHRIS BISHOP

Published by Silverdale Books
an imprint of Bookmart Ltd
Registered Number 2372865
Trading as Bookmart Ltd
Blaby Road
Wigston
Leicester LE18 4SE

ISBN 1-84509-303-8

Editorial and design by
Amber Books Ltd
Bradley's Close
74–77 White Lion Street
London N1 9PF
www.amberbooks.co.uk

Project Editor: Michael Spilling
Design: Jerry Williams

Printed in Singapore

PICTURE CREDITS
All artworks courtesy Art-Tech.
Photographs on pages 7 and 8 courtesy TRH Pictures; page 11
courtesy US Department of Defense.

Contents

Introduction

From the dawn of civilization, the sea has held a fascination for humankind. Over the centuries, men have sought to navigate the seas with a myriad of ships and sailing craft for an equally diverse range of purposes. Ships, even in the earliest days, could carry cargos farther and faster than any type of overland transport.

Long before the Iron Age, when Northern Europeans were building simple plank boats that were suitable for use on rivers and lakes, the pharaohs of Egypt were building sophisticated ships able to operate in the open waters of the Mediterranean. From this period two distinct types of ships evolved, with cargo vessels possessing hull forms designed for carrying capacity while warships developed as fast, manoeuvrable fighting platforms able to mount and use a range of weapons.

The vessels of the Bronze Age were limited in their abilities, but by about 700BC the Greeks, copying and improving upon Phoenician designs, had developed fast, rowed fighting ships with several banks of oars. This was typical of the type of fighting ship that fought at Salamis (480BC) and remained the standard type for a long time after the end of the Peloponnesian War (431–404BC). Manned by large crews, oarsmen were able to propel these agile vessels at high speed under favourable conditions. It would be centuries before sailing ships could reach such speeds over short distances. Naval battle tactics were developed in this period, notably by the Greek admiral Phormio in 400BC, whose skill enabled him to defeat superior forces.

Though Roman merchant ships had sailed the Mediterranean since the beginning of the third century BC, the Romans were traders by sea, not fighters. While the Roman Legions demonstrated the Roman mastery of warfare on land, the development of a fighting navy had been neglected.

Carthage, originally a colony of the Phoenicians, possessed a strong navy because of the necessity to seek its livelihood around the Mediterranean. When commercial rivalry finally caused a war between Rome and Carthage in 264BC, the Romans soon saw the need to develop their navy and modelled their warships upon those captured from Carthage. Although the Romans were originally defeated they soon perfected their tactics, developing the boarding bridge, which enabled their soldiers to storm onto the decks of the Carthaginian vessels.

For the best part of a millenium, there was little development in shipbuilding in the Mediterranean, where the lateen rig held sway. This had been copied from the Arabian Gulf and Indian Ocean, where it was used by Arab traders because it had good sailing qualities, especially in coastal waters. Such a rig, however, was not suitable for long ocean voyages where the fore and aft rig gave a better performance.

With the end of Roman seapower in the Mediterranean the development of shipbuilding underwent further changes, especially in northern waters. From the ninth to the eleventh centuries, the exploits of Viking raiders began to have an effect upon surrounding countries who had no navies of any importance but relied mostly upon their armies for defence.

Sail Takes Over

In northern Europe the warship underwent its own distinct development. By AD1300 high castles were added to the ends of the vessel to give bowmen a height advantage in battle. Over the next 300 years or so these castles grew in size; however, as the gun became the main weapon, housed in the hull for better stability, so the castles were reduced to a low poop and forecastle. As the fore and aft rig gained predominance so the galleys with their banks of oars fell from favour. The need to have the hull sides left clear for the many rowers meant that only the extreme ends could carry guns, making these lightly built vessels no match even for the lightly-armed frigates.

From the beginning of the fifteenth century warships and merchant vessels continued to develop along different lines. Ships would no longer need to carry a single mast but two- and

John Paul Jones' frigate **Bonhomme Richard** *(launched 1765) was typical of the fighting ships that dominated the last days of sail.*

later three-masted vessels were built that proved reliable on long voyages. The early practice of steering with a single large oar at the stern gave way to the rudder right aft on the centre line of the vessel, so giving more positive control on the steering. Other improvements in technology occurred, notably with the development of the compass and the hour glass and these, combined with the log that measured speed, made navigation by dead reckoning possible. Europeans were now able to explore and trade in far off places, which in turn led to colonization in North and South America, Africa and beyond.

By 1800 the sailing ship had reached the peak of its development. Over the preceeding few hundred years many countries developed their navies to a high degree, with England Spain, France and Holland leading the way. Indeed, one of the prime factors in the development of these countries' naval forces was the need to protect the merchant ships trading in far-flung colonies. By 1800 America was also in the forefront of technology, producing some of the world's finest frigates.

The new generation of ocean liners like the **Columbia**, *entering service in 1902, offered well-heeled travellers speed and luxury undreamed of in previous eras.*

The Steam Revolution

Vessels were still built of wood and carried ever greater spreads of sails, but by the end of the eighteenth century the first experiments were being made with steam propulsion, a method that would free ships from being reliant on the wind and eventually, once the steam engine reached a degree of perfection, enable ships to make faster passages along more direct routes. The Industrial revolution ushered in other changes, such as the use of iron, and later steel, in shipbuilding.

Laughed off by the conservative-minded, not least those in high naval office, the smoky, clanking ships were taken up first by the merchant marine, who wanted to shorten journey times. The new steam propulsion, and the new materials provided by the industrial revolution, especially iron plate in mass quantities, wrought more change in the 50 years between 1800 and 1850 than all the developments of the previous 500 years. Yet in the 1850s a full-rigged ship with the wind behind her could still overtake the average packet steamer.

By the mid-1800s the new technologies of the industrial revolution had begun to pick up speed. Marine engineering, based on the twin innovations of the steam engine and metal construction, prospered, and new developments in the field followed one upon another. More efficient machinery and stronger, lighter construction translated into faster ships. In spite of these dramatic developments, the sailing ship continued to play a major role in world commerce. In the 1860s the fast clipper ship appeared, intended for service in the tea, wool and grain trade. The general cargo sailing vessel still prospered amongst the burgeoning steamship fleets; even as late as 1900 well over one third of all merchant ships, 10m tons out of a worldwide fleet of 24m tons, were sailing ships. By 1932 there were still nearly 3000 merchant sailing ships in regular service.

Ironclads

Although early attempts to build iron hulled warships were not successful, the new technologies accelerated warship development. Until 1860, major warships were still built of wood; some of the steam-powered ships carried over 120 guns on three decks. In the late 1850s a major change took place with the laying down of Dupuy de Lome's splendid creation *Gloire* which, although it had a wooden hull, was completely covered in iron armour able to resist the guns of the period. In the 1860s, the broadside ironclad frigates replaced the wooden-hulled two- and three-decker line-of-battle ships, and were soon in turn replaced by turreted ships. As guns became more powerful so armour grew thicker which, because of weight limitations, was restricted to protecting the vitals. Capital ships now carried a mixed armament of larger, quick-firing guns: fewer in number, but by their rapid fire increasing the number of rounds fired per minute.

Machinery and boilers developed rapidly. As engines became more reliable and economical so sail power was dispensed with. Boiler power continued to increase, leading to the triple expansion engine with its good economy. Liquid fuel in the shape of oil began to be used in the 1890s and the turbine first appeared, marking a major step in engineering.

The locomotive torpedo was also adopted by all navies. During this period the submarine slowly evolved, and with the development of the battery by 1900, became a practical weapon. By the turn of the twentieth century the battleship had reached its peak, but by 1906 the all-big-gun *Dreadnought* was on the scene and, like the Warrior before her, immediately eclipsed existing capital ships, thus heralding another new era. HMS *Dreadnought* made all other warships obsolete overnight, and led to a naval construction race that contributed to the outbreak of World War I.

It was a time of innovation, a period that saw the debut of the battlecruiser, a hybrid warship that was to make its mark on the sea battles of the twentieth century. The years that led up to World War I witnessed Great Britain's naval supremacy challenged first by Germany and then Japan, but at the end of that conflict the German High Seas Fleet had ceased to exist and the principal maritime powers were Britain, Japan and the United States.

The Nuclear Age

The years between 1906 and 1935 were marked by undreamed of technological innovation. Destroyers, once little more than coastal craft, were turned into hardy, seaworthy vessels with a role to play on the world's oceans, and World War I proved the destructive capability of the submarine beyond all doubt. During that war, Britain took the first tentative steps in the development of the aircraft carrier, the vessel that was to become the capital ship of the future.

The carrier, perhaps, was the most significant naval design to emerge from the period; not only did it enable fleets to engage one another at distances far beyond visual range but it also became a primary tool in hunting down the two greatest naval threats of World War II, the commerce raider and the submarine. The six years of World War II put an end to centuries of conventional thinking on naval forces. The gun-armed capital ship was no longer the master of war at sea. In the North Atlantic and in the Pacific, the supremacy of the battleship ended when air power defeated sea power. The aircraft carrier brought a whole new dimension to naval warfare and it has been the dominant element of every major application of sea power since 1945.

Since the 1950s, the advent of nuclear power has revolutionized underwater warfare, enabling submarines to remain submerged for many months at a time. In the shape of the ballistic missile submarine, it has made possible the ultimate in weapons.

Progress in merchant shipping since 1900 has also been tremendous. Steam propulsion gave way to the more efficient diesel, and the resultant decline in the number of seafarers was multiplied by the development of automated ship handling systems, while the introduction of containerization and the streamlining of bulk cargo handling changed the nature of port operation beyond recognition. Such changes were vital to accommodate the increase in worldwide trade, of which 90 percent still moves by sea, and the world's mercantile fleet grew to keep pace with the demand, going from 130m tons in 1960 to over 500m tons in 2000 – a twenty-fold increase since 1900. Older styles of cargo boats have almost disappeared with bulk cargo carriers and container ships taking their place.

Ocean liners disappeared in the 1950s and 1960s as a result of expanding air travel but now their successors are cruise ships whose passengers are sailing the oceans for pleasure; these huge floating hotels include in their number some of the largest vessels in the world today.

The US Navy's attack submarine **Seawolf** *(SSN 21) puts to sea in the Narragansett Bay operating area for her first sea trial in July 1996.*

The Cheops ship

The Cheops ship, the oldest preserved ship from antiquity, was found in 1954 close to the Great Pyramid in Egypt. It is built almost entirely of imported cedar. The ship was clearly a ceremonial vessel, yet compression marks of rope show that it was definitely used in the water.

Dating from 2500 BC, the 'shell-first' design of the Cheops ship shows that the hull was shaped before the internal members were added. It has no keel, and the side planking is lashed with rope for security. Built as a ceremonial vessel, rope compression marks show that it was used on water. Two cabins stand on the ship's deck, the two-roomed main one covered by a canopy for added coolness. The ship was equipped with oars plus steering oars. Contemporary Egyptian warships were of similar construction.

Length: 43.6m (143ft)
Beam: 5.7m (18ft 7in)
Depth: 1.45m (4ft 9in)
Displacement: 94t
Rigging: single mast
Complement: 12 plus officers

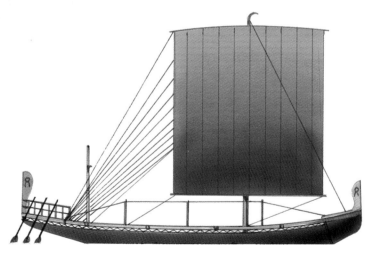

Phoenician cargo ship

The Phoenicians were a great trading nation and practical seafarers. Our evidence for this vessel comes from now-destroyed Egyptian tomb murals dating back to around 1500 BC.

It is the first vessel to show such features as a masthead rope ladder and lookout point. The horse-head prow may have

been a standard motif. There is no suggestion of rope bracing, implying that the vessel, even without a keel, had sufficient rigidity to withstand the sea. The wicker fencing was probably to separate deck cargo from the oarsmen. Timber was an important cargo, and one ancient relief from almost 700 years later shows timber being towed. The Egyptian source showed

a very large amphora attached to the prow of the ship – possibly for the crew's water or wine. Ships at this time possessed no metallic fixings at all. Everything would be made of wood, rope or cloth, apart from pottery utensils. King Solomon may well have used vessels like this to import Lebanese timber to be used in building his temple in Jerusalem.

Length: 16.8m (55ft)

Beam: 3.7m (12ft)

Depth: 1.5m (5ft)

Displacement: not known

Rigging: single mast stayed fore and aft; square sail with upper and lower yards

Complement: 8–12

Main routes: eastern Mediterranean

Cargo: timber, grain, fish, metals

Greek war galley

The trireme was the heavy battleship of the classical world, representing weight, speed and turning circle combined to form an optimum for the operation of an oared vessel.

It has been likened to 'a giant spear, 50 tonnes in weight'. The rowers sat in three banks, one man to each oar. The type appears to have originated in the Greek city of Corinth around 650 BC, and was quickly copied by other maritime states. Remarkably few details of the design survive, and there has been much controversy about how the trireme was laid out and rowed. The essence of the first trireme design was to incorporate an extra bank of oarsmen without making the ship much longer or heavier; better use was simply made of the hull space. The result was 170 oars powering the ship, 31 in the uppermost bank and 27 in each of the lower two banks.

Length: 32.5m (106ft 7in)
Beam: 4.6m (15ft)
Depth: 1.1m (3ft 6in)
Displacement: 50t
Rigging: two masts; square sails
Armament: ram; archers, marines
Complement: 170 rowers

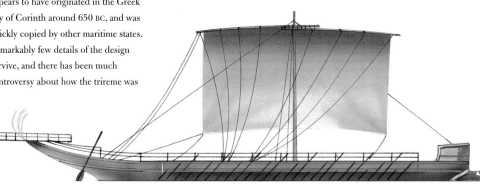

Roman war galley

Quinqueremes are referred to from as early as the fourth century BC and remained a powerful element in naval warfare for several centuries.

The name refers to the number of rowers in each file. Thus on a three-banked ship, rowers were two to an oar on the two lower levels; one to an oar on the upper level. There is no evidence of more than three levels. Some ships were 'sixes', with two men to an oar also on the topmost level (these vessels were normally flagships), and even larger ships were built, with three or four men to an oar on the lower banks. Fives and sixes fought by coming together and boarding. Broad-beamed ships had the advantage of being good platforms for catapults and for carrying marines, but their lack of manoeuvrability must always have been a disadvantage, as was their heavy expense and upkeep compared with smaller warships.

Length: not known
Beam: 5m (16ft 4in)
Depth: not known
Displacement: not known
Rigging: single dismountable mast; square sail
Armament: catapults; marines
Complement: 300 oarsmen, 120 marines

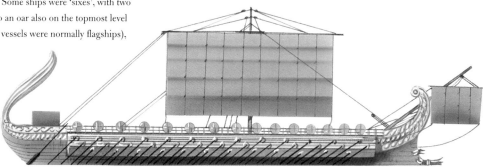

Mediterranean cargo ship

Vessels of this type plied the waters of the Mediterranean around the ninth century AD. Although the basic hull was that of the old Roman cargo ship, its look above the freeboard was very different.

The steering oars were still brought within an extension of the upper hull; however, the stern and prow were far simpler, and the bowsprit gone completely. The ship's mast, stayed by shrouds, had a forward tilt to accommodate the double-sparred yard of a lateen sail, a feature probably copied from Arab vessels. Lateen sails could be trimmed much closer to the wind.

Length: 24.4m (80ft)

Beam: 7.6m (25ft)

Depth: 2.7m (9ft)

Displacement: not known

Rigging: single mast stayed laterally; lateen rig

Complement: 5–8

Main routes: trans-Mediterranean, Atlantic coast of Europe

Cargo: wine, grain, wood, hides, oil

Viking longship

Using longships, the Vikings were able to raid Britain, Ireland and northern France in the ninth and tenth centuries, and to voyage as far as Constantinople in the eleventh.

The celebrated tenth-century Gokstad ship preserved at Oslo, although shorter than a true longship, nevertheless shows the constructional style of these vessels. They were clinker-built of oak on a strong keel, and directed by a steering oar set at the starboard side. The mast stock rested directly on the keel, and could be dismounted. The yardarm, made of a single spar, supported a homespun square sail. There was no cover for the crew; whenever possible, they spent the night on shore, with the boat hauled up on the beach. The longships were fine sea boats, and the Vikings who sailed them appreciated their qualities.

Length: 36.6m (120ft)

Beam: 6.1m (20ft)

Depth: 1.1m (3ft 6in)

Displacement: not known

Rigging: single mast; square sail

Armament: personal weapons – swords, axes, spears, bows

Complement: 50

Main routes: North Sea and Baltic Sea; North Atlantic to Faroe Islands and Iceland

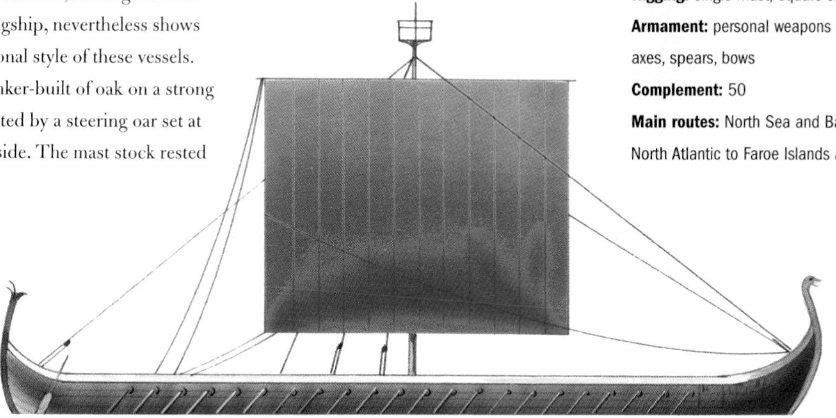

English warship

At the beginning of the fourteenth century, the English Cinque Port towns maintained a fleet of vessels such as this – clinker-built with forecastles and aftercastles for fighting purposes, and with a wide, clear deck. Vessels of this type were not limited only to coastal defence. Illustrated manuscripts show that they also accompanied crusading forces to Palestine.

The steering oar is still employed, but the mast is stayed laterally by shrouds, kept taut by deadeyes and lanyards. The decorative prow has also now become a functional bowsprit, the sheets attached to it helping to hold the sail to the wind. Within half a century, warships would become much more seaworthy, and would include a built-in aftercastle.

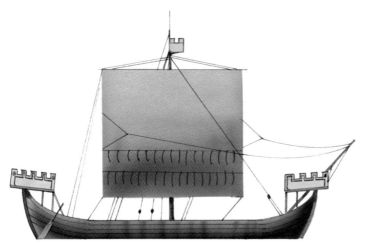

Length: 12.8m (42ft)
Beam: 3.7m (12ft)
Depth: 2.1m (7ft)
Displacement: 180t
Rigging: single mast stayed fore and aft, port and starboard; square sail with bowlines attached to bowsprit
Armament: machines to project arrows and stones; archers, marines
Complement: 6

Hanseatic cog

The Hanseatic League established many of the medieval trade routes around the Baltic and the North Sea, and the mainstay of that trade for more than a century after 1200 was the cog. As with most merchant ships throughout history, the cog was built to maximize cargo capacity, and not for performance.

In 1962, a well-preserved ship was found at Bremen, Germany. It is a fine example of the cog. The lowest part of the hull was flush-built, the upper parts clinker-built, and the hull was rounded out between a pointed stem and stern to increase carrying capacity to its optimum. A rudder was fitted, with the tiller housed below the built-out stern platform.

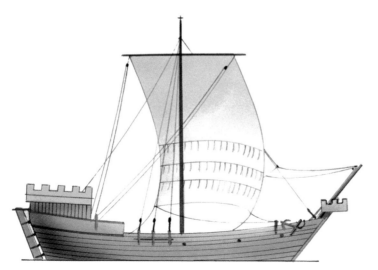

Length: 24m (78ft 9in)
Beam: 8m (26ft 3in)
Depth: 3m (10ft)
Displacement: 120t
Rigging: single mast; square sail, sometimes fitted with a bonnet, sometimes with reefpoints
Complement: 6
Main routes: North Sea, southern Baltic
Cargo: wood, coal, hides, wine

Chinese junk

The junk, in its various guises, has had a long career. By 1350, it was the product of a centuries-long history of Chinese ship design.

As in other sciences, ancient China made many discoveries and innovations in shipbuilding techniques which were to come much later in the West. Notable features include a single stern rudder and a pontoon-type hull-divided into as many as 20 watertight compartments, with the deck built up above its arched top. The planking was flush, with heavy rubbing strakes, and the vessel's bottom was flat, enabling it to sit level if beached. The sails were composed of fibre matting, woven in an interlocking pattern, and strengthened by lateral bamboo battens.

Length: 54.9m (180ft)

Beam: 9.1m (30ft)

Depth: 5.5m (18ft)

Displacement: not known

Rigging: four unstayed masts; lugsail-type rig, reefed from top downwards

Complement: 8-10 seamen

Main routes: coast and main rivers of China

Cargo: timber, rice, metals, cloth, foodstuffs

Nao

In 1350 the Portuguese used *nao*, a generic word like the Italian *nave*, to describe a larger seagoing vessel. Today, the ship, or *nao*, illustrated here would be classed as a carrack, of an early sort with two masts.

The type was soon to be developed and enlarged – Portugal at this time led the world in shipbuilding. Although a quarter deck has replaced the aftercastle, the deck beam ends still protrude from the sides, as in much earlier ships. The yard is supported by topping lifts, a feature of the square rig not found in north European ships for almost another century.

Length: 21.9m (72ft)

Beam: 6m (20ft)

Depth: 3.6m (12ft)

Displacement: 65t

Rigging: two masts; square sail on main, lateen-mizzen

Complement: 10–20

Routes: Iberian coast, northwest Africa

Cargo: wine, grain, manufactured goods, baled and barrelled goods

Caravel

The caravel emerged in the fifteenth century from the form of an earlier Iberian fishing boat, enlarged, decked and fitted with two (later three) masts.

It was a ship that was seaworthy enough to be able to undertake oceanic voyages of unprecedented length. With the encouragement of Portugal's Prince Henry the Navigator, the development of the type was driven, rather than evolutionary. The caravel was originally lateen-rigged. It was in a caravel that Bartholomew Diaz rounded the Cape of Good Hope in 1487.

The later three-masted caravel was the finest sailing ship of its time. Its capacity, sailing qualities and weatherliness gave its captains the confidence to undertake long voyages in unknown waters. Many caravels were converted to square rig on the foremast and mainmast, notably the *Pinta* and the *Niña*, two of the ships in which Christopher Columbus sailed to the New World in 1492. The limited size of the caravel was, over time, to lead to its replacement by larger vessels.

Length: 22.8m (75ft)

Beam: 7.6m (25ft)

Depth: 3m (10ft)

Displacement: 60t

Rigging: (redonada) three masts; square sail on fore and main; lateen-mizzen

Complement: 12–20

Routes: African coast; Atlantic after 1492

Cargo: trading goods, bullion, timber, ores

Carrack

The three-masted ship began to be built in Europe from the early years of the fifteenth century.

Genoa has been suggested as the most likely port to begin building and using the type, as it specialized in bulk cargoes such as timber, alum and ore. Although the name 'carrack' is apparently derived from the Italian word *caracca*, the Italians simply called it *nave* ('ship'). The design was a radical change from what had gone before, and ship sizes doubled within a few years. *Santa Maria*, the largest of Columbus's vessels, was called a nao, meaning a square-rigged vessel larger than a caravel; in fact, what was soon to become known as a carrack. Her carrying capacity was 100 tons – equivalent to 100 double hogsheads or tuns of wine. The rig was standard for a carrack: three masts, square-rigged on fore and main with a lateen sail on the mizzen.

Length: 34.1m (112ft)
Beam: 10m (33ft)
Depth: 5.18m (17ft)
Displacement: 180t
Rigging: three masts; square sail on fore and main; lateen-mizzen
Complement: 20
Routes: long-distance trading routes
Cargo: hides, oil, ore, wine, iron

Great Harry

Known familiarly as 'Great Harry', the *Henry Grace à Dieu* was launched in 1514. She was King Henry VIII's flagship or 'admiral', and she was intended to display the power and splendour of the monarch.

Up to this time, English warships had been converted merchantmen, with all the difficulties involved in the hiring and refitting of them in time of war. *Henry Grace à Dieu*, a large carrack, was purpose-built as a warship, as were her sister ships, the ill-fated *Mary Rose* (1505) and the *Great Galley* (1513). Very heavily armed, she carried the heavier guns in the waist behind watertight gunports, which were opened only in action.

Length: 57.9m (190ft)
Beam: 15.2m (50ft)
Depth: not known
Displacement: c1500t
Rigging: four masts; square-rigged on fore and main; lateen-rigged mizzens
Armament: 43 heavy guns, 141 light pieces
Complement: 700

Galleon

As is often the case with historic nautical terms, the origin of the name 'galleon' is obscure. It is first found in English use in 1529, and it is likely that the first ships of galleon type were built in Spain. The vessel depicted here is the *San Martin*, flagship of the Spanish Armada in 1588.

The crucial new feature was the hull shape: the somewhat greater length in relation to beam helped in sailing to windward, but more significant was the complete redesign of the forecastle. This no longer projected over the bow, as in the carrack, but was pulled back, lightening and raising the bows, and making control of the ship's head easier.

Length: 37.3m (122ft 3in)

Beam: 9.3m (30ft 5in)

Depth: not known

Displacement: 1000t

Rigging: three masts; square-rigged on fore and main; lateen-mizzen

Armament: 48 guns

Complement: 350 seamen and gunners, plus more than 300 soldiers armed with muskets and arquebuses

Mediterranean galley

An important change in the traditional means of Mediterranean galley propulsion took place at the start of the sixteenth century. Previously, oars and oarsmen had been grouped in sets of two or three, one man to each oar.

Now the oars, typically 24 to a side, were spaced evenly along the sides, with each one drawn by a team of up to seven men – the unfortunate galley slaves. Around the same time, guns were begun to be mounted on galleys, sometimes a single heavy gun firing forward from the bows. These superseded the ram, which was mounted well above the waterline, and was used more as a boarding bridge. Although galleys were used throughout the Mediterranean, it seems likely that the innovations came from Italy, and more specifically Venice. The traditional lateen rig remained unchanged; the majority of galleys had only one mast, but a number had two as seen here, and a few large galleys had three masts.

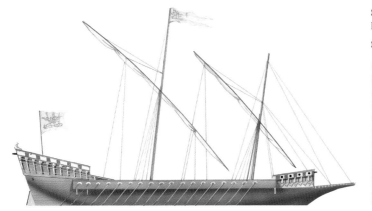

Length: 36.5m (120ft)

Beam: 5.5m (18ft)

Depth: 2.7m (9ft)

Displacement: not known

Rigging: one to three masts; lateen-rigged

Armament: up to five bow-mounted cannon

Complement: 240 oarsmen, 20–40 seamen, 8 gunners, plus soldiers

Ark Royal

The English galleon of 1588 had fine underwater lines and handled well. The lower forecastle and aftercastle improved stability, the armament was carefully thought out and the sails were cut to be taut and responsive.

Intended for Sir Walter Raleigh, the English galleon *Ark Raleigh* was taken over while being built by the government of Queen Elizabeth I. She was launched at Deptford and renamed *Ark Royal*. As the flagship of the English fleet under Lord Howard of Effingham, she met the Spanish Armada on 30 July 1588, and was the first ship to engage the enemy. Rebuilt in 1606, she sank at Tilbury in 1636.

Length: 42.6m (140ft)
Beam: 11.2m (37ft)
Depth: 4.5m (15ft)
Displacement: 690t
Rigging: four masts; square-rigged apart from lateen-mizzens
Armament: 38 guns, plus 17 small pieces
Complement: 270 sailors, 34 gunners, 126 soldiers

Slave carrack

During the sixteenth century the Portuguese, with their large Brazilian possessions, were dominant in the transatlantic slave trade. Speed at sea was essential, as the mortality rate in the slave hold was very high.

Slave ships would moor in creeks on the West African coast in order to rendezvous with their agents in the grim trade. In turn these agents would acquire slaves inland, often from the winners of tribal conflicts where the losers were sold to the highest bidder. At this time there was no ban on slaving in Europe, but official licences were needed. Many captains did without them, as they were expensive to procure. This fast carrack was typical of the vessels involved in the trade, being longer and slimmer in line than a conventional cargo ship.

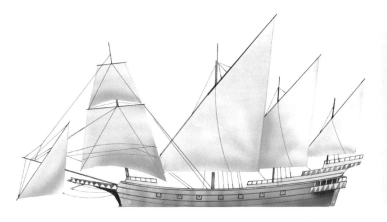

Length: 36m (120ft)
Beam: 8.4m (27ft 6in)
Depth: not known
Displacement: 400t
Rigging: four masts; square-rigged on foremast, others lateen-rigged
Complement: not known
Routes: West Africa to the West Indies and Central America
Cargo: slaves

St Louis

In the second quarter of the seventeenth century, the French, conscious of their lack of seapower, set about establishing a fleet to rival those of the Dutch and English.

The first of the ships, including the *Saint Louis*, were built in Dutch yards; other European navies had responded to the English by building English-style ships. The *Saint Louis* had a much reduced superstructure compared with previous galleons. She had a square stern, known as a transom stern, with a partly closed-in gallery for the main cabin. Gratings were built over the open main deck; these were removable to allow for stowage of boats and supplies. The internal arrangements included a whipstaff to ease steering, and hand-powered bilge pumps.

Length: 36.5m (120ft)
Beam: c12.8m (42ft)
Depth: not known
Displacement: 1000t
Rigging: three masts; square-rigged with topgallants on fore and main; lateen-mizzen with square topsail; spritsail and bowsprit topsail
Armament: 60 guns
Complement: 700

Sovereign of the Seas

Launched in 1637, *Sovereign of the Seas* was the most lavishly decorated vessel ever to sail in the Royal Navy. The king's favourite artist of the time, Van Dyck, is believed to have prepared the designs of her many carvings, statues and decorations.

It was at the direct command of King Charles I that *Sovereign of the Seas* was built. The masterwork of the shipwright Phineas Pett, she was intended to display the naval might of England and the prestige of the English-Scottish king. On a larger scale than *Prince Royal*, she had three complete gun decks and was the first man-of-war to carry 100 heavy guns. In the three Anglo-Dutch wars between 1652 and 1674, this great ship saw action at the Battles of Kentish Knock (1652), Orfordness (1666), Sole Bay (1672), Schoonveld (1673) and the Texel (1673). She also fought at Beachy Head (1690) and at Barfleur (1692).

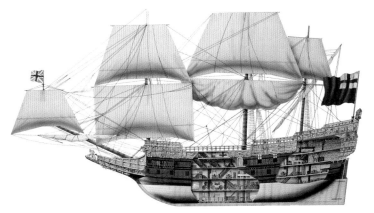

Length: 70.7m (232ft)
Beam: 14.2m (46ft 6in)
Depth: 7.1m (23ft 6in)
Displacement: 1141t
Rigging: three masts; square-rigged fore and main, with topgallants; lateen-mizzen with topsail; spritsail and bowsprit topsail
Armament: 102 guns
Complement: 250 sailors, plus gunners and soldiers

Fluyt

Economics has always had an effect on merchant shipping. Greater capacity, simpler operation, fewer crew and faster sailing times have been goals from the dawn of history.

The *fluyt* was a seventeenth-century accountant's dream ship. The first vessel definitely of the type was built in 1595, at Hoorn in Holland. Long in relation to beam, with a vast hold beneath a single deck, and almost vertical stem and stern, the low prow reduced her exposure to the wind. The rounded stern helped to maintain the course. Intended to sail in peaceful waters, the *fluyt* was lightly built and unarmed, factors which reduced the cost of building and maintenance. The masts were often on the short side, and the sail area no more than adequate.

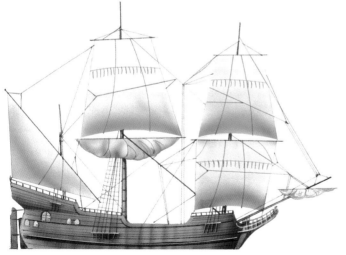

Length: 32m (105ft)
Beam: 8.5m (28ft)
Depth: 4.26m (14ft)
Displacement: 300t
Rigging: three masts; square-rigged on fore and main; lateen-mizzen
Complement: 20-30
Routes: North Sea and Baltic trading routes
Cargo: timber, ore, baled and barrelled goods

Galleass

Despite the fact that the sail had proved vastly more efficient than oarsmen over long distances, oars were never wholly abandoned; even large men-of-war in the nineteenth century carried long sweeps, to turn the vessel in a calm.

Although oceanic nations had long abandoned galleys, many maintained the smaller galleass, powered by both sail and oar, for coastal or local defence. In 1627, 10 small English galleys, known as 'lion's whelps', were launched; they do not appear to have been successful. The Venetians and Turks persisted, largely because, although ineffective against sailing ships which could mount more and heavier guns, the galleass had some value in fighting pure galleys, which had lighter armament. As the light winds and calms of the Mediterranean favoured oared vessels, they were still being built in substantial numbers into the seventeenth and eighteenth centuries.

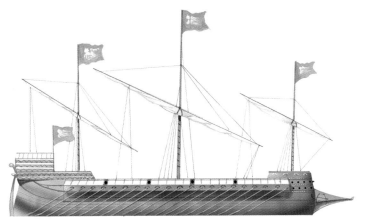

Length: 48.7m (160ft)

Beam: 9.1m (30ft)

Depth: 3.6m (12ft)

Displacement: not known

Rigging: three masts; lateen-rigged

Armament: 20 guns, plus 20–30 light swivel cannon

Complement: 350 oarsmen, 40 gunners, 30 seamen, plus soldiers

Dutch frigate

Like so many other older ship terms, 'frigate' was not used with precision: its conventional seventeenth-century sense was a full-rigged warship with a single gun deck.

Both the Dutch and the English were building ships of this type from the mid-seventeenth century. Usually armed with about 36 guns, the frigate was inferior to the lowest-rated ship of the line. Its role

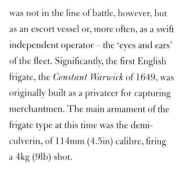

was not in the line of battle, however, but as an escort vessel or, more often, as a swift independent operator – the 'eyes and ears' of the fleet. Significantly, the first English frigate, the *Constant Warwick* of 1649, was originally built as a privateer for capturing merchantmen. The main armament of the frigate type at this time was the demi-culverin, of 114mm (4.5in) calibre, firing a 4kg (9lb) shot.

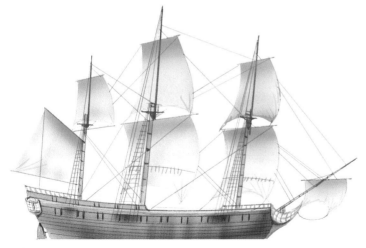

Length: 35.9m (118ft)

Beam: 7.6m (25ft)

Depth: 4.26m (14ft)

Displacement: 270t

Rigging: three masts; square-rigged; lateen-mizzen with square topsail; spritsail and bowsprit topsail

Armament: 30 guns

Complement: 135

Le Soleil Royal

As flagship of the navy of the 'Sun King', Louis XIV, *Le Soleil Royal*, classified as a *vaisseau*, equivalent to a first rate, was one of the largest and most powerful warships of her time.

Painted in royal blue and sumptuously decorated in gold, she must have been a spectacular sight. Launched at Brest in 1669, she was refitted in 1689. In 1690, at Bevéziers, she was the flagship of Admiral Count Tourville when the French triumphed over the English. Damaged at Barfleur in 1692, she was destroyed by English fireships.

Length: 37.3m (122ft 3in)
Beam: 9.3m (30ft 5in)
Depth: not known
Displacement: c1000t
Rigging: three masts; square-rigged on fore and main with topgallants; lateen-mizzen with topsail; spritsail and bowsprit topsail
Armament: 104 guns
Complement: c150 seamen, 120 gunners, 150 soldiers

Xebec (Chebeck)

The xebec, or chebeck, originated in the western Mediterranean during the seventeenth century. The name stems from the Arabic *sabak*. This suggests that the Barbary pirates, who were closely associated with this type of vessel, may have developed it.

Xebecs were designed to emerge from shallow harbours, using their great speed to intercept merchantmen, few of which would be able to outrun or outmanoeuvre the freebooters. The original North African designers of the xebec borrowed from both the galley and the caravel traditions. The Spanish and French were quick to follow, if only to have a ship that could match the fine sailing qualities of the xebeck. Three-masted, and originally with full lateen-rig, it carried 18 oars to assure mobility during calms, and had a distinctive built-out stern platform to stay the mizzen. Although of shallow draught, the xebeck was far from being tub-like, having fine underwater lines. It carried 12 to 15 guns, including four 12pdr guns mounted on the bow.

Length: 31m (103ft 9in)

Beam: 6.7m (22ft)

Depth: 2.5m (8ft 2in)

Displacement: 190t

Rigging: three masts; lateen-rigged

Armament: 12–15 guns

Complement: 24, plus fighting men

Bucintoro

The state barge of the Doge of Venice was used every year on Ascension Day in the re-enactment of Venice's symbolic marriage with the sea.

A ring, blessed by the Patriarch of Venice, would be dropped into the waters of the Adriatic by the Doge, accompanied by the words: 'We wed you, Adriatic, as the sign of our true and perpetual dominion.'

The ceremony probably goes back to the twelfth century. A succession of state barges bore the name *Bucintoro*, which means 'man-ox', probably referring to the first craft's figurehead. The last of the series was launched at the Venice Arsenal in 1728 and was used until 1797; the French captured Venice, and the city's long career as 'bride of the sea' came to an end. At the orders of Napoleon, the barge's ornamentation was stripped and destroyed; the hull was eventually used as a floating battery by the Austro-Hungarian navy and was finally broken up in 1824.

Length: 34.7m (114ft)
Beam: 7.2m (23ft 9in)
Depth: 2.3m (7ft 6in)
Rigging: one flagpole mast
Complement: 168 oarsmen

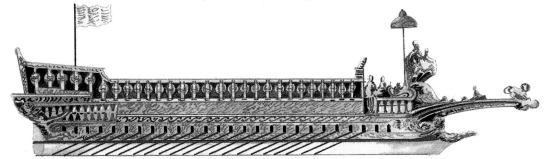

Boston

Considering the lack of a naval building tradition in the North American colonies, the construction of the *Boston* was a remarkable achievement, and many important lessons were quickly learned.

The *Boston* was the first frigate to be built in the American colonies; she was laid down at Newburyport, Massachusetts, in 1747 and launched in the following year. Availability of cheap wood supplies led to rapid growth in the shipbuilding industry along the American coast, although prior to 1776 the products were chiefly merchant vessels. Although classified as a frigate, the *Boston* was on the small side and probably lacked the speed of later American-built frigates, which were built with wider yards and carried a greater spread of sail; she was built for coastal patrol and convoy escort duties. The *Boston*'s career was brief. In 1752, she was broken up, probably because she had been constructed of unseasoned wood.

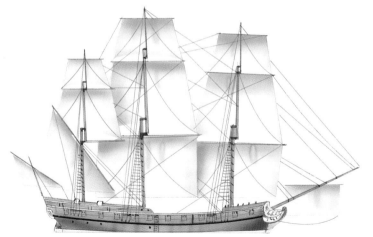

Length: 34.8m (114ft 3in)
Beam: 9.6m (31ft 6in)
Depth: 3.1m (10ft 3in)
Displacement: 514t
Rigging: three masts; square rig
Armament: 24 guns
Complement: c200

Endeavour

Launched at Whitby in 1764 as the collier barque *Earl of Pembroke*, she was purchased by the British Admiralty and fitted out as the *Endeavour* for a scientific journey to the South Seas to observe the transit of Venus from Tahiti and ascertain whether a southern continent really existed.

In command was Lieutenant James Cook, and the expedition left Plymouth on 25 August 1768. It discovered New Zealand to be two islands and explored the eastern coast of Australia. *Endeavour* returned to England on 12 July 1771, almost three years after setting sail, and was then used for three voyages to the Falkland Islands. In March 1775, sold by the Admiralty, she resumed her first occupation as a collier and later became a French-owned whaler.

Length: 29.7m (97ft 8in)

Beam: 8.9m (29ft 4in)

Depth: 3.4m (11ft 3in)

Displacement: 366t burthen

Rigging: three masts; square rig

Armament: six swivel guns

Complement: 85

Routes: South Seas

Victory

Immortalized as Nelson's flagship at Trafalgar, the *Victory* had already had a long and illustrious career before that famous victory.

Laid down in 1759 at Chatham Dockyard and launched in 1765, *Victory*, a first rate of 100 guns, was not put into commission until 1778, when France allied herself with the American colonists. For three years she was flagship of the Channel Fleet under Admiral Keppel; under Admiral Lord Howe she was flagship when the British raised the siege of Gibraltar in 1782. With the end of the War of American Independence she was laid up until 1792. In that year *Victory* went to the Mediterranean as flagship, first to Admiral Hood, then in 1793 to Sir John Jervis, who won a victory over the Spanish off Cape St Vincent.

Between 1800 and 1803, she was rebuilt, and on 18 May 1803, ready to return to the Mediterranean under Captain Hardy, she hoisted the flag of Admiral Lord Nelson. Between 30 July 1803 and the Battle of Trafalgar, Nelson spent only 25 days off the ship. Nelson was shot on her deck during the decisive victory at Trafalgar; she went on to serve as flagship for Admiral Saumarez in the Baltic. Preserved at Portsmouth, the *Victory* remains the flagship of the commander-in-chief.

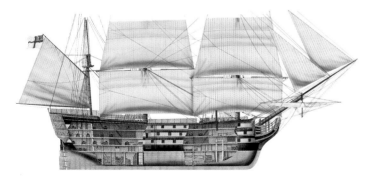

Length: 56.7m (186ft)

Beam: 15.8m (51ft 10in)

Depth: 6.5m (21ft 6in)

Displacement: 2162t burthen

Rigging: three masts; square rig

Armament: 100 guns

Complement: 850

Santissima Trinidad

Built at Havana in 1769, *Santissima Trinidad* was the largest warship of the eighteenth century, the only four-decker to see extensive service.

She took part in the Battle of Cape St Vincent, when a daring manoeuvre by Nelson, then a commodore on HMS *Captain*, effectively detached her and two other first rates from the battle. Captain Saumarez in HMS *Orion* actually compelled her to strike her colours, but Admiral Jervis signalled to his fleet to wear and come to the wind, and *Santissima Trinidad* was able to break away. Her next fleet action was at Trafalgar on 21 October 1805, where she flew the flag of Rear Admiral Cisneros; she was formed in the French–Spanish line just ahead of the flagship *Bucentaure* and was in the thick of the battle when the British ships broke through the line. Towards the close of the battle, *Santissima Trinidad*, dismasted and out of control, was boarded by HMS *Africa*, at 64 guns the smallest ship in Nelson's fleet. The boarders were informed that the ship was still in action and were politely sent back. *Santissima Trinidad* struck her colours only after the battle was over, to HMS *Prince*.

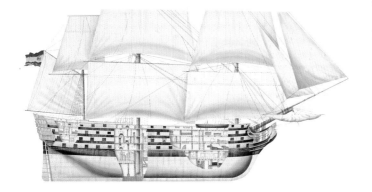

Length: 60.1m (200ft)

Beam: 19.2m (62ft 9in)

Depth: not known

Displacement: 4572t

Rigging: three masts; square rig

Armament: 130 guns

Complement: 950

South Carolina

The Dutch-built *South Carolina* represented a considerable increase in dimensions on frigates of the Hancock class, and gave American ship designers a number of pointers in the design of large frigates, which they would use to great effect.

Built in Amsterdam in 1776 as *L'Indien*, the vessel was originally intended for French service. American purchasing agents, looking for ships in a hurry during the War of American Independence, arranged to acquire her, but the French sold her to the Grand Duke of Luxembourg (who had no coastline); he then lent her to the state of South Carolina in 1777. On 19 December 1782, she was captured by HMS *Astrea* (32 guns), *Diomede* (44 guns) and *Quebec* (32 guns), after an 18-hour chase. *South Carolina*'s hull had hogged (sagged in the middle) because her guns were too heavy, and she was not taken into service in the Royal Navy. A lesson was learned by American warship builders, who put much more longitudinal strength into their own home-built frigates.

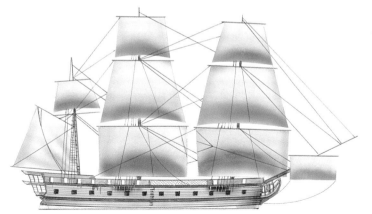

Length: 46.9m (154ft)
Beam: 12.2m (40ft)
Depth: 5m (16ft 6in)
Displacement: 1186t
Rigging: three masts; square rig
Armament: 28 36pdr guns; 12 12pdr guns
Complement: not known

Turtle

Like 'two upper tortoise shells of equal size, joined together', her shape and underwater purpose explain the name of this early submersible, built by brothers David and Ezra Bushnell at Saybrook, Connecticut, in 1776.

Intended to attack the British in the War of American Independence, *Turtle* carried a 68kg (150lb) gunpowder charge that could be secured to a target by an auger operated from within the vessel. Volunteer crewman Ezra Lee failed to attach the mine to the British flagship, HMS *Eagle*, off Staten Island on 6 September 1776 and abandoned the attempt. Although called a failure, *Turtle* forced the British to move their fleet to a safer anchorage.

Length: 2.3m (7ft 6in)
Beam: not known
Depth: 1.8m (6ft)
Displacement: c2000lb (900kg)
Machinery: hand-cranked vertical and horizontal screws
Armament: one mine
Complement: 1

Bounty

The *Bounty* began as the merchant vessel *Bethia*, a ship-rigged craft of 220t, built in the English port of Hull in 1784; three years later the British Admiralty purchased her.

Cook's voyages to the South Pacific had shown that the breadfruit grown in the Society Islands could be use to keep slaves in the West Indies well nourished cheaply. Under the command of Lieutenant William

Bligh, *Bounty* was sent to ship breadfruit plants from the South Pacific to the Caribbean. While at Tahiti, her crew revelled in the easy-going life. On the way back, on 28 April 1789, the crew mutinied under the leadership of Fletcher Christian. The captain and 18 loyal men were set adrift in the ship's launch, making an epic 5800km (3600 mile) voyage to safety while *Bounty* was sailed by the mutineers to the isolated Pitcairn Island and burned.

Length: 27.7m (91ft)

Beam: 7.5m (24ft 4in)

Depth: 3.5m (11ft 4in)

Displacement: 220t

Rigging: three masts; square rig

Armament: four guns

Complement: 45

Routes: South Pacific–Caribbean

Vanguard

The 74-gun ship-of-the-line was the mainstay of most major European fleets throughout the second half of the eighteenth century and into the Napoleonic wars.

Launched at Deptford in 1787, *Vanguard* was one of the most numerous class of big ships; her designer was Sir Thomas Slade. In 1796, she was in the Mediterranean as flagship of Rear Admiral Nelson, under Lord St Vincent. Detailed to watch the French fleet at Toulon, *Vanguard* was totally dismasted in a gale. In 1798 she was Nelson's flagship at the Battle of the Nile. In December 1798, *Vanguard* took the Bourbon royal family from Naples to safety in Sicily. She returned to England in 1800. *Vanguard* saw no further action in the war, and in 1812 she was converted to a prison ship, then became a powder hulk in 1814. She was broken up in 1821.

Length: 51.2m (168ft)
Beam: 14.25m (46ft 9in)
Depth: 6m (19ft 9in)
Displacement: 1604t
Rigging: three masts; square rig
Armament: 28 32pdr guns; 28 18pdr guns; 18 9pdr guns
Complement: 550

Constitution

One of a trio of exceptionally large and well-armed frigates, the Boston-built *Constitution*, with her sisters *President* and *United States*, were the most powerful frigates in the world.

Although classed as 44-gun vessels, they carried as many as 60 guns and carronades. Launched in 1797, *Constitution* gave valuable service against the Barbary States, where she was more than a match for the corsairs' ships. In the British–American War of 1812, the American frigates outclassed their British counterparts, which were much smaller and had less than half the American broadside weight. Under the command of Isaac Hull, *Constitution* defeated HMS *Guerrière* on the Grand Banks. In December 1812, under Captain William Bainbridge, she made similarly short work of the 38-gun HMS *Java* off Brazil. She remains preserved as a commissioned vessel in the US Navy.

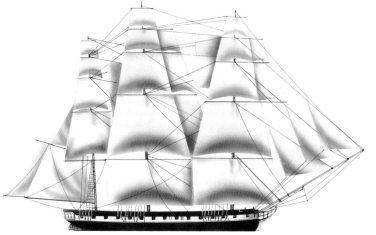

Length: 53.3m (175ft)

Beam: 13.3m (43ft 6in)

Depth: 6.9m (22ft 6in)

Displacement: 2200t

Rigging: three masts; square rig

Armament: 20 32pdr guns; 34 24pdr guns

Complement: 450

Essex

Built at Salem, Massachusetts, *Essex* was a 46-gun frigate which saw extensive service far from the coasts of the United States. Her first voyage in 1800 was to escort a Dutch East India convoy across the Indian Ocean.

In 1801, *Essex* was part of the US Navy squadron sent to the Mediterranean which compelled the Barbary corsairs to cease their attacks on American shipping. Laid up between 1806 and 1809, she was refitted and had a distinguished career in the British-American War of 1812, on both the east and west coasts of America, under Captain David Porter. Between July and September 1812, she took 10 prizes, including the 18-gun vessel HMS *Alert*. At the beginning of 1813, Essex sailed for the Pacific, where, in a 'lone wolf' campaign, she raided British shipping. Fifteen prizes were taken in the course of the year. In February 1814, *Essex* was taken by the Royal Navy frigate *Phoebe* and the 18-gun sloop *Cherub*.

Length: 42.7m (140ft)

Beam: 9.4m (31ft)

Depth: 3.7m (12ft 4in)

Displacement: 850t

Rigging: three masts; square rig

Armament: 40 32pdr guns; six 18pdr guns

Complement: 319

Fulton steamboat

The development of the steam engine in the eighteenth century was one of the main spurs to the Industrial Revolution. It would not be long before engineers would be looking for ways to use the new technology in marine propulsion.

The Marquis de Jouffroy d'Abbans was one of the earliest pioneers, his vessel *Pyroscaphe* giving a working demonstration on the Saône River on 15 July 1783. In 1801, Scottishman William Symington's *Charlotte Dundas* paddle steamer towed two barges up the Forth and Clyde canal against a strong headwind, but canal officials felt that the wash thrown out by steam vessels would erode the banks, and it was not a commercial success. The American entrepreneur-engineer Robert Fulton, probably the most famous of the steam pioneers, constructed two early sidewheel steamships in Paris. The first one sank, but the machinery was retrieved and installed in a stronger hull. Tried out on 9 August 1803, Fulton's steamboat caused a considerable sensation, towing two barges against the current. Fulton's hull was long and narrow, with the engine installed on the deck. Despite his success with this project, Fulton found little support in France or England. He returned to America in 1806, where he continued to build innovative ships.

Length: 27.4m (90ft)
Beam: 4.9m (16ft)
Depth: 1.5m (5ft)
Displacement: not known
Rigging: not applicable
Machinery: sidewheels, steam

Claremont

Outperforming both land coaches and river sloops, the New York-built *Clermont* was one of the first commercially successful steam vessels. She was capable of carrying up to 140 passengers; a second steamer joined her on the Hudson River service in 1809.

Originally known as *Steam Boat*, then *North River Steamboat*, *Clermont* can claim to be the first steamship in regular service; she was built at Corlear's Hook, New York, in 1807 and designed by the prolific Robert Fulton. The engine was made by Boulton & Watt in England, and the vessel also had two masts – she was square-sailed on the main and had a gaff mizzen. Nicknamed 'Fulton's Folly', she actually operated very successfully between New York and Albany until 1814, when she was retired from service.

Length: 40.5m (133ft)
Beam: 4m (13ft)
Depth: 2.1m (7ft)
Displacement: 100t
Rigging: two masts; square sail on main, gaff on mizzen
Complement: not known
Cargo: 90 passengers
Routes: Hudson River

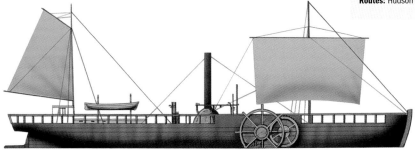

Astrolabe

Originally built for the French Navy in 1811 as the corvette *Coquille*, she was renamed in 1825 in memory of La Pérouse's frigate *L'Astrolabe*, lost in the South Pacific in 1788.

After the end of the Napoleonic wars, the *Astrolabe* became the base for a number of important expeditions. The most notable of this corvette's three great voyages of exploration with the scientist Jules

Dumont d'Urville was that to locate the South Magnetic Pole in 1837–40, which took her – although lacking any sort of reinforcement against ice – deep into the Antarctic ice pack. She had already been twice to the South Seas and had brought back more data and specimens of natural history than any vessel before her. Her post-1840 history is unknown.

Length: not known

Beam: not known

Depth: not known

Displacement: 380t

Rigging: three masts; square rig

Complement: 79

Routes: South Seas; Antarctic

Role: exploration vessel

Demologos

The *Demologos*, the US Navy's first full-size steam warship, was also known as 'Fulton the First'. She was the last ship designed by pioneering engineer Robert Fulton.

The US Navy's first steamship has been variously described as a floating battery and a steam frigate. She was double-ended and double-ruddered, with a twin-pontoon hull and a single paddle wheel mounted between the two hulls. Her wide gundeck supported 24 heavy guns, but she was completed in 1815, at the end of the War of 1812 with the British. Although she proved to be a satisfactory performer on test voyages, she became operational too late to see any action in the war. The engine of the *Demologos* was removed in 1821. On 6 June 1829, she blew up at Brooklyn Navy Yard.

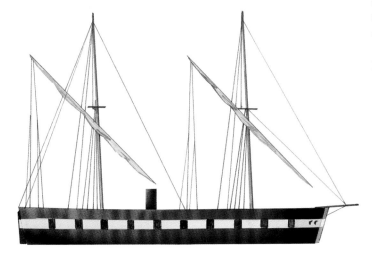

Length: 47.5m (156ft)

Beam: 17.1m (56ft)

Depth: 3.4m (11ft)

Displacement: 2475t

Rigging: steadying sails

Machinery: centre wheel, inclined

Armament: 24 32pdr guns

Complement: 200

Morris

A product of the New York Navy Yard which was completed in 1830, *Morris* was a very swift 'clipper schooner' designed as a revenue cutter for the US Customs Service.

From the beginning of the nineteenth century, the Americans had a reputation for building the finest schooners, and much thought and planning went into the design of the Morris to ensure that she was the best chasing and interception ship of her time. Morris was among the first US government vessels to be fitted with a geared steering wheel. As built, she was pierced to carry 14 guns, but as a cutter she carried only six. The design was a highly successful one, and Morris replaced earlier designs for US revenue cutters. However, subsequent cutters based on her lines had a straight stem, rather than her curved naval-style stem.

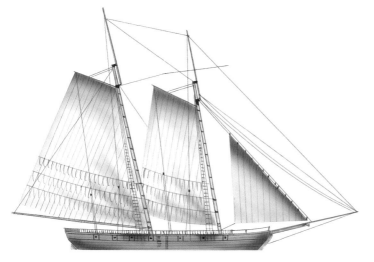

Length: 22.3m (73ft 4in)
Beam: 8.9m (29ft 2in)
Depth: 2.2m (7ft 4in)
Displacement: 147t
Rigging: two masts; square-rigged on foremast with boom and gaff mainsail
Armament: six guns
Complement: not known

Sirius

This Scottish-built paddle steamship, launched at Leith in 1837, was the first vessel to cross the Atlantic under sustained steam power. On the outward Atlantic run, *Sirius* made an average speed of 6.7 knots, compared with the rival *Great Western*, which averaged 8.8 knots.

Although intended for work between the Irish city of Cork and London, she was chartered by a rival company to steal the thunder from Brunel's *Great Western* and by making the first all-steam Atlantic crossing. Having started in London, *Sirius* left Cork on 4 April 1838 and reached New York in 18 days and 10 hours.

Having departed three days later, *Great Western* arrived the day after *Sirius*. *Sirius* was wrecked off the south coast of Ireland, on 29 January 1847, while en route from Glasgow to Cork.

Length: 63.4m (208ft)

Beam: 7.9m (25ft 10in)

Depth: 4.6m (15ft)

Displacement: 703t

Rigging: two masts; brig rig

Machinery: sidewheels, side lever

Complement: 35

Cargo: 60 passengers, light freight

Routes: transatlantic, Irish Sea routes

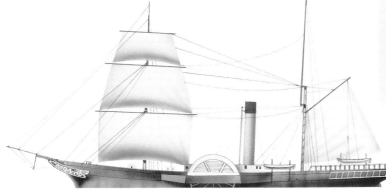

Great Western

Isambard Kingdom Brunel's first steamer, Bristol-built, was a maritime extension of the Great Western Railway, which he had engineered. Passengers would take a fast train to Bristol to connect with the steamer, a combination that provided the fastest route between London and New York.

Launched in 1837, *Great Western* carried 148 first-class passengers. In April 1838, she left Bristol for New York, crossing the Atlantic in 15 days. An engine-room accident on arrival caused the death of the engineer, but *Great Western* went on to make almost 70 crossings. Her best time was 12 days and 9 hours eastbound.

Length: 71.9m (236ft)

Beam: 10.7m (35ft 4in)

Depth: 5.1m (16ft 6in)

Displacement: 2300t

Rigging: four masts; foremast square-rigged, remainder fore-and-aft-rigged

Complement: not known

Cargo: passengers, general cargo

Routes: transatlantic

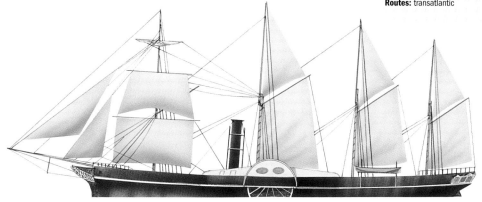

Jane Gifford

In its early days at the end of the eighteenth century, Australia was used as a penal colony by the British. By the nineteenth century, however, the original convicts and their descendants were being joined by migrants looking for a new life.

From around 1840 the flow of migrants from the United Kingdom steadily increased, being carried in small bluff-bowed slow sailing ships that also carried general cargo to Australia and New Zealand. Among the first of the migrant ships was *Jane Gifford* of 1840 which,

after landing her human cargo, and because a full return cargo could not be obtained in the newly established colonies, would often sail on to the Far East or India, to pick up a return cargo. By the 1860s and 1870s sufficient trade became available in the colony to set up regular lines serving Australia. In 1842, *Jane Gifford* would have carried the migrants in the hold, divided off from the ship's cargo. As was usual, the ship's officers were berthed aft, with the crew forward.

Length: 35m (117ft)

Beam: 9.4m (31ft)

Depth: not known

Displacement: 500t

Rigging: ship

Complement: not known

Cargo: migrants, mixed cargo

Congress

By the 1840s, the United States was playing a part in global affairs, and its modest fleet was widely deployed, serving in both the North and South Atlantic, the Mediterranean and in the Pacific.

A product of the final US sailing frigate design, *Congress* was launched in 1841 and saw service in the Mediterranean and at the siege of Montevideo in Uruguay. She served as flagship of the Pacific Squadron before taking part in the Mexican War of

1846–48. On the outbreak of the Civil War in 1861, she formed part of the squadron blockading the Confederate ports. On 8 March 1862, *Congress* was engaged by the newly completed Confederate ironclad ship *Virginia* (formerly USS *Merrimac*) in Hampton Roads. Run aground on the Union side of the Roads, under Signal Point, *Congress* was pounded by incendiary shells, and after some hours she blew up when her magazine was ignited.

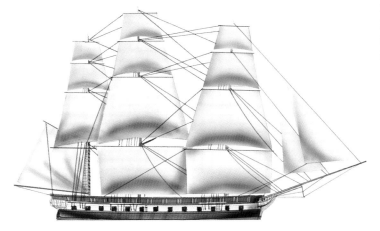

Length: 50m (164ft)

Beam: 12.5m (41ft)

Depth: 4.1m (13ft 4in)

Displacement: 1867t

Rigging: three masts; square rig

Armament: 49 32pdr guns;

four 8pdr guns

Complement: 480

Great Britain

Like all Isambard Kingdom Brunel's ships, *Great Britain* was an epoch-making achievement: the biggest iron ship built up to that time (1843), the first to be intended for deep-sea voyaging, the first to be driven by a screw propeller rather than paddles, and the first screw steamer to cross the Atlantic.

On 26 July 1845, *Great Britain* made her first voyage from Liverpool to New York, in 14 days and 21 hours. In 1852, following a three-year lay-up, *Great Britain* was redirected to the Australia run. Hulked in the Falklands in 1866, she was returned to Britain and restored to her original specification in the 1970s, and is now a museum ship in Bristol.

Length: 98.1m (322ft)
Beam: 15.4m (50ft 6in)
Depth: 4.9m (16ft)
Displacement: 3270t
Rigging: six masts; second mast square-rigged, all others fore-and-aft-rigged
Machinery: single screw; four-cylinder engine
Complement: 350 passengers, 300 crew
Cargo: 260 passengers; general goods
Routes: transatlantic; Great Britain –Australia, Great Britain–San Francisco

Bertha

Thought to have been designed by Isambard Kingdom Brunel and built of rivetted iron by Lunel & Co in Bristol, the dredger *Bertha* is thought to be the oldest steam vessel in the world that is still afloat.

Bertha's official designation was that of a 'drag boat' because she hauled herself along on chains fixed to the quaysides. She was what would now be called a dredger. Built in 1844, her long working life was spent scraping mud from Bridgwater docks in Somerset with a dozer blade fixed to the end of a long pole mounted aft. The docks were opened by the Great Western Railway in 1841, and were later operated by British Rail. *Bertha* was retired in 1968 after 124 years of service, when the docks were converted by Somerset County Council into a marina. *Bertha* was taken over by the International Sailing Craft Association, and is on display at Eyemouth in the Scottish Borders as one of the 'core collection' of British heritage ships.

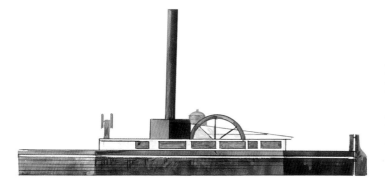

Length: 16.4m (54ft)

Beam: 4.2m (13ft 9in)

Depth: 0.9m (3ft)

Displacement: 64t

Rigging: not applicable

Machinery: single-acting

Complement: not known

Routes: River Parrett, England

Washington

In 1846, when the US government subsidized the transatlantic mail service, American companies began to compete with the established British lines on the Atlantic run.

The wooden-hulled paddle steamer *Washington*, launched at New York in 1847 for the Ocean Steam Navigation Company, was the first American liner. She operated successfully until 1857, when Congress stopped the mail subsidy and she was withdrawn. *Washington* and her sister ship *Herman* ran a regular service between New York, Cowes on the Isle of Wight and the German port of Bremen.

Length: 70.1m (230ft)

Beam: 12.2m (40ft)

Depth: 9.4m (31ft)

Displacement: 1750t

Rigging: three masts, square-rigged on fore and main; spanker on mizzen

Machinery: sidewheels, side lever

Complement: not known

Cargo: passengers, light freight, mails

Routes: New York–Bremen

Agamemnon

The first British warship built with screw propulsion, *Agamemnon* was launched at Woolwich in 1852. She was the prototype for a generation of steam-powered warships.

Her original design was drawn up in 1847 as a direct response to the French 90-gun *La Napoléon*. In the Crimean War, she was flagship of the British Black Sea Fleet, taking part in the shelling of Sevastopol in October 1854 and of Fort Kinburn at the mouth of the Dnieper River in 1855. She laid part of the first transatlantic telegraph cable in 1858, during which her screw was protected by an outrigger. *Agamemnon* returned to normal duties later in 1858 and served on the Caribbean and North American stations. She was paid off in 1862, lay unused for several years, and was finally sold in 1870.

Length: 70.2m (230ft 4in)
Beam: 16.9m (55ft 4in)
Depth: 7.3m (24ft 1in)
Displacement: 5080t
Rigging: three masts; square rig
Machinery: single screw, trunk; 2268hp
Armament: 34 203mm (8in) guns; one 68pdr gun; 56 32pdr guns
Complement: 860

Powhatan

***Powhatan* (1852) was the largest of the US Navy's paddle-wheel frigates. She served as flagship to Commodore Perry in his second Japanese mission of 1854, and the trade treaty of Kanagawa was signed on her deck.**

The imposing sight of US steam-powered warships played its own part in the 'opening' of Japan to international trade in the 1850s. During the American Civil War, *Powhatan* took part in blockades and coastal bombardments of the Confederate States. She then served in the Pacific and Atlantic, until she was broken up in 1887.

Length: 77.3m (253ft 10in)
Beam: 13.7m (45ft)
Depth: 5.6m (18ft 6in)
Displacement: 3479t
Rigging: three masts; barque rig
Machinery: sidewheels, steam
Armament: one 279mm (11in) gun; 10 228mm (9in) guns; five 12pdr guns
Complement: 289

Bretagne

Launched at Brest on 17 February 1855, the mighty steam-powered three-decker *Bretagne* put France firmly in the lead for capital ship design, if only for a few years.

For the first time, sail was used as an auxiliary to steam in a capital ship. *Bretagne* was based with the Mediterranean Fleet at Toulon. She was converted to a training vessel in 1866.

Length: 81m (265ft 8in)

Beam: 18.1m (59ft 4in)

Depth: not known

Displacement: 6770t

Rigging: three masts; square rig

Machinery: single screw, steam; 1200hp

Armament: 130 guns

Complement: c900

Gloire

The success of French armoured batteries in the Crimean War, and the necessity for protecting vessels against shellfire (which had steadily increased in power and accuracy), soon brought about the permanent use of armour in warship construction, resulting in the world's first true ironclad warship.

Construction started in March 1858 at Toulon, and the vessel was named *Gloire*. Because of the greatly increased weight of the armour plating, which covered the entire hull, questions were asked regarding the strength of the vessel. This was solved by fitting a thick layer of sheet metal, nearly 10mm (⅜in) thick, beneath the upper wooden deck and securely fitting

it to the hull side. Original plans to arm *Gloire* with 6.4in (163mm) smoothbores were changed, and rifled versions were carried instead. With the introduction of the ironclad, Napoleon III at last saw a chance to rival Great Britain; *Gloire* and her two sister ships, *Normandie* and *Invincible*, were to form the basis of his powerful French fleet.

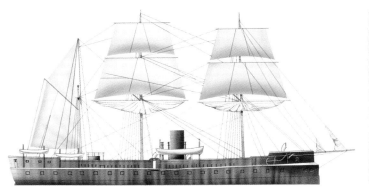

Displacement: 5630t

Dimensions: 77.9m x 17m x 8.5m (255ft 6in x 55ft 9in x 27ft 10in)

Machinery: single screw, horizontal return connecting rod, eight boilers; 2500hp

Armament: 36 162mm (6.4in) guns

Armour: belt 119–110mm (4.7–4in)

Speed: 12.5 knots

Range: not known

Complement: 570

Warrior

In response to the French *Gloire* class, in 1860 Britain launched the *Warrior*, an ironclad broadside frigate intended to overtake and destroy any warship then afloat. The French vessels were wooden-hulled covered in iron: *Warrior* was constructed wholly of iron, which made it possible to be built much larger.

Larger and than any other warship, she was also faster: under sail alone she made 13 knots and once made more than 17 knots under sail and steam. Designed by Isaac Watts, she was the forerunner of a long line of powerful British capital ships. *Warrior* was fully restored in the 1980s and is now a museum ship at Portsmouth Dockyard alongside the *Victory*.

Displacement: 9137t
Dimensions: 128m x 17.8m x 7.9m (420ft x 58ft 4in x 267ft)
Machinery: single screw, horizontal single expansion trunk, 10 boilers; 5267hp
Armament: six 110pdr guns; 26 68pdr guns
Armour: belt 115mm (4.5in); battery 115mm (4.5in); bulkheads 115mm (4.5in)
Speed: 14 knots
Range: 1950km (1210 miles) at 10 knots
Complement: 707

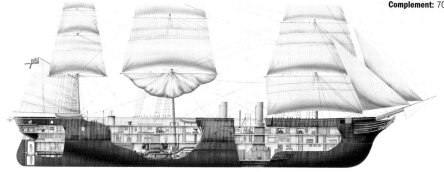

Alabama

One of the most famous commerce raiders in history, the CSS *Alabama* was ordered for the Confederacy from Britain in 1862.

Raphael Semmes took her to sea in August of the same year, narrowly escaping seizure by British officials. Meeting up with her tender *Agrippina*, *Alabama* took on guns, ammunition and stores prior to commencing a 22-month-long cruise covering 120,700km (75,000 miles) without once touching at a Southern port. During this time, *Alabama* destroyed or captured 66 vessels valued at more than $6 million. She was sunk by the sloop-of-war USS *Kearsarge* at Cherbourg, France, in June 1864.

Displacement: 1050t

Dimensions: 67m x 9.6m x 4.2m

(220ft x 31ft 8in x 14ft)

Machinery: single screw

Armament: one 162mm (6.4in) gun;

one 68 pdr gun; six 32pdr guns

Speed: 13 knots

Range: not known

Complement: 145

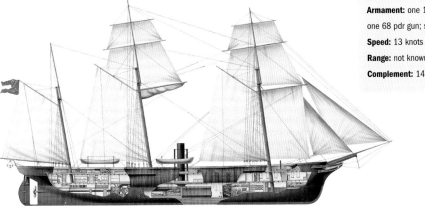

Monitor

At the outbreak of the Civil War, the US Congress asked for proposals for ironclad for the US Navy to counter an ironclad being built for the Confederacy based on the former Union vessel *Merrimac*. Among the 16 submissions was a design from John Ericcson, called the *Monitor*.

Ericcson's vessel, launched on 30 January 1862, had a low freeboard and a hull made up of two halves, one on top of the other. The lower section contained machinery, furnaces, crew quarters and bunkers; the larger upper hull overlapped the lower, forming a large armoured raft with only 457mm (18in) of freeboard, so presenting a small target area. The sides were protected with laminated armour. As an answer to the 178mm (7in) and 203mm (8in) guns likely to be carried by the *Merrimack*, two 280mm (11in) smooth-bores were carried. The single turret, giving all-round fire, was covered with eight 254mm (1in) plates and also acted as a giant ventilating shaft.

Monitor arrived at Hampton Roads on 9 March 1862, a day after the *Merrimack* (now renamed *Virginia*) had destroyed two large Union wooden-hulled frigates and fought a drawn battle. *Monitor* served as a template for larger monitors, as such vessels came to be known, such as the *Monadnock* seen here, which was commissioned in 1864.

Displacement: 3400t

Dimensions: 78.8m x 16m x 3.9m (258ft 6in x 52ft 9in x 12ft 8in)

Machinery: twin screw, vibrating lever, four boilers; 1400hp

Armament: four 381mm (15in) guns

Armour: belt 127mm (5in); turrets 254mm (10in); deck 381mm (1.5in)

Speed: 9 knots

Range: not known

Complement: 150

Banshee

Built for speed alone, the *Banshee* was less successful as a legitimate trader than as a blockade runner for the Confederacy during the American Civil War. She later carried cattle and fruit to and from Cuba.

Launched in 1862 the paddle steamer *Banshee* was the first steel-built ship to cross the Atlantic, leaving Liverpool on 2 March 1863. She was built to operate out of Nassau in the Bahamas, running the blockade imposed by the Union Navy on the ports of the Confederacy, carrying in manufactured goods and munitions, and carrying out cotton. By 21 November 1863, when she was captured by USS *Grand Gulf* near Cape Hatteras, bound for Wilmington, she had already made eight (some reports say 15) return trips.

Tonnage: 325 gross registered tons (grt)
Dimensions: 65.2m x 6.2m x 3m
(214ft x 20ft 3in x 10ft)
Machinery: sidewheels, two-cylinder
oscillating; 120hp
Service speed: 12 knots
Role: cargo carrier (blockade runner)
Route: Bahamas–Eastern Seaboard
Capacity: not known
Constructor: Jones, Quiggin & Co, Liverpool
Material: steel on iron frames
Built for: John T Lawrence & Co

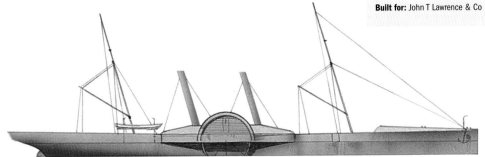

Hope/Savannah

The paddle steamer *Hope* and her sister ship the *Colonel Lamb* were constructed in Liverpool during the American Civil War as blockade runners for the Confederate Navy.

The blockade runners were mostly steel-built to save weight and allow them to carry more cargo, and were some of the fastest ships in service at the time. On trials in 1864, *Colonel Lamb* achieved 16.7 knots, her two oscillating-cylinder engines producing an estimated 1300hp. *Hope* had some initial success, but was captured by USS *Eolus* in 1865. She was sold and became the SS *Savannah* that year, and was sold again the following year to Spain. She was broken up in 1885.

Tonnage: 113 grt

Dimensions: 90.2m x 10.55m (on deck) x 3.35m (296ft x 34ft 7in x 11ft)

Machinery: paddle wheels, oscillating; 1300hp

Service speed: 14 knots

Role: general cargo vessel (blockade runner)

Route: Nassau–Charleston

Capacity: 560t

Constructor: Jones, Quiggin & Co, Liverpool

Material: steel

Built for: not known

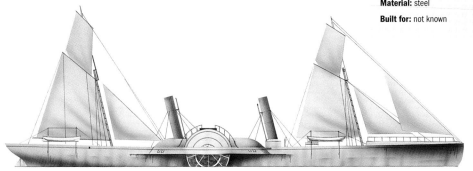

Parramatta

Although the change to iron hulls for oceangoing ships began during the 1840s, relatively large vessels were still being built in wood as late as the early 1870s.

The *Parramatta* was a Blackwall frigate (the type originated in the 1830s at the Blackwall Yard on the Thames). They were called frigates because they were originally designed to escort other 'East Indiamen'. *Parramatta* was the last major ship built by James Laing of Sunderland, and was one of the largest wooden merchant ships ever launched. By the time she was launched in 1866 the cost of iron construction was some 30 per cent lower – around £14 per ton, as opposed to £20 – than that of a wooden ship.

Tonnage: 1521grt
Dimensions: 56m x 12m (185ft x 40ft)
Role: passenger and wool carrier
Route: Great Britain–Australia
Constructor: James Laing
Material: wood

Adelaide

From its beginnings, the paddle steamer was used on rivers as well as on oceanic routes: indeed, the paddle steamer lasted much longer in confined waters than it did on the open seas, where it was replaced by screw-driven vessels.

Adelaide was believed to be the oldest wooden-hulled steamer still operating in 2005, 139 years after she was built in Echuca, Victoria, Australia. One of the earliest economically important industries in Australia was sheep farming, and the *Adelaide* was built for towing barges laden with wool up and down the Murray River in southern Australia. However, for most of her life, from 1872 to 1957, she worked at hauling trains of barges laden with red gum logs to the Echuca sawmills. *Adelaide* was laid up ashore between 1963 and 1984, but was then entirely refurbished and refloated, to operate in conjunction with a restored barge, *D 26*.

Tonnage: 58 grt

Dimensions: 23.3m x 5.2m x 0.7m (76ft 5in x 17ft x 2ft 4in)

Machinery: sidewheels, two-cylinder double-acting; 36hp

Service speed: not known

Role: river tugboat

Route: Murray River

Capacity: not applicable

Constructor: G Link, Echuca, Victoria

Material: wood

Built for: J G Grassie, Echuca, Victoria

Owner: City of Echuca

Canada

The French Compagnie Générale Transatlantique built a number of paddle steamers. All were converted to screw propulsion and most were lengthened in the process.

In 1866, a sidewheel paddle steamer named the *Panama* was launched at St Nazaire for the Compagnie Générale Transatlantique. She operated between France and Central America. In 1876, she was converted to screw propulsion by Leslie on Tyneside, and was renamed *Canada*, for the North Atlantic service; she returned to the Central American service in 1886. Electric lighting was installed in 1888, and in 1892 she received triple-expansion engines to replace the Maudslay compound powerplant. *Canada* was scrapped in 1908.

Tonnage: 3400grt (later 4054grt)

Dimensions: 108.3m x 13.35m
(355ft 5in x 43ft 9in)

Machinery: sidewheels, two side lever; later one-shaft, compound; later triple expansion

Service speed: 12 knots

Role: passenger liner

Route: St Nazaire-Vera Cruz; Le Havre-New York; Le Havre-Panama

Constructor: Chantiers de Penhoët, St Nazaire (under supervision of Scott & Co, Greenock)

Material: iron

Built for: Compagnie Générale Transatlantique

Friedrich Karl

The French-built *Friedrich Karl* was one of the first two modern ironclads to be added to the expanding Imperial German/Prussian Navy. The other vessel was the *Kronprinz*, built by France's major European shipbuilding rival – the British.

The *Friedrich Karl* was completed in 1867, three years before the Franco-Prussian war. Even when the German shipbuilding industry did get under way, heavy forgings and machinery were still imported from Britain. The *Friedrich Karl* was a central battery ship, originally planned to carry 26 72pdr guns, all on the main gun deck. Her wrought-iron armour had 381mm (15in) of teak backing.

Displacement: 6822t

Dimensions: 94.1m x 16.6m x 8m
(308ft 10in x 54ft 6in x 26ft 5in)

Machinery: single screw, horizontal single expansion, six boilers; 3550hp

Armament: 16 210mm (8.2in) guns

Armour: belt 127–115mm (5–4.5in);
battery 115mm (4.5in)

Speed: 13.5 knots

Range: 3560km (2210 miles) at 10 knots

Complement: 531

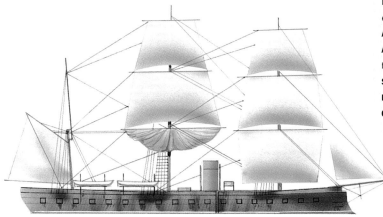

Natchez

In their heyday, the paddle-wheel steamboats on the Mississippi were among the most efficient means of carrying goods and passengers as the United States expanded westwards, until superseded by the railroads.

The *Natchez* of 1869 was the sixth of seven riverboats of the same name built for Thomas P Leathers. Said to be an ungainly-looking craft, she soon had a well-deserved reputation for speed; in 1870, she steamed the 1672km (1039 miles) from New Orleans to St Louis at an average of 11.17 knots, breaking a record which had stood for 25 years. She was perhaps best known for the celebrated (but inconclusive) race against fellow steamboat the *Rob't E Lee* that same year. *Natchez* remained in service until 1879.

Tonnage: 1547grt

Dimensions: 91.7m x 13m (301ft x 42ft 6in)

Machinery: sidewheels; engine type not known

Service speed: 10 knots

Route: New Orleans-St Louis riverboat

Capacity: not known

Material: wood

Built for: Thomas P Leathers

Devastation

***Devastation* was the first of a new type of seagoing mastless turret ship known as the 'breastwork monitor'.**

Designed for the Royal Navy by Sir Edward Reed and completed in 1873, she had a low hull with a greater freeboard than contemporary monitors and a raised armoured redoubt, or breastwork, amidships on which the turrets were mounted, one at each end. The armoured freeboard provided stability, while the guns were placed considerably higher than in the monitor type; the turret-turning gear was also well protected. By dispensing

with rigging, a far greater arc of fire was obtained, and the low freeboard could be used with greater safety. However, even with the raised freeboard *Devastation* was a very wet ship in any kind of sea.

Displacement: 9330t
Dimensions: 93.6m x 19m x 8m (307ft x 62ft x 26ft 8in)
Machinery: twin screws, horizontal direct acting, eight boilers; 6640hp
Armament: four 305mm (12in) guns
Armour: belt 215–305mm (8.5–12in); breastwork 254–305mm (10–12in); turrets 254–356mm (10–14in); deck 52–76mm (2–3in)
Speed: 13.8 knots
Range: 9660km (6000 miles) at 10 knots
Complement: 358

City of Berlin

The Inman Line operating out of Liverpool was one of the pioneers of steam on the North Atlantic route. Its vessels, named after European cities, were among the largest of their era.

The Inman Line's steamer *City of Berlin* entered service on the transatlantic route in May 1875 and was the biggest steamer on the route for some years. In the year in which she entered service, the *City of Berlin* briefly held the Blue Riband, awarded to the ship making the fastest transatlantic crossing, in both directions. In 1887, the ship was re-engined with the newly developed triple-expansion machinery, from Laird Bros of Birkenhead, which proved to be an outstanding success. She was transferred to the American Line in 1893, but also made voyages for the Red Star Line. She was eventually scrapped in 1921.

Tonnage: 5491grt

Dimensions: 149m x 13.4m (489ft x 44ft)

Machinery: one-shaft, compound (later triple expansion); 5200hp (later 6025hp)

Service speed: 15 knots

Role: passenger liner

Route: North Atlantic

Capacity: 202 cabins; 1500 3rd class berths

Constructor: not known

Material: steel

Built for: Inman Line

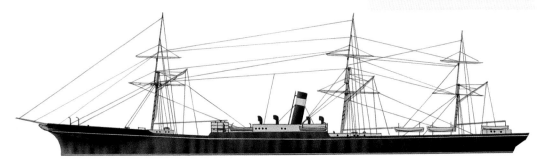

Collingwood

In 1880, HMS *Collingwood* was laid down for the Royal Navy. She was the first of the 'Admiral' class of barbette-ship, designed to compete with the French 'Amiral Duperré' type.

The class had a compound armour belt which was low and short. Above the belt, coal bunkers 3m (10ft) deep were fitted to assist in maintaining stability should the unprotected sides become damaged. The barbettes, one at each end of the superstructure, were polygonal in shape with the sides sloping at 60 degrees.

The main guns were about 6m (20ft) above water, with the secondary battery positioned in the superstructure amidships. *Collingwood* was the first British battleship to have a mixed armament. The overall layout of the *Collingwood* fixed the pattern for future British battleships until the 'all big gun' *Dreadnought* of 1906.

Displacement: 9500t
Dimensions: 99m x 20.7m x 8m (325ft x 68ft x 26ft 4in)
Machinery: twin screws, inverted compound, 12 boilers; 9600hp
Armament: four 12in (305mm) guns; six 6in (152mm) guns; four 14in (356mm) TT
Armour: belt 457-203mm (18-8in); bulkheads 406-178mm (16-7in); barbettes 292-254mm (11.5-10in); deck 76mm (3in)
Speed: 16.8 knots
Range: 15,742km (8500nm) at 10 knots
Complement: 498

Dogali

Laid down in 1885 in Britain as the *Salamis* for Greece, but taken over by Italy, the Italian cruiser *Dogali* was the first warship to be equipped with triple expansion engines.

When first completed, she carried a light fore and aft rig, but this was discarded in the 1890s. The 152mm (6in) guns were placed one on the forecastle, which had a slight turtle back deck, one aft, and one each side in the waist amidships. Designed by Sir William White, she was a good example of the Elswick cruiser in spite of her light build. Sold in 1908 to Uruguay, *Dogali* was discarded in 1914, but she was not scrapped until 1930.

Displacement: 2050t

Dimensions: 76.2m x 11.3m x 4.4m (250ft x 37ft x 14ft 6in)

Machinery: twin screws, triple expansion, four boilers; 5012hp

Armament: four 152mm (6in) guns; four 356mm (14in) TT

Armour: deck 152-52mm (6-2in); shields 115mm (4.5in)

Speed: 19.7 knots

Complement: 224

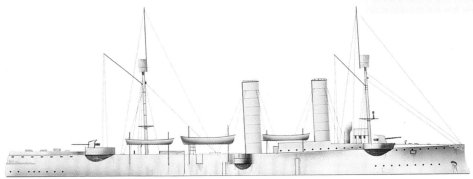

Charleston

In the United States during the mid-1880s there was a lull in the building of warships, to enable the erection of suitable steel-making plant and availability of sufficient work to make it profitable.

Although several warships were authorized in 1885 and 1886, none was laid down until 1887. Plans for the new cruisers were purchased in England, but all construction materials were of domestic manufacture. The first of this group was the *Charleston*, a duplicate of the Japanese *Naniwana*, one of several successful cruisers developed from the *Esmeralda* built for Chile in 1884. Protective armour deck ran the full length of the ship. The main deck was unbroken, and carried one 203mm (8in) gun at each end in a low 54mm (2in) high-plated barbette. The secondary guns were also on this deck, three each side.

Displacement: 4200t

Dimensions: 97.5m x 14m x 5.6m (320ft x 46ft x 18ft 6in)

Machinery: twin screws, horizontal compound, six boilers; 7650hp

Armament: two 203mm (8in) guns; six 152mm (6in) guns

Armour: deck 76–54mm (3–2in)

Speed: 18.9 knots

Range: 4828km (3000 miles) at 10 knots

Complement: 300

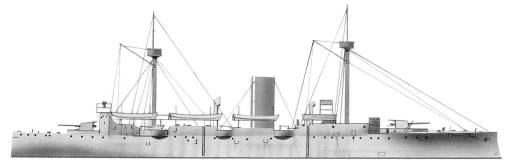

Gymnôte

Interest in submarines grew towards the end of the nineteenth century, when new, more effective power plants became available. A single-hull steel submarine designed by Gustave Zédé, *Gymnôte*, was ordered in 1886 and proved to be a great success.

Power for *Gymnôte* was supplied from batteries made up of 204 cells and weighing nearly one-third of the displacement. Experiments with hydroplanes led to their being incorporated in the design of all subsequent submarines. The French were successful with several of their early submarines built during the late 1880s and 1890s, and *Gymnôte* was no exception, making about 2000 successful dives. The torpedoes were carried in drop collars, one on each beam. *Gymnôte* had a raised conning tower added in 1898, so foreshadowing the shape of submarines to come. *Gymnôte* was modernized in 1898 and stricken in 1909.

Displacement: 30t surfaced; 31t submerged
Dimensions: 17.8m x 1.8m x 1.7m
(58ft 5in x 6ft x 5ft 6in)
Machinery: single screw, electric;
33.4hp/25hp
Armament: two 356mm (14in) TT
Speed: 7.3 knots surfaced; 4.3 knots submerged
Range: 120km (65nm) at 7.3 knots; 57km
(31nm) at 5 knots
Complement: 5

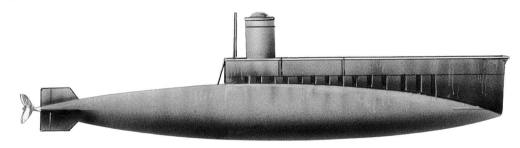

Lawhill

In a career lasting almost half a century, the four-masted barque *Lawhill* made over 50 major voyages.

The *Lawhill* was built in 1892 for the jute trade, but was too late to succeed in it and was given over to general cargo. In 1900, she was sold to the Anglo-American Oil Co to carry case oil (kerosene) to the Far East. She passed into Finnish ownership in 1914. Gustaf Erikson bought her in 1917, and she sailed under his flag until 1941, when she was seized in South Africa. *Lawhill* was later sold to Portuguese interests, but never went to sea again. She was scrapped in 1958.

Tonnage: 2816 grt

Dimensions: 96.7m x 13.7m x 7.6m (317ft 4in x 45ft x 25ft 2in)

Machinery: not applicable

Service speed: not applicable

Role: general cargo vessel; case oil carrier; grain carrier; nitrate carrier

Route: not applicable

Constructor: W B Thompson, Dundee

Material: steel

Built for: Charles Barrie

Texas

Authorized in August 1886 and laid down three years later but not completed until August 1895, *Texas* was the first modern US capital ship.

The design was prepared by the Barrow Shipbuilding Company, England. The short 36m (118ft) waterline belt was of Harvey nickel steel; two complete decks were fitted above the belt to give good seakeeping qualities. Two 305mm (12in) guns in single turrets were mounted on the main deck, *en échelon*, and protected by a redoubt which did not extend down to the waterline armour belt. Four 152mm (6in) guns were positioned on the second deck, and two more on the main deck. The main delay in completing *Texas* was that the armour factory was not ready to make steel until 1891, two years later than planned. However, the delay enabled the designers to improve the ship's protection.

Displacement: 6665t

Dimensions: 94.1m x 19.5m x 6.9m (309ft x 64ft x 22ft 6in)

Machinery: twin screw, vertical triple expansion, four boilers; 8600hp

Armament: two 305mm (12in) guns; six 152mm (6in) guns; four 356mm (14in) TT

Armour: belt 152–305mm (6–12in); turrets 305mm (12in); redoubt 305mm (12in); deck 52–76mm (2–3in)

Speed: 17.8 knots

Range: not known

Complement: 392

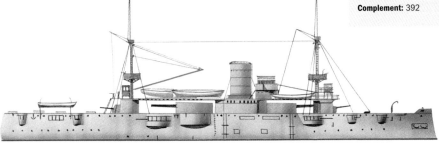

Havock

Completed in January 1894, *Havock* was the world's first torpedo-boat destroyer, later to be known simply as a destroyer.

In the early 1890s, considerable concern was felt in the British Admiralty regarding the rapid growth in size and numbers of French torpedo-boats. Speeds of 25 knots were being attained, and the leading French torpedo-boat builder, Normand, was planning a boat of 30 knots. This prototype vessel eventually became the

Forban. Britain's existing torpedo gun-boats were unable to cope with these torpedo-boats, but in early 1892 Yarrow put forward plans for a super torpedo-boat that would eventually be called a destroyer. Two designs were submitted and four vessels were ordered: steel-hulled, lightly built, with a turtle back deck forward, and armed with one 76mm (3in) gun mounted on a raised platform, and three 6pdrs (one aft and one on each beam). They also carried one bow torpedo tube and two trainable deck tubes.

Displacement: 275t

Dimensions: 56.4m x 5.6m x 2.2m (185ft x 18ft 6in x 7ft 6in)

Machinery: twin screws, triple expansion; 3400hp

Armament: one 76mm (3in) gun; three 6pdr guns; three 14in (356mm) TT

Speed: 26.7 knots

Range: 1610km (1000 miles) at 10 knots

Complement: 43

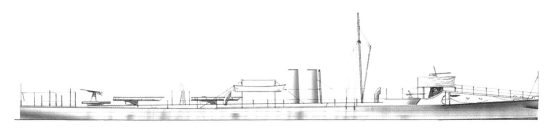

St Louis

The *St Louis* and her sister ship the *St Paul* were the first American-built passenger liners to be fitted with screw propulsion.

St Louis joined the American Line's service between New York and Southampton in 1894, with three classes of accommodation. In 1898, *St Louis* was briefly taken up by the US Navy as an armed merchant cruiser during the Spanish–American War. In 1903, she was reboilered and had her two funnels raised in height. Just before World War I she was refitted, with second- and third-class accommodation only, and was switched to the Liverpool service. She was taken up by the US Navy as the *Louisville* and operated as a troopship from late 1918 until 1920. She caught fire while under refit, and was sold to be converted as an exhibition ship. The transformation was never completed, and she was towed to Genoa and broken up in 1924.

Tonnage: 11,629 grt

Dimensions: 163.2m x 19.2m (535ft 6in x 63ft)

Machinery: two-shaft, triple expansion

Service speed: 19 knots

Role: passenger liner; armed merchant cruiser; troopship

Route: North Atlantic

Capacity: 350 1st, 220 2nd, 800 3rd

Constructor: W Cramp & Co, Philadelphia

Material: steel

Built for: American Line

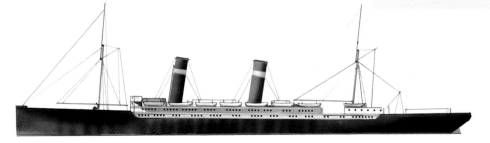

Esmeralda

The Chilean *Esmeralda* of 1894 was typical of the armoured cruisers which were built by the British company Armstrong. She combined high speed, great offensive powers and good protection.

The belt was 106m (350ft) long and 2.1m (7ft) deep. Behind this, the armoured deck sloped down at the sides connecting with the lower edge of the belt, as well as sloping down at the bow and stern. The powerful main armament comprised an 203mm (8in) gun forward and aft, each firing a 114kg (250lb) shell at the rate of four rounds in 62 seconds. The secondary battery spread along the sides behind shields, with eight 152mm (6in) guns per side. A mix of smaller weapons filled the gaps between. A screen was positioned in front of the bridge and over the forecastle to deflect the blast from the forward firing guns. This was the first time such a protective device had been fitted to a warship, and such screens were to be used extensively on all later types of warships.

Displacement: 7000t

Dimensions: 133m x 16.2m x 6.2m (436ft x 53ft x 20ft 3in)

Machinery: twin screw, vertical triple expansion; 16,000hp

Armament: two 203mm (8in) guns; 16 152mm (6in) guns; three 18in (451mm) TT

Armour: belt 152mm (6in); deck 52-38mm (2-1.5in); shields 115mm (4.5in)

Speed: 22.25 knots

Range: not known

Complement: 500

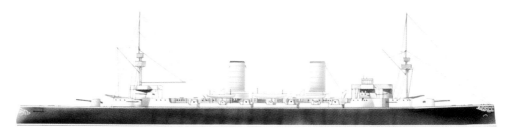

Forban

Early torpedo-boats were armed with spar torpedoes and were usually launches. By the 1870s, they had become specially built light craft of high speed and small size, and without any protection, relying upon surprise for a successful attack.

In 1876, the US Navy ordered a large wooden launch from the Herreshoff Company with a speed of 17.5 knots. One year later, the first torpedo-boat to be equipped with the self-powered Locomotive Whitehead torpedo, the

Lightning, was built by Thornycroft. As the the new torpedo boats developed, so the French began to build them both for coast defence and use with the battle fleet. By 1895, the French Navy had entire flotillas of these nimble craft, totalling over 250 vessels. The French seagoing torpedo-boat *Forban* was launched in July 1895 from the yard of Normand. An improved version of the preceding *Filibustier*, and with more powerful engines, at her trials *Forban* achieved slightly more than 31 knots, making her the fastest vessel in the world at the time.

Displacement: 150t
Dimensions: 44m x 4.7m x 1.3m
(144ft 6in x 15ft 3in x 4ft 5in)
Machinery: twin screw, triple expansion, two boilers; 3260hp
Armament: two 37mm (1.46in) guns; two 356mm (14in) TT
Speed: 31 knots
Range: not known
Complement: 27

Majestic

In 1893, the British decided to construct nine powerful battleships, known as the 'Majestic' class. These were designed to maintain Royal Navy superiority over any two other navies.

An important improvement in the design of the 'Majestic' was made by sloping down the sides of the armoured deck so that it joined the bottom of the belt, greatly increasing the protection of the vital areas. A new type of wire-bound 305mm (12in) gun was installed as the main armament, and was subsequently used in nearly all battleships for the next 15 years. All-round

loading was also introduced as was better protection in the form of hoods. The secondary battery was increased to 12 152mm (6in) guns, all in single casemates, eight on the gun deck and four on the main deck between the main armament. The anti-torpedo battery was also greatly increased by installing 12pdrs instead of 6pdrs.

Displacement: 14,890t

Dimensions: 128.3m x 22.9m x 8.2m (421ft x 75ft x 27ft)

Machinery: twin screws, triple expansion, eight boilers; 12,000hp

Armament: four 305mm (12in) guns; 12 152mm (6in) guns; five 457mm (18in) TT

Armour: belt 229mm (9in); casemate 152mm (6in); bulkheads 356–305mm (14–12in); barbettes 356mm (14in); hoods 254mm (10in); deck 102–64mm (4–2.5in)

Speed: 17.9 knots

Range: not known

Complement: 672

D'Entrecasteaux

A flush-decked protected cruiser built in 1896, designed by Lagane and intended for service overseas, *D'Entrecasteaux* was one of two such vessels planned by the French navy.

The cruiser's 240mm (9.4in) guns were in single turrets fore and aft; eight of the 140mm (5.5in) guns were in casemates on the main deck, with four more behind shields one deck above. The hull sides had a tumble-home, so allowing better axial fire. Each of the secondary guns had an ammunition supply of 200 rounds, with 75 rounds for each of the 240mm (9.4in). The forward boiler room housed four boilers, while the aft boiler room had a single boiler. *D'Entrecasteaux* burnt 15.5t of coal every hour at full power: she carried a maximum coal stock of 1000t.

Displacement: 7995t

Dimensions: 117m x 17.8m x 7.5m (383ft 10in x 58ft 6in x 24ft 7in)

Machinery: twin screws, vertical triple expansion, five boilers; 14,500hp

Armament: two 240mm (9.4in) guns; 12 140mm (5.5in) guns; two 457mm (18in) TT

Armour: deck 102–56mm (4–2.2in); turrets 254mm (10in); casemates/shields 56mm (2.2in)

Speed: 19.2 knots

Range: 2222km (1200nm) at 19 knots

Complement: 559

Fuji

**Designed by the Thames Ironworks,
Fuji and her sister ship *Yashima* were
the templates for future Japanese
battleship designs.**

In the early 1890s, Japan anticipated war
with China, but feared the powerful
Chinese turret ships, *Ting Yuan* and *Chen
Yuan*. Japan ordered her first major

battleships from British yards to an
improved 'Royal Sovereign' design. The
305mm (12in) guns, placed in twin turrets
on the centreline had a rate of fire of one
round every 80 seconds. Delivered after
the end of the 1894–95 war with China,
Fuji played a major part in the war with
Russia in 1904–05. *Yashima* was sunk by
a mine in May 1904.

Displacement: 12,533t

Dimensions: 118.8m x 22.2m x 8m
(412ft x 73ft x 26ft 6in)

Machinery: twin screw, vertical triple
expansion, 10 boilers; 14,000hp

Armament: four 305mm (12in) guns; 10
152mm (6in) guns; five 18in (457mm) TT

Armour: belt 457–356mm (18–14in);
upper belt 102mm (4in); deck 64mm
(2.5in); barbettes 356–229mm (14–9in);
casemates 152–52mm (6–2in)

Speed: 19.2 knots

Range: not known

Complement: 637

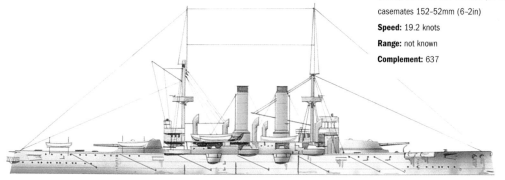

Kaiser Wilhelm der Grosse

The *Kaiser Wilhelm der Grosse* was not only the biggest and fastest liner of her day, but also the first to have four funnels and remotely actuated watertight doors.

By the 1890s, Germany's merchant marine felt that it was ready to challenge the British domination of the North Atlantic. To do so, the Norddeutscher Lloyd Line ordered the largest and most powerful ship built up to that time. The *Kaiser Wilhelm der Grosse*, launched in 1897, narrowly escaped destruction in June 1900, when fire broke out at New York; in 1905 she was rammed by the British freighter *Orinoco* off Cherbourg, France, with the loss of five lives. She was refitted to carry emigrants in 1914 and on the outbreak of war was armed as a merchant cruiser. Coaling in the Spanish Sahara on 21 August 1914, she was surprised by the British cruiser HMS *Highflyer* and was scuttled to avoid capture.

Tonnage: 14,349grt (later 13,952grt)
Dimensions: 191.2m x 20.1m (627ft 5in x 66ft)
Machinery: two-shaft, triple expansion; 14,000hp
Service speed: 22 knots
Role: passenger liner; armed merchant cruiser
Route: Bremen–New York
Capacity: 332 1st, 343 2nd, 1074 3rd
Constructor: AG Vulcan, Stettin (Szczecin)
Material: steel
Built for: Norddeutscher Lloyd Line

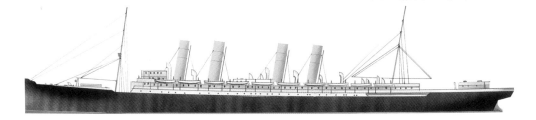

Châteaurenault

A purpose-built commerce raider, the French navy's _Châteaurenault_ of 1898 had good range and high speed, but was lightly armed.

She was designed to resemble an ocean liner – her four equally spaced funnels gave that impression at a distance of 10km (6 miles). Protection was provided by a full-length armoured deck, curving down at the ends and sides. Above this was a cellular layer. The 165mm (6.4in) guns were carried one on the foredeck and one aft, with three 140mm (5.5in) guns on each beam and four in the casemates. Around half of the length of the ship was taken up with machinery. Her maximum speed was 24.5 knots.

Displacement: 7898t

Dimensions: 135m x 17m x 7.4m (442ft 11in x 55ft 9in x 23ft 3in)

Machinery: triple screws, vertical triple expansion, 14 boilers; 24,964hp

Armament: two 165mm (6.4in) guns; six 140mm (5.5in) guns

Armour: deck 76mm (3in); casemates 38mm (1.5in)

Speed: 24.5 knots

Complement: 604

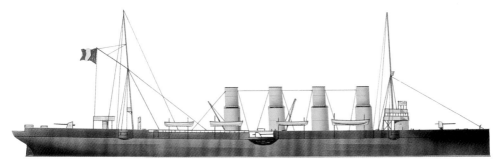

Giuseppe Garibaldi

Severe financial constraints between 1870 and 1890 set back Italy's ambitious plans to replace her fleet of early broadside ironclads.

Several unique warships were delayed in completion due to a lack of funds, and some had to be sold to foreign navies while still under construction. One such group of vessels comprised the powerful armoured cruisers; they were exceedingly well protected for their size, and considered suitable to form in the line with battleships if need be. These were extremely successful cruisers, and the four original ships in this class, launched 1895 to 1897, were sold to Argentina, with one more going to Spain, where she became the *Cristóbal Colón*.

Displacement: 7972t

Dimensions: 111.8m x 18.2m x 7m (366ft 8in x 60ft x 23ft)

Machinery: twin screws, vertical triple expansion, 24 boilers; 14,713hp

Armament: one 254mm (10in) gun; two 203mm (8in) guns; 14 152mm (6in) guns

Armour: belt 203-102mm (8-4in); turrets 203-102mm (8-4in); deck 52mm (2in)

Speed: 19.7 knots

Range: 8149km (4400nm) at 10 knots

Complement: 510

Bayan

Bayan, launched in June 1900, was an armoured cruiser designed in France by Lagane and built for the Imperial Russian Navy at La Seyne.

Bayan was an outstanding design, combining a good balance between offence and defence. She took part in most of the major actions in and around Port Arthur during the Russo–Japanese War in 1904; however, she missed the major battle which took place on 10 August as the Russian Pacific Fleet attempted to reach Vladivostok, after striking a mine in July. *Bayan* was captured by the Japanese in January 1905.

Displacement: 7775t
Dimensions: 137m x 17.5m x 6.5m (449ft 7in x 57ft 6in x 21ft 3in)
Machinery: twin screw, vertical triple expansion, 26 boilers; 17,400hp
Armament: two 203mm (8in) guns, eight 152mm (6in) guns; 20 11pdr guns; two 381mm (15in) TT
Armour: belt 76–203mm (3–8in); casemates and redoubt 76mm (3in)
Speed: 22 knots
Complement: 568

Mikasa

One of the finest examples of a pre-dreadnought battleship, the *Mikasa* combined all the best qualities of the type, and displayed them as Admiral Togo's flagship at the battle of Tsushima.

The last of a group of four battleships laid down under Japan's 1896 announcement of a 10-year naval expansion programme, the *Mikasa* benefited from the earlier improvements in armour and general layout. The *Mikasa* was the flagship of Vice Admiral Togo during the Russo-Japanese War of 1904–05. She blew up in 1905 at Sasebo. Later, after being raised and maintained as a national monument, she was nearly destroyed in World War II. However, she was restored again and is now the last surviving battleship of her era.

Displacement: 15179t

Dimensions: 131.7m x 23.2m x 8.3m (432ft x 76ft x 27ft)

Machinery: twin screws, vertical triple expansion, 25 boilers; 15,000hp

Armament: four 305mm (12in); 14 152mm (6in); four 457mm (18in) TT

Armour: belt 229–102mm (9–4in); battery 152mm (6in); barbettes 356–203mm (14–8in); casemates 152–52mm (6–2in); deck 76–52mm (3–2in)

Speed: 18.6 knots

Range: 14,484km (9000 miles) at 10 knots

Complement: 830

Deutschland

The *Deutschland* of 1900 was Albert Ballin's Hamburg–Amerika Line's only record-breaker; her best Atlantic crossing was made at an average speed of more than 23.5 knots.

The *Deutschland* was built specifically to be the fastest ship across the Atlantic. Her main purpose was to capture the Blue Riband from the rival Norddeutscher Lloyd Line's *Kaiser Wilhelm der Grosse*. In 1900 she accomplished that handsomely, taking the record in both directions on her maiden voyage between Hamburg and New York. She always suffered from excessive vibration and once lost her sternpost and rudder in mid-Atlantic as a result. The *Deutschland* later became a cruise ship and, in 1920, an emigrant ship. She was scrapped in 1925.

Tonnage: 16,502grt (later 16,333grt)
Dimensions: 208.5m x 20.4m
(684ft x 67ft 4in)
Machinery: two-shaft, two six-cylinder
quadruple expansion; 37,800hp
Service speed: 22 knots
Role: liner; cruise ship; emigrant ship
Route: Hamburg–New York
Capacity: 450 1st, 300 2nd, 350 3rd;
487 1st, 36 cb, 1350 3rd
Constructor: AG Vulcan, Stettin (Szczecin)
Material: steel

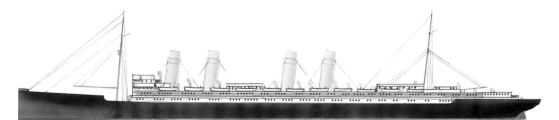

Blücher

The *Blücher* was one of a pair of German ships seized at Pernambuco, where they had taken refuge, when Brazil entered World War I on the side of the Allies in 1917.

The Hamburg–Amerika Line ordered a passenger liner, to be known as the *Blücher*, from Blohm & Voss in Hamburg in 1900. The vessel was launched the following year and entered service between Hamburg and New York in 1902. In 1917, *Blücher* was seized by the Brazilian government at Pernambuco and briefly put into service as the *Leopoldina*. Sold to the French Compagnie Générale Transatlantique and later renamed *Suffren*, she operated between Le Havre and New York until 1928, and was scrapped the following year.

Tonnage: 12,350 grt
Dimensions: 160.2m x 19m
(525ft 7in x 62ft 3in)
Machinery: two-shaft, two eight-cylinder quadruple expansion
Service speed: 15 knots
Role: passenger liner
Route: North Atlantic
Capacity: 500 cb, 250 3rd
Constructor: Blohm & Voss, Hamburg
Material: steel
Built for: Hamburg-Amerika Line

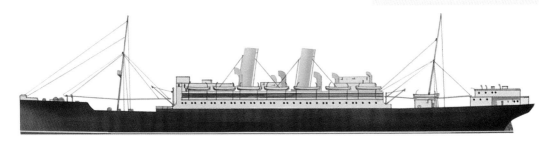

Discovery

The *Discovery* was built in Dundee, Scotland, then a major whaling port as well as a centre for the jute industry, in 1901. Her design was based on an earlier whaling ship of the same name which had carried an 1875 expedition to the Arctic.

Her maiden voyage in 1901, under the command of Robert Falcon Scott, took her to the Ross Sea in Antarctica, where she was to remain until 1904, having been frozen into the ice. She broke free with the help of the supply ship *Morning* and the *Terra Nova*, both of them Dundee whalers; the latter was to carry Scott and his party back south for the fatal polar expedition of 1911–12. Restored by the Maritime Trust in 1986, she is now on display at Dundee.

Tonnage: 1570t displacement

Dimensions: 52.1m x 10.3m x 4.8m (171ft x 33ft 9in x 15ft 9in)

Machinery: one-shaft, auxiliary triple expansion; 450hp

Service speed: 8 knots

Role: research ship; cargo ship; training ship

Route: UK–Antarctica; UK–Hudson Bay; Archangel–Black Sea; UK–Arctic

Constructor: Steven's Yard, Dundee Shipbuilders, Dundee

Material: wood

Built for: British National Antarctic Expedition

Current owner: Dundee Heritage Trust

Bainbridge

Bainbridge was listed as destroyer No. 1 in the US Navy. By the end of World War II, after just over 40 years, the number of destroyers which had been commissioned into the US Navy had reached 890.

Bainbridge, laid down in August 1899 and completed in November 1902, was the lead ship in a class of five. This was the first group of destroyers to have what was to become a characteristic destroyer feature: a raised forecastle to provide better seakeeping qualities. The vessels of the 'Bainbridge' class were also the first group of vessels to be built to a single design, previous destroyers having been built as single units. The four funnels were in two groups, with one torpedo tube between and a second tube right aft. *Bainbridge* and her sister ships spent most of their careers serving with the US Pacific Fleet squadrons forward deployed in the Philippines.

Displacement: 420t

Dimensions: 76.2m x 7.2m x 2m (250ft x 23ft 7in x 6ft 6in)

Machinery: twin screw, vertical triple expansion, four boilers; 8000hp

Armament: two 76mm (3in) guns; two 457mm (18in) TT

Speed: not known

Range: not known

Complement: 73

Thomas W Lawson

The *Thomas W Lawson* was the largest sailing schooner ever built, her seven 58m (190ft) masts each carrying a course, a jib-headed topsail and a topmast staysail plus five headsails.

She was built of steel by the Fore River Ship & Engine Building Company at Quincy, Massachusetts. Launched in 1902, she was employed in the coastal trade originally, carrying 11,000t of coal on each voyage. She was soon converted to carry oil in bulk from the Gulf of Mexico, her draught being too great for the coaling ports. Every halyard, topping lift and sheet aboard the 117.3m-long (385ft) ship was led to one or other of two large steam winches, one forward, the other on the after deckhouse. As a result she needed a crew of just 16 men, but she was unhandy in anything but strong winds. She was lost in heavy weather off the Scilly Isles on 13 December 1907. Only her captain and one of her crewmen survived.

Tonnage: 5218 grt

Dimensions: 117.3m x 15.2m x 10.7m
(385ft x 50ft x 35ft)

Machinery: not applicable

Service speed: not applicable

Role: coal/oil carrier

Route: coastal waters, USA; Atlantic

Capacity: 11,000t (coal)

Constructor: Fore River Ship & Engine
Building Co, Quincy, Massachusetts

Material: steel

Built for: Coastwise Transportation Co

Archibald Russell

Completed in 1905, the four-masted barque *Archibald Russell* was built on the Clyde, which at that time was one of the most important shipbuilding centres in the world. She was laid up on the outbreak of World War II.

Built for the Pacific nitrate and wheat trade, she returned to Falmouth, Cornwall, from Australia in 93 days on her maiden voyage. She was the last square-rigged ship built on the Scottish river Clyde, and one of very few fitted with bilge keels, to reduce roll. She was later sold to Gustaf Erikson of Mariehamn, and continued to carry grain from Australia until 1939.

Tonnage: 2385 grt
Dimensions: 88.8m x 13.2m x 7.3m
(291ft 5in x 43ft 2in x 24ft 1in)
Role: nitrate/grain carrier
Route: Australia/Chile–Europe
Constructor: Scott's Shipbuilding & Engineering Co, Greenock
Material: steel
Built for: John Hardie & Co

Lusitania

Although she was the largest, the fastest and the most luxurious liner in the world, the Cunard Line's 31,500-ton _Lusitania_ is far more famous for her ending than for her qualities as a liner.

Completed in 1906, by October 1907 the _Lusitania_ held both eastbound and westbound Blue Ribands for transatlantic crossing simultaneously; she eventually posted an average speed, westbound, of 25.65 knots over 2890 nautical miles

(5352km). Her younger sister ship the _Mauretania_ was marginally faster, and eventually took both Blue Ribands.

On 7 May 1915, _Lusitania_ was sunk without warning by a torpedo from the German submarine _U-20_ off the Old Head of Kinsale on the south coast of Ireland, with the loss of 1198 (some reports say 1201) men, women and children. Among the dead were 127 (possibly 128) American citizens, and their deaths may have been a factor in the United States' eventual entry into World War I.

Tonnage: 31,550 grt

Dimensions: 232.3m x 26.75m x 10.2m (762ft 3in x 87ft 9in x 33ft 6in)

Machinery: four-shaft, direct-drive turbines; 68,000hp

Service speed: 24 knots

Role: passenger liner

Route: Liverpool–New York

Capacity: 563 1st, 464 2nd, 1138 3rd

Constructor: John Brown & Co, Glasgow

Material: steel

Built for: Cunard Steam Ship Co

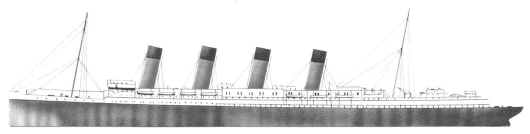

Chester class

USS *Chester* and her sister ships, *Salem* and *Birmingham*, were classed as 'scout cruisers'. *Chester* and *Salem* were the first turbine-engined ships in the US Navy.

Authorized in April 1904, the ships carried very little armour protection, their maximum deck armour being 25mm (1in), with plate protecting the machinery of 50mm (2in). Armament was also very light, the main guns being on the forecastle deck forward and upper deck aft, with secondary armament positioned to port

and starboard on the upper deck. In 1910, a wooden platform was positioned on the bow of *Birmingham* and from this, on 14 November, Eugene B. Ely took off in a Curtiss Golden Flyer, becoming the first aviator ever to fly from a ship. His aircraft struck the water, slightly damaging the propeller, but Ely retained control; he made a flight of 4km (2.5 miles), landing safely at Willoughby Spit, Virginia. *Chester* was renamed *York* in July 1928 to allow her original name to be transferred to a 'Northampton'-class cruiser. She was sold for scrap in 1930.

Displacement: 3750t standard; 4687t full load

Dimensions: 128.98m x 14.34m x 5.1m (423ft 2in x 47ft 1in x 16ft 9in)

Machinery: four screws; turbines; 16,000hp

Armament: two 127mm (5in) guns; two 76mm (3in) guns; two 533m (21in) TT

Armour: belt 50mm (2in); deck 25mm (1in)

Speed: 24 knots

Range: not known

Complement: 359

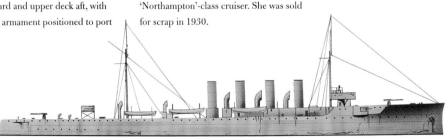

Dreadnought

***Dreadnought* was a brilliant concept, and revolutionized naval warfare. Her introduction, however, sparked off a naval arms race between Britain and Germany that became unstoppable.**

Laid down by Portsmouth Dockyard in October 1905, built in great secrecy and in record time, the vessel was ready for initial sea trials a year and a day later. As well as being the first battleship with main armament of a single calibre, *Dreadnought* was also the first with steam turbines and quadruple screws, machinery that gave her a top speed of 21 knots. Once the concept of the dreadnought had been proven, construction of this revolutionary type of battleship proceeded rapidly, at the rate of three or four per year.

Displacement: 21,845t full load

Dimensions: 160.6m x 25m x 8.1m (527ft x 82ft x 26ft 6in)

Machinery: four screws, turbines; 23,000hp

Armament: 10 305mm (12in) guns; 27 12pdr guns; five 457mm (18in) TT

Armour: belt and barbettes 279mm-102mm (11in-4in); bulkheads 203mm (8in); turrets 279mm (11in); decks 102mm-25mm (4in-1in)

Speed: 21 knots

Range: 6620nm (12,266km) at 10 knots

Complement: 697

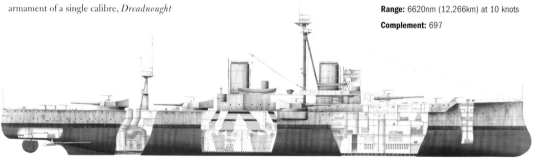

Scharnhorst

***Scharnhorst* and *Gneisenau* were powerful armoured cruisers, enlarged and improved versions of the earlier 'Roon' class, completed in 1907–8.**

From 1911, they were deployed to Tsingtao in China, to form the spearhead of the German Asiatic Squadron under Admiral von Spee. The squadron sailed east for home waters on the outbreak of World War I, and destroyed the British South Atlantic Squadron at Coronel off the Chilean coast. Rounding Cape Horn, the squadron raided the Falklands, but encountered a strong British naval force that included the battlecruisers *Inflexible* and *Invincible*. After a three-hour running fight *Scharnhorst* went down with all hands: *Gneisenau* was battered into a blazing wreck and sank soon afterwards.

Displacement: 11,600t standard, 12,900t full load

Dimensions: 144.6m x 21.6m x 7.9m (474ft 4in x 70ft 10in x 26ft)

Machinery: three screws, vertical triple expansion engines; 26,000hp

Armament: eight 210mm (8.25in) guns; six 150mm (5.9in) guns; four 450mm (17.7in) TT

Armour: belt 150–80mm (5.9–3.2in); turrets 170mm (6.6in); deck 60mm (2.3in)

Speed: 22.5 knots

Range: 9487km (5120nm) at 12 knots

Complement: 764

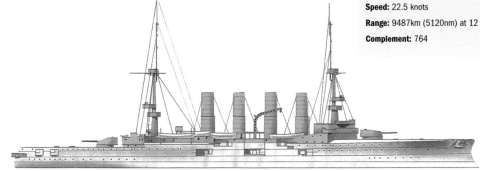

Inflexible

In parallel with Britain's development of the dreadnought, the Royal Navy sponsored another revolutionary warship concept – the battlecruiser.

Armed like a battleship but faster than a cruiser, battlecruisers could scout for the main battle fleet, and be able to destroy any conventional cruiser. They proved their capabilities in destroying *Scharnhorst* and *Gneisenau* at the Falkland Islands in 1914. The first ship of the new class was the *Inflexible*, completed in 1908. She carried eight 305mm (12in) guns, and had

a speed of 26 knots. She had dreadnought firepower, but protection had to be sacrificed in the cause of speed. With a reduced armament, and protection sacrificed for speed, the battlecruisers were inevitably more vulnerable, as events at Jutland in 1916 were to show in a tragic manner: *Invincible*, the sister ship of *Inflexible*, blew up and sank with the loss of 1026 lives after a shell penetrated her deck and exploded in a magazine.

Displacement: 17,250t standard; 20,125t full load

Dimensions: 567ft x 78ft 5in x 26ft 8in (172.8m x 23.9m x 8.1m)

Machinery: four screws, turbines, 31 boilers; 41,000hp

Armament: eight 12in (305mm); 16 4in (102mm); five 18in (457mm) TT

Armour: belt 6in-4in (152mm-102mm); turrets 7in (178mm); decks 2.5in-1.5in (63mm-37mm)

Speed: 25 knots

Range: 3000nm (5559km) at 10 knots

Complement: 784

Emden

Completed in 1908, the German light cruiser _Emden_ served in Far Eastern waters from 1909, providing support for Germany's Asian colonies.

At the outbreak of World War I, she was at Tsingtao in China and, on the orders of Admiral von Spee, sailed immediately to begin independent commerce raiding. In September 1914 she appeared in the Bay of Bengal, where she began her spree of merchant sinkings interspersed with shore bombardments. On 9 November she destroyed the wireless station at the Cocos Islands, but on that same day she was intercepted by the Australian cruiser HMAS _Sydney_ and left ablaze and on the beach. The _Emden_'s surviving crew seized a schooner and were able to reach Arabia, and after an adventurous overland journey they made it to Germany, where they were greeted as heroes.

Displacement: 3664t standard; 4268t full load

Dimensions: 117.9m x 13.5m x 5.5m (386ft 10in x 44ft 4in x 18ft)

Machinery: two screws, vertical triple-expansion engines; 13,500hp

Armament: ten 105mm (4.1in) guns; two 450mm (17.7in) TT

Armour: deck 30-20mm (1.75-0.75in); gunshields 50mm (2in)

Speed: 23.5 knots

Range: 6967km (3760nm) at 12 knots

Complement: 361

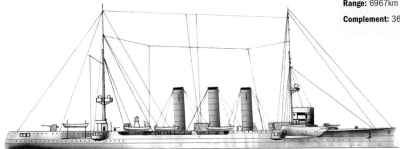

Wyoming

The six-masted schooner *Wyoming*, one of only 10 such ships ever constructed, was probably the biggest wooden ship ever built.

She was constructed in Bath, Maine, in 1909, by which time the coal trade between New England and the ports serving the Pennsylvania coalfield, for which she was built, had largely passed to steamships. She later made longer offshore voyages. The *Wyoming* was sold in 1916 for $350,000; by 1 October 1919, she was reported to have already paid for herself twice over. In March 1924, she was en route from Norfolk, Virginia, to St John, New Brunswick, when she was overtaken by a storm and foundered with the loss of all 13 hands.

Tonnage: 3730grt

Dimensions: 100.4m x 15.3m x 9.3m (329ft 6in x 50ft x 30ft 4in)

Machinery: not applicable

Service speed: not applicable

Role: collier

Route: Eastern seaboard, USA

Capacity: c6500t

Constructor: Percy & Small, Bath, Maine

Material: wood

Built for: Percy & Small

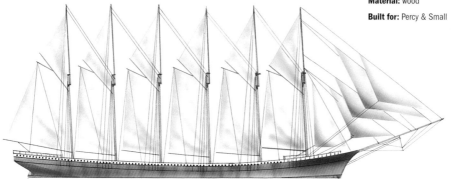

Michigan

The first dreadnoughts built in the United States were the *Michigan* and *South Carolina*. Although laid down after HMS *Dreadnought*, they were designed before the British warship.

They were in fact the first battleships designed with an 'all big-gun' armament comprising eight 305mm (12in) guns and superfiring turrets, features that were copied by all other nations. However, their propulsion system of twin screw, vertical triple expansion engines left much to be desired. The *Delaware* and *North Dakota* suffered similarly, although

they were generally a much more successful class with a larger-calibre secondary armament. *Delaware* (BB-28) was launched on 6 February 1909 and assigned to the Atlantic Fleet. During World War I, she was assigned to the British Grand Fleet. She was decommissioned in 1923, sold and broken up at Philadelphia in 1924.

Displacement: 20,380t standard; 22,060t full load
Dimensions: 158.1m x 26m x 808m (518ft 9in x 85ft 3in x 28ft 10in)
Machinery: two screws, vertical triple expansion; 25,000hp
Armament: 10 305mm (12in) guns; 14 127mm (5in) guns; two 533mm (21in) TT
Armour: belt 279-76mm (11-3in); turrets 305-203mm (12-8in); deck/conning tower 305mm (12in)
Speed: 21 knots
Range: 16,677km (9000nm) at 12 knots
Complement: 945

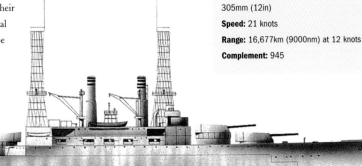

Titanic

The *Titanic* was the second of a trio of ill-fated 45,000t ships constructed in Belfast for the White Star Line; the *Olympic* was involved in four collisions in a 24-year career, and the *Britannic* was sunk by a German mine while serving as a hospital ship.

All three had double bottoms and no fewer than 15 transverse watertight bulkheads, with electrically operated doors, although these only extended to the lower deck.

RMS *Titanic* left Southampton on her maiden voyage, bound for New York via Cherbourg and Queenstown (Cork), on 10 April 1912. On the night of 14 April the ship grazed the underwater spur of an iceberg, buckling her portside hull plates along the riveted seams. Water flooded in above the watertight bulkheads and she sank, with the loss of 1503 of the 2223 people aboard, in less than two and a half hours. Most of those who died had been among the third-class passengers.

Tonnage: 46,328grt
Dimensions: 259.85m x 28.2m x 10.35m (852ft 6in x 92ft 6in x 34ft)
Machinery: three-shaft, triple expansion plus low-pressure turbine; 50,000hp
Service speed: 21 knots
Role: passenger liner
Route: Southampton–New York
Capacity: 1034 1st, 510 2nd, 1022 3rd
Constructor: Harland & Wolff, Belfast
Built for: White Star Line

Courbet

Designed by Lyasse, the 'Courbet' class of battleships of 1910-11 were the first French dreadnoughts.

The four vessels in the class were the *Courbet*, the *France*, the *Jean Bart* and the *Paris*. Their armament was mounted in six turrets, including one on each beam amidships. In an action off Albania on 16 August 1914, *Courbet* sank the Austrian cruiser *Zenta*. Both *Courbet* and *Jean Bart* underwent substantial reconstruction in 1926–29, their two forward funnels being trunked into one, and a tripod replacing the pole mast. *Courbet* was seized by the British at Portsmouth in June 1940, where she was based after lending fire support to Allied forces evacuating Cherbourg, France. She was later returned to the Free French, but was considered obsolete and decommissioned in April 1941. In June 1944 she was sunk as part of an artificial harbour during the Normandy invasion.

Displacement: 23,189t standard; 28,850t full load

Dimensions: 168m x 27.9m x 9m (551ft 2in x 91ft 6in x 29ft 6in)

Machinery: four screws, turbines; 28,000hp

Armament: 12 305mm (12in) guns; 22 137mm (5.4in) guns; four 450mm (17.7in) TT

Armour: belt 300–180mm (11.8–7in); turrets 320mm (12.5in); deck 70mm (2.75in)

Speed: 21 knots

Range: 7782km (4200nm) at 10 knots

Complement: 1108

Gangut

Gangut was named in honour of the great Russian naval battle which was fought on 27 July 1714 during the war with Sweden.

Gangut and her three sister ships, *Petropavlovsk*, *Poltava* and *Sevastopol*, were the first Imperial Russian Navy dreadnoughts. Their original design was modified to include ice-breaking bows. *Gangut* was launched on 7 October 1911, and served with the Baltic Fleet during World War I. Following the Russian Revolution, on 27 June 1925, she was renamed *Oktyabrskaya Revolutsia* and became part of the Red Fleet. She was refitted between October 1934 and April 1935 at the Baltic Shipyard, Leningrad. During World War II she took part in the protracted defence of Leningrad, where she was severely damaged by German bombs. Briefly used as a training ship in 1954, she was broken up between 1956 and 1959.

Displacement: 23,400t standard; 25,850t full load

Dimensions: 182.9m x 26.5m x 8.3m (600ft x 87ft x 27ft 3in)

Machinery: two screws, vertical quadruple expansion engines; 50,000hp

Armament: 12 305mm (12in) guns; 16 120mm (4.7in) guns; four 450mm (17.7in) TT

Armour: belt 279-100mm (10-3.9in); turrets 305-125mm (12-4.9in); deck 76mm (3in)

Speed: 24.6 knots

Range: 7412km (4000nm) at 16 knots

Complement: 1125

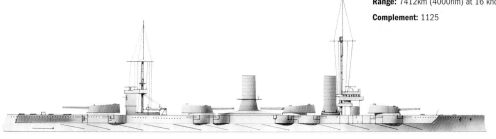

Cap Trafalgar

Thanks to the Imperial German Navy's decision to arm her as an auxiliary cruiser, the *Cap Trafalgar* had one of the shortest careers of any major steamship.

Built to operate on the passenger routes to South America, the Hamburg-Südamerika Line's *Cap Trafalgar* set out on her maiden voyage to Buenos Aires in July 1914 and was there when World War I started. Converted into an auxiliary cruiser, she was armed with two 10cm (3.9in) and four 37mm (1.46in) guns taken from the obsolete gunboat *Eber*, and commissioned on 31 August. Fourteen days later she was intercepted while coaling off Trinidade Island by the British armed merchant cruiser *Carmania*, which had considerably superior armament, and was sunk after a furious hour-long artillery duel, with the loss of 16 of her crew.

Tonnage: 18,805grt

Dimensions: 186m x 21.9m x 8.3m (610ft 3in x 71ft 10in x 27ft 3in)

Machinery: three-shaft, two vertical triple expansion plus one low-pressure turbine

Service speed: 17 knots

Role: passenger liner; auxiliary cruiser

Route: Hamburg–Buenos Aires

Capacity: 400 1st, 275 2nd, 900 3rd

Material: steel

Built for: Hamburg-Südamerikanischen Dampffschiffahrts Gesellschaft

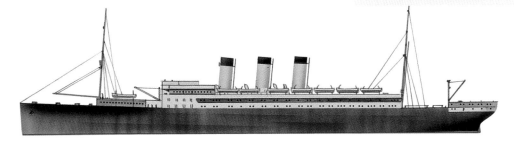

E class

The 'E' class was a mainstay of British submarine operations in World War I. Completed from 1913 through to 1916, the 'E' class ran to 55 hulls.

Five major groups were built, differences being primarily in torpedo layout and the adaptation of six boats to carry 20 mines in place of their midships tubes. *E11*, under the command of Lieutenant Commander Martin Nasmith, was arguably the most famous of them all. She scored many successes, including the sinking of the Turkish battleship *Hairredin*

Barbarossa. For these operations in the Dardanelles, the British submarines adopted a blue camouflage to conceal themselves in the shallow, clear waters. The class was also active in the North Sea and the Baltic. In 1916–17, some of the boats operating in these areas were fitted with high-angle 76mm (3in) or 12pdr guns for anti-aircraft defence. In all, 22 E-class boats were lost.

Displacement: 667t surfaced; 807t submerged

Dimensions: 55.17m x 6.91m x 3.81m (181ft x 22ft 8in x 12ft 6in)

Machinery: two screws, diesels, plus two electric motors; 1600/840hp

Armament: five 457mm (18in) TT; one 12pdr gun

Speed: 14 knots surfaced; 9 knots submerged

Range: 560km (300nm) at 10 knots, surfaced

Complement: 30

Kongo

The battlecruiser *Kongo* and her three sisters, *Hiei*, *Kirishima* and *Haruna*, were designed by an Englishman, Sir George Thurston.

He included some improvements as a result of experience in the building of the 'British Lion' class. *Kongo* was the last Japanese capital ship to be built outside the country while, due to a lack of slipways in Japanese government-owned yards, *Haruna* and *Kirishima* became the first Japanese capital ships to be constructed in private yards (Kawasaki and Mitsubishi, respectively). *Haruna* was launched on

14 December 1913 and completed in April 1915. The class had a new arrangement of main armament turrets, heavy secondary armament, and good protection; they outclassed contemporary ships. All the ships, with the exception of *Hiei*, underwent two periods of extensive reconstruction between the wars (*Hiei* was rebuilt only once), and were then reclassified as battleships. They were named after mountains, and all went on to serve in the Pacific in World War II, where all were sunk by the Allies.

Displacement: 27,500t standard; 32,200t full load

Dimensions: 201m x 28m x 8.4m (659ft 4in x 92ft x 27ft 6in)

Machinery: three screws, geared turbines; 64,000hp

Armament: eight 380mm (15in) guns; 16 152mm (6in) guns; eight 76mm (3in) guns; four 21in (533mm) TT, later removed

Armour: belt 203–76mm (8–3in); turrets 230mm (9in); barbettes 255mm (10in); bulkheads 230–140mm (9–5.5in), conning tower 255mm (10in)

Speed: 27.5 knots

Range: 14,824km (8000nm) at 14 knots

Complement: 1221

Queen Elizabeth

Laid down for the Royal Navy in 1912, the 'Queen Elizabeth' class of dreadnoughts included the *Barham*, *Malaya*, *Valiant* and *Warspite*. A sixth vessel, *Agincourt*, was never built.

Queen Elizabeth was launched on 16 October 1913 and completed in January 1915. Oil-fired and armed with 381mm (15in) guns, she was the most powerful battleship of her time. The class saw extensive action during World War I, including the Dardanelles campaign and the Battle of Jutland. All of the 'Queen Elizabeths' underwent substantial reconstruction in 1926–27, and *Warspite* and *Queen Elizabeth* were further upgraded

between 1937 and 1940, emerging as virtually new ships, having been re-engined, reboilered and rearmed. *Warspite* saw extensive action at Narvik and in the Mediterranean. *Barham* was sunk by a U-boat in 1941. On 19 December 1941, *Queen Elizabeth* and *Valiant* were heavily damaged at Alexandria in a daring attack by Italian frogmen. After service with the Home Fleet, *Queen Elizabeth* was sent to join the Eastern Fleet in the Indian Ocean. All were broken up in the late 1940s.

Displacement: 27,500t standard; 33,000t full load

Dimensions: 195m x 27.6m x 10.4m (640ft x 90ft 6in x 34ft 1in)

Machinery: four screws, turbines; 75,000hp

Armament: eight 381mm (15in) guns; 14 152mm (6in) guns; four 533mm (21in) TT

Armour: belt 330-152mm (13-6in); turrets 330-279mm (13-11in); decks 76-25mm (3-1in)

Speed: 24 knots

Range: 11,952km (6450nm) at 10 knots

Complement: 951 (later 1297)

Fuso

When completed in November 1915, the Imperial Japanese Navy's *Fuso* was the fastest and most powerful battleship in the world.

Her main turrets were all mounted on the centreline and she featured two tripod masts of uneven height. Fire-control platforms were added to these during a refit in 1927–28; new AA armament and searchlights were also fitted. *Fuso* and her sister ship *Yamashiro* were both reconstructed in 1930–35, new engines and boilers being fitted, the forward funnel removed, anti-torpedo bulges added, the elevation of the main battery increased, and the tripod masts replaced by towers fore and aft. The fore tower was so tall it became known as a 'pagoda' mast. Catapults were installed on the 'P' turret of *Fuso* and on the stern of *Yamashiro*. Both were sunk by the US Navy at Leyte Gulf: *Fuso* was sunk by gunfire and torpedoes in Surigao Strait. *Yamashiro* sank after being hit by numerous shells and three torpedoes.

Displacement: 30,600t standard; 35,900t full load

Dimensions: 205.1m x 28.7m x 8.6m (673ft x 94ft x 28ft 3in)

Machinery: four screws, turbines; 40,000hp

Armament: 12 355mm (14in) guns; 16 152mm (6in) guns; five 533mm (21in) TT

Armour: belt 305–102mm (12–4in); turrets 305–114mm (12–4.5in); deck 50mm (2in)

Speed: 22.5 knots

Range: 14,824km (8000nm) at 14 knots

Complement: 1193

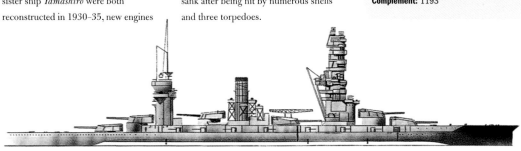

Nevada

Nevada **(BB-36) and her sister ship**
Oklahoma **(BB-37) were second-**
generation American dreadnoughts.
Of revolutionary design, they featured
'all or nothing' protection.

Nevada was launched in 1914. Her
designers decided that, as armour-piercing
shells did not burst when penetrating thin
plating, there was nothing to be gained
from using thin armour, which would
serve only to detonate the missiles. Vital
spaces were protected by the thickest
possible armour; non-vital areas were not

armoured. Rebuilt in 1927–30, *Nevada*
and *Oklahoma* were fitted with new
engines and boilers and their cage masts
were replaced by tripods. *Oklahoma* was
sunk at Pearl Harbor and the *Nevada* was
severely damaged and beached, but was
reconstructed in time to take part in the
Normandy landings. Late in the Pacific
war, *Nevada* was damaged by a kamikaze
and also hit by shore batteries off
Okinawa.

Displacement: 27,500t standard;
28,400t full load
Dimensions: 177.7m x 29m x 8.7m
(583ft x 95ft 3in x 28ft 6in)
Machinery: two screws, turbines; 26,500hp
Armament: 10 356mm (14in) guns; 21
127mm (5in) guns; four 533mm (21in) TT
Armour: belt 343-203mm (13.5-8in);
turrets 457-229mm (18-9in); deck 76mm
(3in)
Speed: 20.5 knots
Range: 18,530km (10,000nm) at 10 knots
Complement: 1049

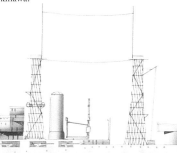

U-21

Strangely enough, at the beginning of the twentieth century the German Naval Staff failed to appreciate the potential of the submarine.

The first submarines built in Germany were three 'Karp'-class vessels ordered by the Imperial Russian Navy in 1904. Germany's first practical submarine, *U-1*, was not completed until 1906. Although the Germans got away to a slow start in their submarine construction programme before World War I, the vessels they did build were well engineered and used double hulls and twin screws from the start. German engineers refused to employ highly inflammable petrol engines in the early boats, preferring to use smellier but safer kerosene fuel. In 1908, suitable diesel engines were designed; these were installed in the U-19 class and used exclusively thereafter. One of the four boats of the U-19 class, *U-21*, was constructed at Danzig and completed in 1913.

Displacement: 650t surfaced; 837t submerged

Dimensions: 64.2m x 6.1m x 3.5m (210ft 6in x 20ft x 11ft 9in)

Machinery: two screws, two diesels, plus two electric motors; 1700/1200hp

Armament: four 508mm (20in) TT; one 86mm (3.4in)

Speed: 15.5 knots surfaced; 9 knots submerged

Range: 14,082km (7600nm) at 8 knots surfaced; 145km (80nm) at 5 knots submerged

Complement: 35

Baden

The German 'Baden' class battleship of 1913 was an upgraded version of the previous König design, carrying a main armament of eight 381mm (15in) guns.

The two Badens were built in response to the Royal Navy's 'Queen Elizabeth' class, but were slower. Laid down in September 1913, *Baden* was launched in February 1915 and was completed the following March. She became the flagship of the High Seas Fleet in April 1916, replacing *Friedrich der Grosse*. Interned at Scapa Flow on 14 December 1918, she was scuttled there on 21 June 1919, but instead of sinking she was towed ashore

and beached. In July 1919, she was refloated for use as a naval gunnery target, and on 16 August 1921 she was sunk by British warships off Portsmouth. Her sister ship, *Bayern*, was also scuttled at Scapa Flow; she was raised and broken up at Rosyth in September 1934.

Displacement: 28,600t standard; 32,200t full load

Dimensions: 180m x 30m x 9.3m (590ft 6in x 98ft 6in x 30ft 6in)

Machinery: triple screws, geared turbines; 35,000hp

Armament: eight 381mm (15in) guns; 16 150mm (5.9in) guns; five 609mm (24in) TT

Armour: belt 350–170mm (13.9–6.7in); turrets 350–254mm (13.9–10in); deck 100mm (3.9in)

Speed: 22 knots

Range: 9265km (5000nm) at 12 knots

Complement: 1171

Pennsylvania

The dreadnoughts *Pennsylvania* and her sister ship *Arizona* were improved developments of the US Navy's 'Nevada' class, with their main guns mounted in four triple turrets.

Neither saw overseas service in World War I due to a shortage of tankers for resupply; *Pennsylvania*, launched on 15 March 1915 and completed in June 1916, was assigned as flagship of the Atlantic Fleet. In 1922 she was assigned to the Pacific Fleet as flagship, undergoing a second period of reconstruction in 1929–31. On 7 December 1941, at Pearl Harbor, she

was badly damaged by Japanese bombs while in dry dock. *Arizona* exploded and sank during the attack. *Pennsylvania* was reconstructed again in 1942. She rejoined the Pacific Fleet in 1943, and took part in all the major naval campaigns. She was badly damaged by a Japanese aerial torpedo in Buckner Bay, Okinawa, on 12 August 1945. Only temporary repairs were made following the end of the war.

Displacement: 31,400t standard; 32,567t full load

Dimensions: 185.3m x 29.6m x 8.8m (608ft x 97ft x 28ft 10in)

Machinery: four screws, geared turbines; 31,500hp

Armament: 12 355mm (14in) guns; 22 127mm (5in) guns; two 533mm (21in) TT

Armour: belt 343-203mm (13.5-8in); turrets 457-229mm (18-9in); deck 102mm (4in)

Speed: 21 knots

Range: 18,530km (10,000nm) at 10 knots

Complement: 1040 (later 1314)

Royal Oak

One of the 'Revenge'-class dreadnoughts, HMS *Royal Oak* was launched on 17 November 1914 and completed in May 1916, just in time to take part in the Battle of Jutland.

She served with the Grand Fleet for the remainder of World War I and, after a refit in 1922–24, was deployed to the Mediterranean, where she served for the best part of a decade. She underwent a second refit in 1934–45, having a tripod mainmast fitted, and was then assigned to the Home Fleet. At the outbreak of World War II, *Royal Oak* was on patrol duty in northern waters. Detached from the Home Fleet to guard the Fair Isle Channel, she made her way to the anchorage at Scapa Flow. On the night of 13/14 October 1939, the German submarine *U-47*, commanded by Kapitanleutnant Günther Prien, penetrated the defences of Scapa Flow and sank the *Royal Oak* with three torpedo hits. The daring attack in such a heavily defended anchorage came as a severe shock to the Royal Navy, and to the British public.

Displacement: 27,500t standard; 31,200t full load

Dimensions: 190.3m x 27m x 8.7m (624ft 3in x 88ft 6in x 28ft 7in)

Machinery: four screws, turbines; 40,000hp

Armament: eight 381mm (15in) guns; 14 152mm (6in) guns; four 533mm (21in) TT

Armour: belt 330–102mm (13–4in); turrets 330–127mm (13–5in); decks 102mm–25mm (4–1in)

Speed: 23 knots

Range: 12,600km (6800nm) at 10 knots

Complement: 936

Courageous

***Courageous* was the first major British warship loss of World War II, being sunk by the *U-29* in September 1939, with the loss of 514 crew.**

Although they were defined as large light cruisers, *Courageous* and her sister ship, *Glorious*, were actually light battlecruisers armed with four 381mm (15in) guns. Ordered early in 1915, at a time when the British War Cabinet was reluctant to fund the building of more capital ships, they were the brainchild of Admiral Fisher, who was drawing up plans to invade the German-occupied Baltic states and who

needed the ships to provide fire support. The operation never took place, and *Courageous* was decommissioned for conversion as an aircraft carrier in 1924. *Glorious* was also converted to be an aircraft carrier in the 1920s, and both ships became early World War II losses: *Courageous* was torpedoed by *U-29* on 17 September 1939, and *Glorious* was sunk by the gunfire of *Scharnhorst* and *Gneisenau* while ferrying aircraft from Norway to Scotland on 8 June 1940.

Displacement: 19,230t standard; 22,690t full load

Dimensions: 239.7m x 24.7m x 7.1m (786ft 3in x 81ft x 23ft 4in)

Machinery: four screws, geared turbines; 90,000hp

Armament: four 381mm (15in) guns; 18 102mm (4in) guns; two 533mm (21in) TT

Armour: belt 3-2in (76–50mm); bulkheads 76–50mm (3–2in); turret faces 330–280mm (13–11in); decks 38–20mm (1.5–0.75in)

Speed: 32 knots

Range: 5929km (3200nm) at 19 knots

Complement: 828–842

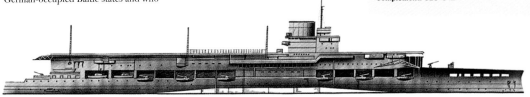

Furious

Launched on 15 August 1916, the British light battlecruiser *Furious* was originally completed as a modified *Courageous*-type vessel, designed with two massive 457mm (18in) guns in two single turrets.

In 1917, in the course of a refit, one of her 457mm guns was removed, together with her mainmast, and a hangar and flightdeck installed aft. Recommissioned in March 1918, her aircraft successfully attacked the Zeppelin sheds at Tondern on 19 July. In 1921–25, *Furious* was fully converted to aircraft carrier status with the fitting of a complete flightdeck. During World War II, after two refits in the 1930s, she served in northern waters, including the Norwegian campaign. Later, she ferried vital aircraft reinforcements to the besieged island of Malta, and formed part of the covering force during the Allied invasion of North Africa in November 1942. After further operations in northern waters against the battleship *Tirpitz*, she was placed in reserve in 1944 and broken up in 1948.

Displacement: 19,513t standard; 22,890t full load

Dimensions: 239.7m x 26.8m x 6.4m (786ft 6in x 88ft x 21ft)

Machinery: four screws, geared turbines; 90,000hp

Armament: two 457mm (18in) guns; 11 140mm (5.5in) guns; two 533mm (21in) TT

Armour: belt and bulkheads 75–50mm (3–2in); turret faces 230mm (9in); decks 76–20mm (3–0.75in)

Speed: 31.5 knots

Range: 11,118km (6000nm) at 12 knots

Complement: 880

M1

In 1917, British experiments with very large, steam-powered submarines of the 'K' class, fast enough to operate with the battlefleet, encountered major technical difficulties.

As a result, the British Admiralty suspended construction work on four K-boats and revised plans to turn them into more conventionally powered 'submarine monitors'. They became known as M-boats and featured a single 305mm (12in) gun mounted in the front part of an extended conning tower. The gun could be fired from periscope depth within 30 seconds of a target being sighted, or in 20 seconds if the submarine was surfaced. The *M1* was the only M-boat to see war service. The second of the M-boats, *M2*, was converted to the role of seaplane carrier in April 1928 and foundered off Portland, Dorset in 1933. A principal drawback with the 'M'-class submarines was that the gun could not be reloaded under water, so the submarine had to surface after each round was fired – earning the M-boats the nickname 'Dip Chicks'.

Displacement: 1594t surfaced; 1946t submerged

Dimensions: 90.1m x 7.5m x 4.9m (295ft 7in x 24ft 7in x 16ft)

Machinery: two screws, diesel/electric motors; 2400/1600hp

Armament: four 533mm (21in) TT; one 305mm (12in) gun

Speed: 15 knots surfaced; 9 knots submerged

Range: 18,530km (10,000nm) at 10 knots, surfaced; 185km (100nm) at 5 knots, submerged

Complement: 65

Idaho

One of three 'New Mexico'-class dreadnoughts, USS *Idaho* (BB-42) was launched on 30 June 1917. She underwent a major reconstruction programme in 1931–34.

Among other refinements, her cagemasts were removed, a tower superstructure was added, her AA armament was increased, anti-torpedo bulges were fitted, and she was re-engined and reboilered. After a brief assignment to the Atlantic Fleet in 1941, *Idaho* returned to the Pacific, her service in World War II taking her to Attu, the Gilbert Islands, Kwajalein, Saipan,

Guam, Palau, Iwo Jima and Okinawa. On 13 June 1945, she ran aground off Okinawa, effectively bringing her operational career in the Pacific to a close. In September that year, together with other US battleships, she sailed for the United States with high-priority personnel on board. *Idaho* was decommissioned in July 1946, to be sold and broken up in the following year.

Displacement: 32,000t standard; 33,000t full load

Dimensions: 190.2m x 29.7m x 9.1m (624ft x 97ft 5in x 30ft)

Machinery: four screws, geared turbines; 32,000hp

Armament: 12 356mm (14in) guns; 14 127mm (5in) guns; two 533mm (21in) TT

Armour: belt 343–203mm (13.5–8in); turrets 457–229mm (18–9in); deck 152mm (6in)

Speed: 22 knots

Range: 18,530km (10,000nm) at 10 knots

Complement: 1080

Eagle

Britain's Royal Navy was the first to embrace the idea of the aircraft carrier, and in the years after 1918 it developed many of the standard features of such vessels.

One of the first carriers to enter service was HMS *Eagle*. Originally laid down as a battleship for Chile, and acquired in 1917 for conversion to an aircraft carrier, *Eagle* was extensively modified after trials and rebuilt in 1922–23, when she was fitted with a full-length flightdeck and heavy armament. She was the first aircraft carrier

with an island superstructure. In the early months of World War II, *Eagle* was in the West Indies, subsequently deploying to the Mediterranean where she was used to support convoy operations. *Eagle* met her end while providing support for Operation Pedestal, the attempt to run a supply convoy to Malta during August 1942. On 11 August she was torpedoed and sunk by the German submarine *U-73*.

Displacement: 22,600t standard; 26,400t full load

Dimensions: 203.3m x 28.3m x 8.2m (667ft x 92ft 9in x 27ft)

Machinery: four screws, geared turbines; 50,000hp

Armament: nine 152mm (6in) guns; five 102mm (4in) AA

Armour: belt 114mm (4.5in); deck 38mm (1.5in)

Speed: 24 knots

Range: 8153km (4400nm) at 10 knots

Complement: 748

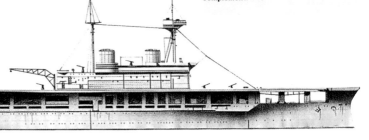

Hood

HMS *Hood* owed her existence to the threat posed by the German 'Mackensen'-class battlecruisers – which were never completed.

At the time of her launch on 22 August 1918, *Hood* was the largest warship in the world. In 1923–24 she undertook a much-publicized world cruise. She remained the largest warship afloat throughout the inter-war years – and, with a speed of 32 knots, she was also one of the fastest, deck armour having been sacrificed to produce a higher speed. Her armour was increased after an analysis of British battlecruiser losses during the Battle of Jutland, but she still remained poorly protected. A major reconstruction, scheduled for 1939, was cancelled on the outbreak of war. She took part in the bombardment of French naval bases in North Africa in July 1940. In May 1941, together with the battleship *Prince of Wales*, the *Hood* sailed to intercept the German battleship *Bismarck* and the heavy cruiser *Prinz Eugen* in the Denmark Strait. A German salvo penetrated her deck and exploded in her magazine. *Hood* blew up and sank with the loss of 1338 lives, leaving only three survivors.

Displacement: 45,200t full load

Dimensions: 262.3m x 32m x 9.6m (860ft 7in x 105ft x 31ft 6in)

Machinery: four screws, geared turbines; 144,000hp

Armament: eight 381mm (15in) guns; 12 140mm (5.5in) guns; four 102mm (4in) guns; six 533mm (21in) TT

Armour: belt/barbettes 305-127mm (12-5in); turrets 381-279mm (15-11in); conning tower 279-229mm (11-9in); bulkheads 127-102mm (5-4in); decks 76-26mm (3-1in)

Speed: 32 knots

Range: 11,674km (6300nm) at 12 knots

Complement: 1477

Hermes

At the end of World War I, Great Britain was significantly ahead of the rest of the world in the development of vessels which could be truly defined as aircraft carriers.

The first vessel to be designed from the outset as an aircraft carrier, with a full flight deck and a large island, was HMS *Hermes*. Laid down on 15 January 1918, she was launched on 11 September 1919 and fully fitted out by February 1925. She served mainly in the Far East. At the outbreak of World War II, she was in the South Atlantic, and her aircraft were involved in the attack on the French base at Dakar in July 1940. In 1941 she was involved in convoy protection in the Indian Ocean and South Atlantic. Early in 1942, *Hermes* was part of the Royal Navy's Eastern Fleet, based in Ceylon. On 8 April that year, air reconnaissance reported a Japanese carrier task force approaching Ceylon; *Hermes* was ordered to put to sea, along with the Australian destroyer *Vampire*, the corvette *Hollyhock* and two tankers. The ships were attacked by some 80 Japanese aircraft and all five were sunk. *Hermes* had no aircraft on board and was defenceless. Over 300 of her crew died.

Displacement: 10,850t standard; 12,900t full load
Dimensions: 182.3m x 21.3m x 6.6m (598ft x 70ft x 21ft 6in)
Machinery: two screws, geared turbines; 40,000hp
Armament: six 140mm (5.5in); four 3pdr AA
Armour: belt 76mm (3in); deck 25mm (1in)
Speed: 25 knots
Range: 7783km (4200nm) at 14 knots
Complement: 664

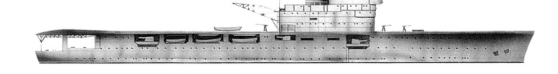

Java

The Dutch navy, while not as large as the British or French navies, nevertheless had worldwide colonial commitments in the inter-war years.

Java and her sister cruisers, *Sumatra* and *Celebes*, were built to a Dutch design, but with materials, technical supervision, and some labour supplied by Krupp. They were planned for completion by 1918, but construction was delayed by World War I; by 1925–26, when they were finished, they were already obsolete. The class was to be equipped with two seaplanes (Fairey IIIDs). *Java*'s sister ship *Sumatra* was laid up at Portsmouth and used as a breakwater at Normandy; *Celebes* was cancelled while incomplete. *Java* was torpedoed and sunk by the Japanese heavy cruiser *Nachi* in the Battle of the Java Sea early in 1942.

Displacement: 6670t standard; 7050t full load

Dimensions: 155.3m x 16.0m x 5.5m (509ft 6in x 52ft 6in x 18ft)

Machinery: three screws, turbines; 72,000hp

Armament: 10 150mm (5.9in) guns

Armour: belt 76-50mm (3-2in); deck 50-38mm (2-1.5in)

Speed: 31 knots

Range: 6300km (3400nm) at 14 knots

Complement: 480

Kaga

Launched on 17 November 1920, *Kaga* was originally laid down as an improved Nagato-type dreadnought, with increased armour protection and an enlarged main battery.

She was cancelled in February 1922 to comply with the terms of the Washington Naval Treaty, but instead of scrapping her the Japanese Naval Staff decided to complete her as an aircraft carrier. *Kaga* was completed in March 1928 and joined the Combined Fleet in 1930. Reconstructed in 1934–35, she gained a full-length flight deck and island. Recommissioned in June

1935, *Kaga* was assigned to the 1st Carrier Division with the *Akagi*, which had been converted from a battlecruiser while under construction. Kaga's World War II career was short but spectacular. In December 1941, her aircraft attacked Pearl Harbor, and subsequently operated over Rabaul, Darwin and Java. She then formed part of the Japanese carrier task force assembled for the assault on Midway Island. Concentrating on destroying Midway's air defences, the Japanese carriers were caught unprepared when US dive-bombers launched their counterattack; *Akagi*, *Kaga*, *Hiryu* and *Soryu* were sunk.

Displacement: 26,000t standard; 33,693t full load

Dimensions: 240.48m x 32.91m x 9.44m (789ft x 108ft x 31ft)

Machinery: four screws, geared turbines; 91,000hp

Armament: 25 20mm (0.79in) guns; 30 13.2mm (0.52in) AA

Armour: belt 279mm (11in); deck 58.5mm (2.3in)

Speed: 27.5 knots

Range: 10,191km (5500nm) at 16 knots

Complement: 1340

William G Mather

Trade on the Great Lakes of North America called for a number of unusual types of vessel to be built to meet local needs and requirements.

The size of the Great Lakes and the large amount of bulk carriage of cargo meant that vessels designed for operations along their lengths had to be as large as their seagoing contemporaries. Two of the biggest users of shipping were the iron-ore trade and the grain trade. It was more economical to ship iron ore from the vast open-cast mines of Minnesota through the port of Duluth on Lake Superior than to move it eastwards by train. Similarly, grain from the Midwest could be transported through the lakes to Chicago. The *William G Mather* was typical of the bulk carriers built to operate on the North American Great Lakes, with the command position right forward and engines right aft. She was equally at home carrying grain from the prairies or iron ore. She had four holds, each of them served by four large hatches to speed loading and discharging. Built in 1925, she had a long career before being acquired as a floating museum.

Tonnage: 8662grt

Dimensions: 183.2m x 18.9m x 55.5m (601ft x 62ft x 18ft)

Machinery: one-shaft, geared turbine; 5500hp

Service speed: 12 knots

Role: bulk carrier

Route: Great Lakes

Capacity: c10,000t

Constructor: Great Lakes Engineering Works, River Rouge, Michigan

Material: steel

Built for: Cleveland-Cliffs Steamship Co

Owner: Great Lakes Historical Society, Vermilion, Ohio

Saratoga

In 1916–17, as a counter to the powerful Japanese 'Kongo' class, the US Naval Staff ordered six new battlecruisers. Under the 1922 Washington Naval Treaty, construction was suspended.

It was decided to complete two vessels as the world's largest aircraft carriers, the *Constitution* (renamed *Lexington*) and the *Saratoga*. The *Lexington* was given the designation CV-2; the *Saratoga* was designated CV-3. As finally completed, both ships were armed with 203mm (8in) guns to match heavy cruisers which were similarly armed, although during the war these were replaced by 127mm (5in)

mounts aboard *Saratoga*. After Pearl Harbor, *Lexington*'s air group was involved in the battle for Wake Island. In May 1942, *Lexington* was assigned to Task Force 11, formed to counter a Japanese move on New Guinea. In the Battle of the Coral Sea, *Lexington* was hit by two torpedoes and three bombs, and had to be abandoned, being sunk later by the destroyer USS *Phelps*. *Saratoga* survived the war, despite being twice torpedoed in 1942 and hit by four kamikazes in 1945, only to be expended in the atomic bomb tests at Bikini in 1946.

Displacement: 37,681t standard; 43,055t full load

Dimensions: 270.66m x 32.12m x 10.15m (888ft x 105ft 5in x 33ft 4in)

Machinery: four screws, turbines; 180,000hp

Armament: eight 203mm (8in) guns; 12 127mm (5in) guns; 63 aircraft

Armour: belt 178-127mm (7-5in); deck 50mm (2in)

Speed: 33.25 knots

Range: 19,456km (10,500nm) at 15 knots

Complement: 2327

Nelson

The principal aim of the 1922 Washington Treaty, the first disarmament treaty in history, was to limit the size of the navies of the five principal maritime powers.

Britain's capital ships were less heavily armed than those of the United States, so she was therefore permitted to build two new 35,000-ton vessels as replacements for older vessels. The new vessels were the battleships *Nelson* and *Rodney*, both laid down in December 1922. They adopted the same design as the G3 class of four unnamed battlecruisers, cancelled due to the Washington Treaty. They were the only British ships to mount 406mm (16in) guns in triple turrets. To reduce the weight of armour, an internal inclined armour belt was used. All main armament was concentrated forward, while all machinery and secondary armament was concentrated aft. Slow but powerfully armed, both saw extensive action in the Mediterranean, and *Rodney* helped batter the *Bismarck* to destruction in May 1941.

Displacement: 33,950t standard; 38,000t full load

Dimensions: 710ft x 106ft x 30ft (216.4m x 32.3m x 9.1m)

Machinery: two screws, geared turbines; 45,000hp

Armament: nine 16in (406mm); 12 6in (152mm); six 4.7mm (120mm); two 24.5in (622mm) TT

Armour: belt 14in–11in (355mm–279mm); turrets 16in-9in (406mm-229mm); deck 6.5in (165mm)

Speed: 23 knots

Range: 16,500nm (30,574km) at 12 knots

Complement: 1314

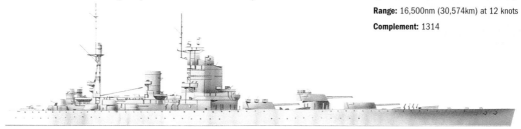

Maya

The 'Nachi'-class cruisers were Japan's first generation of 10,000-ton vessels built under the restrictions of the Washington Treaty. Their advanced design and the techniques used in their construction combined to produce warships able to attain the highest possible speeds while mounting the maximum armament.

The cruiser *Maya* was one of four laid down in 1927–28, the others being *Takao*, *Atago* and *Chokai*. They were a slightly improved version of the previous 'Nachi' class, the main alterations being a larger bridge structure, torpedo tubes in a rotating mount on the upper deck, and an upright second funnel. As built, all four carried three seaplanes for general reconnaissance. These cruisers were among the most powerful of World War II. Following bomb damage in November 1943, 'C' turret on *Maya* was removed and replaced by two twin 127mm (5in) AA turrets. Only *Takao* survived the war after being scuttled in shallow water. *Maya* was sunk by four torpedoes from the US submarine *Dace* on 23 October 1944.

Displacement: 9850t standard; 12,781t full load
Dimensions: 203.76m x 18.03m x 6.11m (668ft 6in x 59ft 2in x 20ft 1in)
Machinery: four screws, geared turbines; 130,000hp
Armament: 10 203mm (8in) guns; four 120mm (4.7in) guns; eight 609mm (24in) TT
Armour: belt 100mm (3.9in); magazines 125mm (4.9in); deck 38mm (1.5in)
Speed: 35.5 knots
Range: 9265km (5000nm) at 14 knots
Complement: 773

Köln

The three 'K'-class light cruisers were among the first major warships built for the German Navy after the end of World War I.

Konigsberg was laid down in July 1926 and was completed in April 1929. Hit by Norwegian coastal artillery during the landings at Bergen in 1940, she was damaged beyond repair by British carrier aircraft. *Karlsruhe* was completed later in 1929. On 9 April 1940 she was torpedoed and damaged by the submarine HMS *Truant*, and the hulk was later sunk by the German torpedo-boat *Grief* off Kristiansand, Norway. The third vessel, the *Köln* was completed in January 1930. *Köln* had a

much longer combat career than her sisters. She served with the neutrality patrol during the Spanish Civil War, and was in action from the very first day of World War II. She served in northern waters until 1943, when she was transferred to the Baltic Fleet. During the closing months of the war, she provided fire support for German forces on the Eastern Front. On 30 March 1945, while refitting at Wilhelmshaven, she was badly damaged in an Allied air attack. She was decommissioned on 6 April and her guns used for local defence. *Köln* was scrapped in 1946.

Displacement: 6650t standard; 8130t full load

Dimensions: 174m x 15.3m x 5.56m (570ft 10in x 50ft 2in x 18ft 3in)

Machinery: two screws, geared turbines; 65,000hp

Armament: nine 150mm (5.9in) guns; 12 500mm (19.7in) TT

Armour: belt 68.58mm (2.7in); deck 38mm (1.5in); turrets 25mm (1in)

Speed: 32 knots

Range: 8338km (4500nm) at 14 knots

Complement: 850

Infanta Beatriz

After the Spanish Civil War, the *Infanta Beatriz*, named after Spain's crown princess, was renamed after the city of Seville.

Infanta Beatriz was the first motor passenger ship built for Spain. Completed in 1928, she was built by Krupp of Kiel, with the design following closely two successful motor ships built for a major German shipping firm. *Infanta Beatriz* was a major addition to a fleet of more than 60 vessels, many of them older and smaller. Passenger accommodation was to a high standard, with an unusually large number of single cabins. Cargo holds were fitted out for the banana trade, as she was intended for service between Germany and the Canary Islands. Cargo capacity was 5200dwt. While alongside at Barcelona in January 1939, during the Spanish Civil War, *Ciudad de Sevilla*, as she had recently become, was bombed and sunk. Later raised and repaired, she served until the 1960s.

Tonnage: 6279grt
Dimensions: 125m x 15.8m x 6.4m (410ft x 52ft x 21ft 6in)
Machinery: two-shaft, diesel; 4340hp
Service speed: 14 knots
Role: passenger/cargo liner
Route: Germany–Canary Islands
Capacity: 134 1st, 38 2nd, 60 3rd; 5200dwt
Constructor: Krupp AG (Germaniawerft), Kiel
Built for: Cia Trasmediterranea

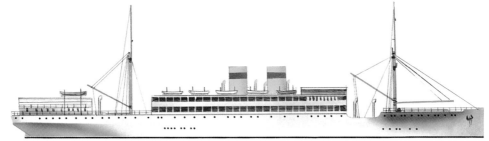

Ardent

In 1918, at the end of World War I, the Royal Navy had a huge inventory of destroyers on strength, and it would be some time before any new building plans were proposed.

HMS *Ardent* was one of a class of eight units with which the Royal Navy began a new era of destroyer construction, after a gap of eight years from the end of World War I. The design was derived from the final 'V' and 'W' class vessels in service at the end of the Great War. Laid down in 1929 and completed in 1930–31, the class introduced quadruple torpedo tubes, and had full shields for their 120mm (4.7in) guns. The 'A'-class destroyers were the first to introduce quadruple torpedo tubes. Four of the eight ships constructed were lost in action during World War II. *Ardent* and her sister ship *Acasta* were sunk in June 1940 by the German battlecruisers *Scharnhorst* and *Gneisenau*, while escorting the aircraft carrier *Glorious*, which also fell victim to the German guns.

Displacement: 1360t standard; 1747t full load

Dimensions: 95.1m x 9.8m x 3.7m (312ft x 32ft 3in x 12ft 3in)

Machinery: two screws, geared turbines; 34,000hp

Armament: four 120mm (4.7in) guns; eight 533mm (21in) TT

Armour: belt 76mm (3in)

Speed: 35 knots

Range: 4632km (2500nm) at 18 knots

Complement: 138

Exeter

Launched in 18 July 1929, the British cruiser HMS *Exeter* became famous for her part in the action with the German 'pocket battleship' *Graf Spee* off Montevideo in December 1939.

During this engagement she received direct hits from seven 280mm (11in) shells, and took splinter damage from several more which dropped short. She was out of action for 14 months, returning to service just in time to take part in the hunt for the German battleship *Bismarck* in May 1941. She later deployed to the Far East, and took part in combined naval operations against the Japanese in the Dutch East Indies, forming part of the Allied Eastern Force under Admiral Doorman. During the Battle of the Java Sea, she was hit in the aft boiler room by a 203mm (8in) shell, reducing her speed to 16 knots; two days later on 1 March 1942, she became trapped between two Japanese naval forces. Together with the destroyer *Encounter*, the *Exeter* was sunk by gunfire and torpedoes from the destroyer *Inazuma*.

Displacement: 8390t standard; 10,490t full load

Dimensions: 175.25m x 17.68m x 6.17m (575ft x 58ft x 20ft 3in)

Machinery: four screws, geared turbines; 80,000hp

Armament: six 203mm (8in) guns; four 102mm (4in) guns; six 533mm (21in) TT

Armour: box protection to ammunition spaces 100-25mm (4-1in); side 76mm (3in); turrets 25mm (1in)

Speed: 32 knots

Range: 9635km (5200nm) at 12 knots

Complement: 630

Amerigo Vespucci

Designed to resemble an early nineteenth-century frigate, *Amerigo Vespucci* was actually a sophisticated twentieth-century design.

The Italian navy's principal sail training ship during much of the second half of the twentieth century was the *Amerigo Vespucci*, which was purpose-built for the task at the beginning of the 1930s with accommodation for a large crew (228 men) in addition to 170 cadets. Superficially a nineteenth-century design, in fact she had a modern rig with a total sail area of 2800sq m (30,140sq ft) and a clipper bow. Somewhat unusually for a sail training ship, she had a fairly sophisticated diesel-electric powerplant. The *Amerigo Vespucci* was the second of two almost identical ships; the other, the *Cristoforo Colombo*, was transferred to the Soviet Union in reparation after the end of World War II, but was eventually scrapped.

Tonnage: 3545t displacement

Dimensions: 82m x 15.5m x 6.55m (269ft x 50ft 9in x 21ft 6in)

Machinery: one-shaft, auxiliary diesel-electric; 1900hp

Service speed: not applicable

Role: sail training ship

Constructor: Cantiere di Castellamare di Stabbia

Material: steel

Built for: Italian navy

Owner: Italian navy

Zara

Originally classed as light, then armoured and finally as heavy cruisers, the Italian navy's 'Zara' class was an improvement on the earlier 'Trento' class, completed in the 1920s.

However, the intended increase in armour, speed and firepower pushed displacement 1500t beyond its nominal treaty limit of 10,000t. The four ships in the class were *Zara*, *Fiume*, *Gorizia* and *Pola*, each equipped with a launch catapult and a hangar capable of accommodating two spotter aircraft which fitted beneath the forecastle. The ships were capable of

more than 33 knots, even with a weight of armour three times that of the 'Trento' class. *Zara* was launched on 27 April 1930 and completed on 20 October 1931. *Zara*, *Fiume* and *Pola* were sunk at the Battle of Cape Matapan in March 1941 by the radar-equipped British battleships *Warspite* and *Barham*, and the cruiser *Ajax*, in a close-range night engagement. In 1944 the *Gorizia* was sunk by British 'human torpedoes' at La Spezia.

Displacement: 11,680t standard; 14,300t full load

Dimensions: 182.8m x 20.62m x 7.2m (557ft 2in x 62ft 10in x 21ft 11in)

Machinery: two screws, geared turbines; 95,000hp

Armament: eight 203mm (8in) guns; 16 100mm (3.9in) guns

Armour: belt 150–100mm (9–4in); decks 70–20mm (2.75–0.75in)

Speed: 32 knots

Range: 7412km (4000nm) at 15 knots

Complement: 841

Conte di Savoia

The orders for the *Rex* and the *Conte di Savoia* were announced almost simultaneously, but there was no rivalry between the two – *Rex* was built for speed; *Conte di Savoia* for style and grace.

The *Conte di Savoia* was launched in October 1931 and began sea trials just over a year later, proving herself able to sustain 29 knots. She left Genoa for New York on 30 November. All went well until, some 1450km (900nm) off her destination, an outlet valve stuck and blew a hole in her hull below the waterline. A superhuman effort saw it patched, and she continued on her way, her passengers unaware of how close they had come to disaster. Repaired, she continued in service until 1940 when Italy entered World War II, and was then laid up near Venice. She was sunk by Allied aircraft in September 1943, salvaged in 1945 and broken up five years later.

Tonnage: 48,502grt

Dimensions: 248.3m x 30m
(814ft 8in x 96ft 2in)

Machinery: four-shaft, geared turbines

Service speed: 27 knots

Role: passenger liner

Route: Genoa–New York

Constructor: Cantieri Riuniti dell'Adriatico, Trieste

Material: steel

Built for: Lloyd Sabaudo Line

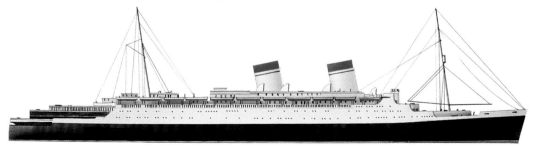

Rex

In 1927, Navigazione Generale Italiana ordered the biggest passenger liner ever built in Italy to supplement the *Roma* and *Augusta* on its Genoa – Côte d'Azure–New York run.

At the same time the rival Lloyd Sabaudo Line announced almost simultaneously that it had ordered the *Conte di Savoia*. In fact there was no real competition between the two, for the former was to be built primarily for speed and the latter as a showpiece of Italian style, and by the time they were ready to enter service the two lines had merged with Cosiluch to become the Italia Line. From the outset the *Rex* was meant to win the Blue Riband, though on her maiden voyage she developed major engine problems. *Rex* was laid up in the spring of 1940, and there were reports that she was to be converted to an aircraft carrier. In the event she fell victim to air attack by the RAF in September 1944 and sank in the Gulf of Muggia.

Tonnage: 51,062grt

Dimensions: 268m x 29.25m x 8.55m (879ft x 96ft in x 28ft)

Machinery: four-shaft, geared turbines; 136,000hp

Service speed: 28 knots

Role: passenger liner

Route: Genoa–New York

Capacity: 604 1st, 378 2nd, 410 tr, 866 3rd

Constructor: Ansaldo, Genoa

Material: steel

Built for: Navigazione Generale Italiana

Indianapolis

Indianapolis and Portland were improved 'Northampton'-class cruisers of the US Navy. They had more armour around the magazines and above the machinery spaces.

In trials *Indianapolis* achieved 32.86 knots at a displacement of 11,144t and an output of 108,317shp. *Indianapolis* was launched on 7 November 1931, some six months before *Portland*. During the early months of the Pacific War, she took part in attacks on Japanese-held objectives. She carried out a number of bombardment missions in 1943, and formed part of the naval force supporting the landings in the Gilbert Islands. Early in 1944,

Indianapolis undertook similar operations at Kwajalein and Eniwetok, and in June and July lent her firepower to the assault on the Marianas. In 1945 she was escorting carriers raiding Tokyo. In March she was at Iwo Jima. As flagship of the Fifth Fleet she was damaged by a kamikaze off Okinawa on 30 March. After repair she transported the first atomic bomb to Tinian. She was proceeding to Leyte, when she was torpedoed by the Japanese submarine *I-58*, sinking with heavy loss of life. Only 316 of her 1199 crew survived.

Displacement: 10,258t standard; 12,755t full load

Dimensions: 185.93m x 20.12m x 6.4m (610ft x 66ft x 21ft)

Machinery: four screws, turbines; 107,000hp

Armament: nine 203mm (8in) guns; eight 127mm (5in) guns

Armour: belt 57mm (2.25in); deck 146–63mm (5.75-2.5in)

Speed: 32.5 knots

Range: 18,530km (10,00nm) at 15 knots

Complement: 917/1199

Achilles

A cruiser of the 'Leander' class, the only single-funnelled cruisers to be built for the Royal Navy since the 1880s, HMS *Achilles* was launched on 1 September 1932.

By the early 1930s, British naval thinking had come to the view that smaller ships carrying the newer 152mm (6in) guns, with a higher rate of fire and improved armour penetration, were a match for older 533mm (8in) gunned heavy cruisers. *Achilles* was loaned to the Royal New Zealand Navy from 1937–43. She became famous for her part in the Battle of the River Plate in December 1939. *Achilles* served in New Zealand waters 1940–43, home waters 1943–44, and joined the Pacific Fleet in 1945. She was sold to India and became INS *Delhi* in 1948. Three of the eight cruisers in the 'Leander' class, *Neptune*, *Sydney* (RAN) and *Perth*, were lost in action during World War II.

Displacement: 6985t
Dimensions: 169.01m x 16.97m x 5.99m (554ft 6in x 55ft 8in x 19ft 8in)
Machinery: four screws, geared turbines; 72,000hp
Armament: eight 152mm (6in) guns; eight 533mm (21in) TT
Armour: belt 76mm (3in); bulkheads 38mm (1.5in)
Speed: 32.5 knots
Range: 8338km (4500nm) at 15 knots
Complement: 570

Astoria

The USS *Astoria* was one of a class of seven heavy cruisers launched in 1933–36. These vessels were based on the Northampton class of 1927, which had set the pattern for all US Navy heavy cruisers over the next decade.

Their silhouette was altered, but they retained the same armament and machinery as the older class. *Astoria* (CA.34) was launched on 16 December 1933. In May 1942, she took part in the Battle of the Coral Sea and the Battle of Midway. In August *Astoria* was part of the Northern Covering Force which supported the landings by US Marines on the island of Guadalcanal; during a night action with Japanese cruisers off Savo Island, she was badly damaged, and so was abandoned, then sank. Two of her sister ships, *Quincy* (CA.39) and *Vincennes* (CA.44) were also sunk during this action, but the rest of the class survived the war, having taken part in almost every major Pacific engagement.

Displacement: 10,136t standard; 12,463t full load

Dimensions: 179.22m x 18.82m x 6.93m (588ft x 61ft 9in x 22ft 9in)

Machinery: four screws, geared turbines; 107,000hp

Armament: nine 203mm (8in) guns; eight 127mm (5in) guns; four aircraft

Armour: belt 127mm (5in); deck 57mm (2.25in)

Speed: 32.7 knots

Range: 18,530km (10,000nm) at 15 knots

Complement: 868

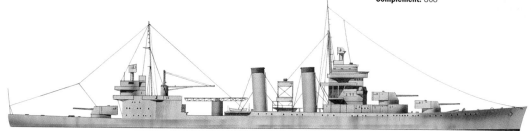

Fantasque

The 'Fantasque' class of six destroyers was the penultimate class in a French series of *contre-torpilleurs* that set new standards of performance.

Launched in 1932 and 1933, the ships had little real influence on destroyer construction abroad because they stemmed largely from naval rivalry with the Italians. The rivalry took the form of an obsession with speed, and though the 'Fantasques' were among the fastest vessels of their size ever built, they were virtually unarmoured. Although the design speed of the 'Fantasque' class was 37 knots, all six vessels in fact exceeded 40 knots during trials. Unlike other superfast vessels, the 'Fantasques' could maintain their high speeds for long periods. At the height of the Norwegian campaign, *Le Triomphant*, *L'Indomptable* and *Le Malin* carried out an audacious raid into the Skagerrak, engaging a force of German patrol boats. *L'Audacieux* was badly damaged at Dakar, and *L'Indomptable* was scuttled at Toulon in 1942. The four survivors were refitted in the United States later in the war, and remained operational through the 1950s.

Displacement: 2569t standard; 3300t full load
Dimensions: 132.4m x 12.35m x 5m (434ft 4in x 40ft 6in x 16ft 4in)
Machinery: two screws, geared turbines; 81,000hp
Armament: five 139mm (5.46in) guns; three triple 533mm (21in) TT
Armour: belt 76mm (3in); turret faces and decks 25mm (1in)
Speed: 37 knots
Range: 5559km (3000nm) at 14 knots
Complement: 210

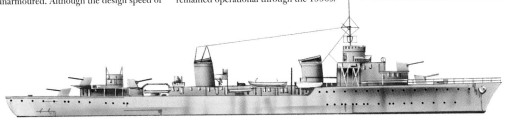

Town class

In 1933, the Royal Navy began work on a new class of light cruiser. The 'Town' class, also known as Southamptons after the lead ship, were to be substantially bigger than British cruisers then in service.

The first five ships were to provide a basic pattern for future classes. Although they were protected for the length of their machinery space by an armoured belt, brought up to the upper deck level to cover the boiler rooms, only box protection of similar thickness was provided for the magazines. Their

four-shaft machinery was enough to give them a maximum speed, on trial, of 32 knots, which was comparable with most of their contemporaries. All saw extensive service during World War II. The second series of three 'Towns', beginning with HMS *Gloucester* in 1937, had better armour and more powerful machinery. They were succeeded by two 'Belfast' class cruisers, based on the 'Towns', but enlarged. HMS *Belfast* was completed on 3 August 1939, and survives as a museum ship in London.

Displacement: 11,350t/12,190t) full load

Dimensions: 180.3m x 18.8m x 6.20m – later 6.55m (591ft 6in x 61ft 8in x 20ft 4in – later 21ft 6in)

Machinery: four-shaft, Parsons geared turbines; 75,000hp

Armament: 12 152mm (6in) guns; eight 102mm (4in) AA; four 3pdr guns; eight (later 28) 2pdr pom-poms; six 533mm (21in) TT; three aircraft

Armour: belt 114mm (4.5in); ammunition spaces 114mm (4.5in); bulkheads 64mm (2.5in); turrets 25mm (1in)

Speed: 32 knots

Range: 11,100km (6000nm) at 14 knots

Complement: 748

Queen Mary

The *Queen Mary*, which was completed in 1936, was built to take the Blue Riband and was to hold the record, both ways, until 1952.

Although a genuine speedster, she was far from austere – she was a fitting successor to the *Aquitania*, with which she operated pre-war. Laid down in 1931, she was due to be launched in 1932, but the Great Depression forced Cunard to suspend construction. She was eventually launched in September 1934. Wartime service as a troopship was marred by her colliding with and sinking the cruiser HMS *Curacoa* in October 1942; she was forbidden to stop to render assistance to the cruiser's crew, all but 26 of whom perished. The *Queen Mary* completed 1001 Atlantic crossings in her three decades of mercantile service. She was sold to the City of Long Beach, California, as a museum and hotel in 1967. To reach her new home she had to round Cape Horn, being too wide – by 1m (39in) – to pass through the Panama Canal.

Tonnage: 80,744grt (later 81,237grt)
Dimensions: 310.75m x 36.15m (1019ft 6in x 118ft 7in)
Machinery: four-shaft, geared turbines; 160,000hp
Service speed: 29 knots
Role: passenger liner; troopship
Route: Southampton–New York
Capacity: 15,000 troops; 711 1st, 707 cb, 577 tr
Constructor: John Brown & Co, Glasgow
Built for: Cunard-White Star Line

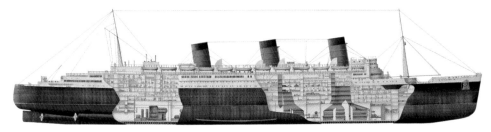

Graf Spee

Popularly known as 'pocket battleships' due to their combination of light and heavy armament, the *Admiral Graf Spee* and her two sister ships, *Deutschland* and *Admiral Scheer*, were properly designated Panzerschiffe, or armoured ships.

Designed for Germany's Kriegsmarine as commerce raiders with a large radius of action, their hulls were electrically welded and their armour plating reduced to the minimum considered necessary, achieving a substantial saving in weight, and permitting a higher maximum speed. *Graf Spee* was the last of the three constructed,

and completed in January 1936. She carried out blockade duty off Republican ports during the Spanish Civil War. At the beginning of World War II she sank or captured nine British merchant vessels in the South Atlantic before being brought to battle by a British naval force comprising the cruisers *Exeter*, *Ajax* and *Achilles* off the estuary of the river Plate. On 17 December 1939, *Graf Spee* was scuttled off Montevideo; her captain, Hans Langsdorff, committed suicide.

Displacement: 12,100t standard; 16,200t full load

Dimensions: 186m x 21.7m x 7.2m (610ft 3in x 71ft 2in x 23ft 9in)

Machinery: two screws, diesel; 55,400hp

Armament: six 280mm (11in) guns; eight 150mm (5.9in) guns; eight 533mm (21in) TT

Armour: belt 80–50mm (3–2in); turrets 140mm (5.5in); deck 40–18mm (1.5–0.71in)

Speed: 26 knots

Range: 18,530km (10,000nm) at 20 knots

Complement: 926

Mogami

The four Japanese light cruisers of the 'Mogami' class were in effect 'mini battleships', designed to mount the heaviest possible armament on the restricted tonnage set by the London Naval Treaty of 1930.

They featured triple gun turrets and, like Germany's 'pocket battleships', their hulls were electrically welded to save weight. At an early stage in the trials of the first two ships, *Mogami* and *Mikuma*, they were found to be top-heavy and had to be withdrawn for modification. Launched on 14 March 1934, *Mogami* took part in the Battle of Midway in June 1942, where she was severely damaged by carrier aircraft from the USS *Yorktown*. After a lengthy period of reconstruction she was returned to service in 1943, having been fitted with a flight deck on which it was intended to carry 11 seaplanes. *Mogami* was sunk by air attack in the Battle of the Surigao Strait on 25 October 1944. None of the ships of the 'Mogami' class survived the war.

Displacement: 8500t standard; 10,993t full load
Dimensions: 201.5m x 18m x 5.5m (661ft 1in x 59ft 1in x 18ft 1in)
Machinery: four screws, geared turbines; 152,000hp
Armament: 15 152mm (6in) guns; eight 127mm (5in) DP; 12 609mm (24in) TT
Armour: belt 100mm (3.9in); magazines 124mm (4.9in); deck 61-31mm (2.4-1.4in)
Speed: 37 knots
Range: 8153km (4400nm) at 14 knots
Complement: 850

Normandie

The *Normandie*'s story is one of superlatives. When launched in 1935 she was the biggest liner of her day, the most expensive, the most powerful, the fastest and the most extravagantly decorated.

Aesthetically she was superb, her three funnels raked and reducing in height, moving aft. The third funnel was actually a ventilator. Mechanically she was plagued by vibration which was cured only by substituting four-bladed for three-bladed propellers, but she certainly lived up to expectations concerning her performance, taking both westbound and eastbound Blue Ribands on her maiden voyage. She was to lose the record to the new Cunarder, the *Queen Mary*, and although she won it back again in March 1937, she lost it for good in August 1938. Laid up in New York in August 1939 and taken over by the US Navy as the USS *Lafayette* in December 1941, she was destroyed just days before she was due to enter service in February 1943, by a fire.

Tonnage: 79,280grt (later 83,423grt)

Dimensions: 313.6m x 35.7m x 10.2m (1029ft x 117ft 10in x 33ft 6in)

Machinery: four-shaft, turbo-electric; 165,000hp

Service speed: 29 knots

Role: passenger liner

Route: Le Havre–New York

Capacity: 848 1st, 670 tr, 454 3rd

Constructor: Chantiers et Ateliers de l'Atlantique, St Nazaire

Material: steel

Built for: CGT

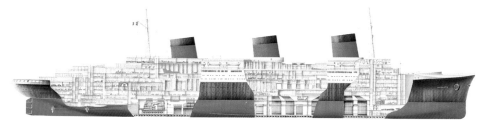

Condottiere

There were 12 'Condottieri'-class light cruisers in all, named after great generals and mercenary captains of Italian history.

The *Emanuele Filiberto Duca d'Aosta*, together with her sister ship *Eugenio di Savoia*, formed the fourth group. They were very fast, but in general the minimal armour of the 'Condottieri' was inadequate against gunfire from slower but tougher British cruisers. Five were sunk in World War II: three by submarines, one in a naval gunnery action and one by aerial bombing. Both *Duca d'Aosta* and *Eugenio di Savoia* saw a great deal of war service, much of

their activity involving convoy escort and running essential supplies to the Axis forces in North Africa. Both vessels survived World War II. *Duca d'Aosta* was ceded to the Soviet Union early in 1949 under the designation Z.15. She was renamed *Stalingrad* and later became the *Kerch*. She was discarded around 1957. Her sister ship *Eugenio di Savoia* was transferred to Greece in July 1951 and renamed *Helle*. She was removed from the active list in 1964.

Displacement: 8317t standard; 10,374t full load

Dimensions: 186.9m x 17.5m x 6.5m (613ft 2in x 57ft 5in x 21ft 4in)

Machinery: two screws, geared turbines; 110,000hp

Armament: eight 152mm (6in) guns; six 100mm (3.9in) AA; six 533mm (21in) TT

Armour: belt 70mm (2.75in); bulkheads 50-30mm (2-1.2in); turrets 90mm (3.5in)

Speed: 36.5 knots

Range: 7968km (4300nm)

Complement: 578 (694 during war service)

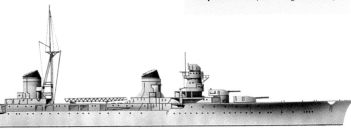

Dunkerque

With main armament concentrated forward like the Royal Navy's 'Nelson' class, *Dunkerque* and her sister ship *Strasbourg* were the French Navy's fastest battleships at the outbreak of World War II.

They formed the nucleus of a fast raiding force, based at the Atlantic port of Brest, that also included seven heavy cruisers, three light cruisers and some 50 destroyers. These French warships were capable of a sustained speed of 30 knots which, at that time, could not be matched by any other naval force in the world.

Dunkerque was launched on 2 October 1935. After the fall of France, she joined other French warships at Mers-el-Kebir in North Africa where, on 3 July 1940, she was attacked and heavily damaged by British warships. Three days later, she was damaged again and partly sunk by Swordfish torpedo-bombers. She was refloated and sailed to Toulon, where she was blown up in dry dock on 27 November 1942, when German forces occupied the port.

Displacement: 33,000t full load

Dimensions: 214.5m x 31.1m x 9.6m (703ft 9in x 102ft x 31ft 6in)

Machinery: four screws, geared turbines; 100,000hp

Armament: eight 330mm (12.9in) guns; 16 130mm (5in) DP; eight 37mm (1.46in) AA

Armour: belt 225-125mm (8.8-4.9in); turrets 345-330mm (13.5-13in); deck 140-130mm (5.5-5in)

Speed: 30 knots

Range: 13,897km (7500nm) at 15 knots

Complement: 1431

Gloire

The French Navy had too little time to play a major part in World War II, but individual French ships escaping to the Allies fought as part of the Free French forces.

French naval designers had every reason to be proud of the six 'La Galissonniere'-class light cruisers of the mid-1930s, of which *Gloire* was one. They were an outstanding success, with excellent seagoing characteristics and splendid armament. On completion in 1936, *La Galissonniere* joined the 2nd Light Squadron in the Mediterranean until the remaining five ships entered service in 1937. In October of that year she formed the 3rd Cruiser Division at Toulon, together with *Jean de Vienne* and *Marseillaise*. All three were scuttled at Toulon in November 1942 to prevent their capture by the Germans. The *Georges Leygues*, *Montcalm* and *Gloire* fought as Free French vessels on the Allied side, supporting the landings in France in 1944. All three surviving light cruisers served in the post-war French fleet. *Gloire* was sold for scrap in 1958.

Displacement: 7600t standard; 9120t full load
Dimensions: 179.5m x 17.48m x 5.35m (588ft 11in x 57ft 4in x 17ft 7in)
Machinery: two screws, geared turbines; 84,000hp
Armament: nine 152mm (6in) guns; eight 89mm (3.5in) guns; four 550mm (21.7in) TT
Armour: belt 120–76mm (4.7–3in); turret faces 102mm (4in); deck 38mm (1.5in)
Speed: 31 knots
Range: 10,080km (5440nm) at 15 knots
Complement: 540

Brooklyn

The US Navy's 'Brooklyns' were of roughly the same size as the heavy cruisers which had preceded them into service, but were very much more modern in their appearance.

They had an all-new hull form, flush-decked with a high transom stern which housed a hangar capable of accommodating four aircraft, accessible via a sliding hatch. They were the first of the American 'large light cruisers', and were to provide a model for the later 'Cleveland' class. Before the design was finalized, however, Japan launched the first of the 'Mogamis', which mounted 15 155mm (6.1in) guns on a reported standard displacement of 8500t, (although in reality the 'Mogamis' topped 11,000t) and this caused a hasty revision of the 'Brooklyns' weapons plan, the weight of an extra 152mm (6in) triple being 'stolen' from the hull. When they began entering service from 1937, there was some speculation that the 'Brooklyns' were too lightly constructed, but all but one of the nine-strong class survived the war, and most continued for many decades more in foreign service. *Brooklyn* was sold to Chile in 1951 to serve as the *O'Higgins*. She was finally decommissioned in 1992.

Displacement: 9770t standard; 12,210t full load

Dimensions: 608ft 4in x 61ft 9in x 22ft 9in (185.4m x 18.8 x 6.95m

Machinery: four-shaft, Parson geared turbines; 100,000hp

Armament: 15 152mm (6in) guns; eight 127mm (5in) guns; eight 12.7mm (0.5in) MG (later 28 40mm/1.57in and 20 20mm/0.79in); four aircraft

Armour: belt 127mm (5in); deck 51mm (2in); turret faces 166mm (6.5in); conning tower 127mm (5in)

Speed: 32.5 knots

Range: 18,500km (10,000nm) at 15 knots

Complement: 868

Scharnhorst

Hitler originally wanted the 'Scharnhorst'-class battleships to be similar to the 'Deutschland'-class 'pocket battleships', but with much-improved protection.

The German Navy eventually persuaded Hitler that a bigger ship, mounting nine guns, would be more satisfactory. *Gneisenau* entered service on 21 May 1938, six months before her sister ship, the *Scharnhorst*. The following year both received the so-called 'Atlantic' bow, which increased overall length by 5.1m (16ft 9in) and made them more satisfactory sea-boats. *Gneisenau* and *Scharnhorst* sank the carrier *Courageous* in 1940, and

in 1941 broke out into the North Atlantic attacking merchant convoys before running into Brest. The two battleships, plus the cruiser *Prinz Eugen*, made the celebrated 'Channel dash', arriving in Wilhelmshaven on 13 February 1942. *Scharnhorst* was sunk by the British battleship *Duke of York* at the end of 1943. *Gneisenau* was damaged beyond repair by an RAF raid on the floating dock at Kiel. Her guns were removed, and she was towed to Gotenhafen (Gdynia), where she was scuttled in March 1945.

Displacement: 38,100t full load

Dimensions: 753ft 11in x 98ft 5in x 27ft 3in (229.8m x 30m x 8.3m)

Machinery: three-shaft, Germania geared turbines; 165,000hp

Armament: nine 11in (280mm); 12 5.9in (150mm); 14 4.1in (105mm); 16 37mm; eight 20mm; three or four aircraft

Armour: belt 13.75in–6.75in (350mm–170mm); deck 2in (50mm); armoured deck 4in–3in (100mm–75mm); main turret faces 14in (355mm); secondary turret faces 5.5in (135mm); conning tower 350mm (13.75in)

Speed: 32 knots

Range: 6200nm (11,450km) at 19 knots

Complement: 1670–1840

Type II U-Boat

The German Type II U-boats were small coastal submarines, the first constructed in numbers for the Kriegsmarine from 1934.

They were based on the Finnish Vesikko, built with German assistance in 1932. They were single-hull types, divided into three watertight compartments, with an operating depth of 80m (260ft) and crush depth of 150m (490ft). Only six of the first group, the Type IIAs, were produced, and the three units which survived were all stricken before the end of World War II, in August 1944. Later groups were increased

in size, but retained the same powerplant and armament. Six Type IIBs were laboriously transported to the Black Sea via the Elbe and the Danube. They were cut into three sections, removing all the heavy components, and loaded aboard 50t pontoons. They were transported overland on specially built vehicles between Dresden and Linz in Austria. Here they were reassembled, to continue their journey between two barges.

Displacement: 250t surfaced; 374t submerged

Dimensions: 40.9m x 4.1m x 3.8m (134ft x 13ft 5in x 12ft 5in)

Machinery: two-shaft, MWM diesel engines, plus Siemens-Schuckert electric motors; 700bhp/360hp

Armament: three 533mm (21in) TT (bow: six torpedoes); one 20mm (0.79in) gun

Speed: 13 knots surfaced; 7 knots submerged

Range: 2950km (1600nm) at 8 knots surfaced

Complement: 25

Type VII

The Type VII submarines, known as the 'Atlantic' boats, were the most common by far in German service during World War II, a total of 715 being produced in five variants.

They were saddle-tank boats, divided into six watertight compartments, with an operating depth of 100m (330ft), and they proved to be highly seaworthy and very manoeuvrable. After 1943 many boats lost their 88mm (3.5in), and had extra light AA guns added. The 'Atlantic' U-boats were actually not well suited to oceanic operations at all, having been designed for service in the North Sea and the western approaches. Their design was the minimum acceptable for open-ocean work by reason of their limited torpedo capacity in particular. Nonetheless, their one vital attribute was that they were available and they worked – reason enough to ensure the boat's employment (and even continuing construction), even after it was functionally obsolete. Type VIIs were used by Germany's early aces, and one of the most famous was Guenther Prien's *U-47*, with which he sank the *Royal Oak* in 1939.

Displacement: 741t surfaced; 1021t submerged

Dimensions: 66.5m x 6.2m x 4.7m (218ft 2in x 20ft 4in x 15ft 5in)

Machinery: two-shaft, Germaniawerft diesel engines, plus AEG electric motors; 2800bhp/750hp

Armament: five 533mm (21in) TT (four bow, one stern; 14 torpedoes); one 88mm (3.5in) gun; one 20mm (0.79in) gun

Speed: 18 knots surfaced; 8 knots submerged

Range: 16,100km (8700nm) at 10 knots surfaced

Complement: 44

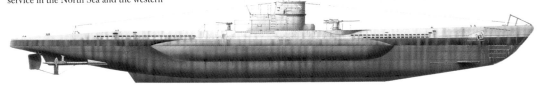

Yorktown

**The US Navy was limited by the 1922
Washington Treaty to a total of
135,000t of aircraft carriers.
Lexington and *Saratoga* consumed
66,000t, and the less-than-satisfactory
Ranger took another 14,000t.**

Washington decided to build two more
carriers at 20,000t each. The first of these
was the *Yorktown*, completed in September
1937 and the *Enterprise* which followed
six months later. These ships were to
define the form of the modern aircraft
carrier and become legends in their own
lifetimes, but they were not fault-free.

The carriers' lightweight hangars and
superstructures proved vulnerable to
enemy attack, although they did allow the
carriers to operate with much bigger air
groups than similar-sized British carriers.
Apart from the Coral Sea, USS *Enterprise*
was involved in almost every carrier battle
of World War II. At Midway, her aircraft
and those of her two sister ships sank four
Japanese carriers and inflicted a blow from
which Japan never recovered. *Yorktown*
was sunk after the same battle.

Displacement: 19,875t standard;
25,485t full load
Dimensions: 251.4m x 25.35m x 7.9m
(824ft 9in x 109ft 6in x 26ft)
Machinery: four-shaft, Parsons geared
turbines; 120,000hp
Armament: eight 127mm (5in) guns; 16
28mm (1.1in) guns; 24 12.7mm (0.5in)
guns (later 60 40mm/1.57in); 32
20mm/0.79in); up to 96 aircraft
Speed: 32.5 knots
Range: 22,200km (12,000nm) at 15 knots
Complement: 1890 (1938); 2175 (1942)

Giulio Cesare

The *Giulio Cesare* was one of Italy's 'Cavour'-class battleships, launched in 1911, but extensively modernized between the wars.

As constructed, she mounted 13 305mm (12in) guns and had a top speed of 21.5 knots at a displacement of around 24,000t. From October 1933, she was rebuilt from a stripped-out hull and re-engined with two-shaft machinery, giving 75,000hp for 27 knots under normal conditions, and 93,000hp for 28 knots under forced draught, a speed she exceeded marginally

on trial. Her main armament was reduced to 10 guns. The guns themselves were bored out and relined, and the mountings were modified to allow them to elevate to 27 degrees. New secondary and anti-aircraft batteries were added.

Recommissioned into the Italian navy as a virtually new ship on 1 October 1937, she survived World War II. In 1948 she was transferred to the Soviet Union as war reparations where, renamed *Novorossiisk*, she was either sunk after hitting a mine or badly damaged, then broken up, in 1955.

Displacement: 29,032t full load
Dimensions: 186.4m x 28m x 10.5m (611ft 6in x 91ft 10in x 34ft 5in)
Machinery: two-shaft geared turbines; 75,000hp/93,000hp forced draught
Armament: 10 320mm (12.6in) guns; 12 120mm (4.7in) guns; eight 100mm (3.9in) AA; 12 37mm (1.46in) guns; 12 13.2mm (0.52in) MG (later 12, and later again 16, 20mm/0.79in)
Armour: belt 254mm (10in); deck 112–80mm (4.4–3.15in); barbettes 280mm (11in); turrets 254mm (10in); conning tower 260mm (10.2in)
Speed: 28 knots
Range: 12,000km (6500nm) at 13 knots
Complement: 1235

Tromp

HNLMS *Tromp* and her sister ship *Jacob van Heemskerck* were originally conceived in 1931 as 2500t flotilla leaders, but when they were authorized in 1936 they had gained more than 50 per cent displacement and evolved into conventional scout cruisers.

They had comparatively heavy armament, concentrated forward, at the cost of reduced protection consisting of a splinter-proof box enclosing the machinery and magazines, something like the citadel found in ships of an earlier generation, but much lighter. It had always been intended that these cruisers would operate in the Dutch East Indies, but when war broke out in Europe only *Tromp* had been completed. She and her sister ship escaped to Britain in 1940, where *van Heemskerck* was completed as an AA cruiser, with 10 102mm (4in) HA guns of British design and British gunnery directors, and extra light weapons. Both ships survived the war and were to be the mainstay of the Royal Netherlands Navy immediately post-war. On being stricken in 1958, they became accommodation ships.

Displacement: 4860t full load

Dimensions: 132m x 12.4m x 4.2m (433ft x 40ft 8in x 13ft 9in)

Machinery: two-shaft, Parsons geared turbines; 56,000hp

Armament: six 150mm (4.9in); (later four 76mm/3in AA); eight (later 12) 40mm (1.57in); (later two 20mm/0.79in); four 12.7mm (0.5in) MG; six 533mm (21in) TT; one aircraft

Armour: belt 15mm (0.7in); sides and bulkheads 30mm (1.2in); decks 25mm (1in); gunshields 15mm (0.7in)

Speed: 33.5 knots

Range: 18,500km (10,000nm) at 15 knots

Complement: 309

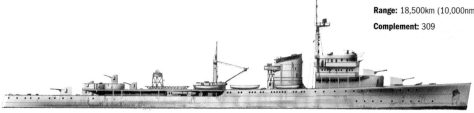

Ark Royal

HMS *Ark Royal* was the first large aircraft carrier to be built for the Royal Navy. Constructed by Cammell Laird at Birkenhead, 'The Ark' was commissioned on 16 November 1938 and had a short but eventful wartime career.

One of her Blackburn Skua aircraft scored the first aerial victory of the war, and another, a Fairey Swordfish, crippled the *Bismarck* with a torpedo, forcing her into a fatal gunnery duel. *Ark Royal* did sterling service as part of Force 'H' in the Mediterranean. She was sunk there on 14 November 1941, by a single torpedo fired from *U-81*. The torpedo opened a 40m x 9m (130ft x 30ft) hole in her starboard side and bottom, abreast of the starboard boiler room; she capsized and went down after 14 hours. It was something of a lucky shot: accidentally or on purpose, the German torpedo was set to run very deep and thus evaded both her armoured belt and the cellular system within the hull itself. The three boiler rooms, connected by unbaffled smoke ducts – allowing them all to be flooded at an angle of list of just 10 degrees – was perhaps the only serious mistake *Ark Royal*'s designers made, but it was to prove fatal.

Displacement: 22,000t standard; 27,700t full load
Dimensions: 243.8m x 29.3m x 8.5m (800ft x 96ft x 27ft 9in)
Machinery: three-shaft, Parsons geared turbines; 102,000hp
Armament: 16 114mm (4.5in) guns; 32 2pdr pom-poms; four 3pdr; 72 aircraft
Armour: belt 114mm (4.5in); bulkheads 76mm (3in); decks 89mm (3.5in)
Speed: 31 knots
Range: 14,100km (7600nm) at 20 knots
Complement: 1580

Hiryu

The *Hiryu* was built at Yokosuka Navy Yard and completed in July 1939. She was a slightly enlarged version of the *Soryu*, the ship which set the style for Japanese fleet carriers in the years before the start of World War II.

Hiryu's 1m (3.3ft) greater beam increased her bunkerage by 20 per cent and so increased her unrefuelled range. Although protection was minimal, consisting of an armoured waterline belt and flight deck, the *Hiryu* had a two-level hangar, the upper some 20 per cent longer than the lower, which connected to the flight deck by three lifts, and could operate up to 64 aircraft. Her island was positioned to port, and served to balance the horizontal funnels to starboard, just below the level of the flight deck. *Hiryu* took part in the attacks on Pearl Harbor, the East Indies and Darwin, and also in the Indian Ocean raid. She was one of the four Japanese carriers sunk at the Battle of Midway in early June 1942 – but not before her aircraft had crippled the US carrier *Yorktown*. *Hiryu* was hit four times by dive-bombers, sustained insupportable damage to flight deck and hangars, and was abandoned, then torpedoed by the destroyer *Mikagumo*.

Displacement: 17,300t standard; 21,900t full load

Dimensions: 745ft 11in x 73ft 3in x 25ft 9in (227.4m x 22.3m x 7.85m)

Machinery: four-shaft, geared turbines; 153,000hp

Armament: 12 5in (127mm) DP; 31 25mm; 64 aircraft

Armour: belt 5.9in–3.6in (150mm–90mm); deck 1in (25mm)

Speed: 34.5 knots

Range: 9500nm (17,600km) at 18 knots

Complement: 1100

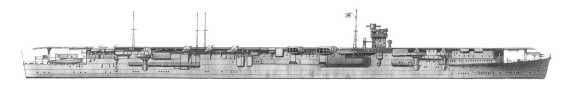

Mohawk

The large 'Tribal' class destroyers were a new departure for the Royal Navy. They were inspired by France, Germany, Japan and the United States, who already had heavily armed destroyers at sea or being built.

The Admiralty's decision was to mount new models of 119mm (4.7in) guns in five twin mountings in the belief that their faster rate of fire would make up for their lighter weight. A design review later replaced the central 'Q' mount with a pair of quad 2pdr pom-poms. The Tribals

were thus the first British destroyers to have an effective light AA armament. All the British Tribals were laid down during 1936–37 and took about two years to complete. They saw hard service during the war. HMS *Mohawk* was built by Thornycroft at Portsmouth and entered service in October 1938. She was sunk in the course of a fierce battle on 16 April 1941 with the Italian 'Navigatori'-class destroyer *Luca Tarigo*, which managed to

torpedo *Mohawk* while under fire from her and her sister ship *Nubian*, as well as the two 'J'-class destroyers *Jervis* and *Janus*, before succumbing herself.

Displacement: 1960t standard; 2520t full load
Dimensions: 114.9m x 11.15m x 3.95m (377ft x 36ft 6in x 13ft)
Machinery: two-shaft, Parsons geared turbines; 44,000hp
Armament: eight 120mm (4.7in); eight 2pdr pom-poms; four 533mm (21in) TT; DC racks
Speed: 36 knots
Range: 11,100km (6000nm) at 20 knots
Complement: 190

Vittorio Veneto

Pride of the Regia Marina Italiana during World War II were the three brand-new fast battleships of the 'Littorio' class.

The first to enter service was the *Vittorio Veneto*, followed by the *Littorio* and the *Roma*. The *Impero* was laid down and launched at Trieste, but never completed. The Littorios were of a thoroughly modern design, the work of Umberto Pugliese, and were the first new battleships laid down since the British Nelsons of 1922. Although supposedly within the 35,000t treaty limit, by the time they were authorized in 1934 the planned weight was around 40,000t. *Vittorio Veneto* entered service in April 1940; she was hit by an aerial torpedo at the Battle of Matapan in March 1941, and repairs took five months. She was torpedoed again in December 1941, this time by the British submarine *Urge*, and was out of action until March 1942. She was interned in the Bitter Lakes on the Suez Canal from late 1943, and returned in 1946. *Vittorio Veneto* was given to Britain as a reparation in 1947 and was later broken up.

Displacement: 45,030t full load

Dimensions: 237.75m x 32.8m x 10.5m (780ft x 107ft 7in x 34ft 6in)

Machinery: four-shaft, Belluzzo geared turbines; 128,200hp

Armament: nine 381mm (15in); 12 152mm (6in); four 120mm (4.7in); 12 90mm (3.6in) AA; 20 37mm (1.46in); 16 20mm (0.79in)

Armour: belt 280mm (11in); bulkheads 210mm (8.25in); decks 162–45mm (6.4–1.8in); barbettes 350–280mm (13.8–11in); turret faces 350mm (13.8in); conning tower 260mm (10.2in)

Speed: 30 knots

Range: 8500km (4600nm) at 16 knots

Complement: 1830

Nieuw Amsterdam

The Dutch contribution to the great age of the transatlantic ocean liner was the *Nieuw Amsterdam*, completed for the Holland–America line in the late 1930s.

The *Nieuw Amsterdam* was the second vessel of that name; like her predecessor, she operated on the Rotterdam–New York service. She made her last pre-war Atlantic crossing in September 1939, then sailed as a cruise ship out of New York before converting to a troopship a year later. She returned to mercantile service in October 1947 after a refit, having sailed more than 800,000km (half a million miles) as a troopship. She was used for cruising from 1971 and was scrapped in 1974. The *Nieuw Amsterdam* was designed and constructed with economy, rather than record breaking, in mind and enjoyed a long useful career as a result.

Tonnage: 36,287grt
Dimensions: 231.2m x 26.9m
(758ft 6in x 88ft 4in)
Machinery: two-shaft, geared turbines
Service speed: 20.5 knots
Role: passenger liner; troopship; cruise ship
Route: Rotterdam–New York
Capacity: 556 cb, 455 tr, 209 3rd; postwar 552 1st, 426 cb, 209 tr
Constructor: Rotterdamsche Droogdok Mij
Material: steel
Built for: Holland America Line

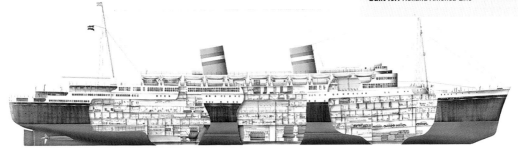

Atlantis

Germany made extensive use of heavily armed and disguised merchant raider against British shipping in distant waters during the early years of World War II.

In 1937, AG Vulcan, Bremen, laid down a motor ship, the *Goldenfels*, of 7862grt. She was to have a very different career than that envisaged for her; on 30 November 1939 she was impressed into the Kriegsmarine as *Schiff 16*, armed as a Hilfskreuzer (auxiliary cruiser, or commerce raider). The captains of such vessels were allowed to name them themselves, and under Captain Bernhard Rogge she became the *Atlantis*.

For 601 days she cruised the Atlantic, the Indian Ocean and the Pacific, sinking 22 vessels of 146,000 tons of shipping (this was about the same tonnage as that sunk by the two 32,000-ton battleships *Scharnhorst* and *Gneisenau* in Operation Berlin). In November 1941 the *Atlantis* was sunk by the British heavy cruiser HMS *Devonshire*.

Displacement: 17,600t full load

Dimensions: 508ft 6in x 61ft 4in x 28ft 6in (155m x 18.7m x 8.7m)

Machinery: one-shaft, two MAN double-acting 6-cyl. diesels; 7600bhp

Armament: six 5.9in (150mm); one 75mm; two 37mm; four 20mm; four 21in (533mm) TT; two aircraft

Speed: 16 knots

Range: 12,000nm (22,200km) at 12 knots

Complement: 351

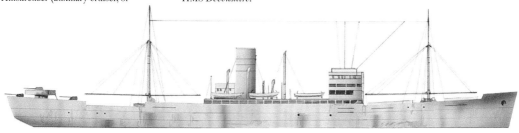

Hipper

The Kriegsmarine completed just three heavy cruisers of the 'Hipper' class, which massively contravened the 10,000t displacement limit of the 1935 Anglo–German Agreement.

There was considerable opposition to the 'Hipper' class in German naval circles; their range was thought to be nowhere near sufficient for a commerce raider. The Hippers were built in two groups. *Hipper*, which entered service in 1938, achieved some success as a commerce raider in the early years of World War II. *Blücher* was sunk in Oslofjord in 1940. *Prinz Eugen* was marginally longer and broader, and proportionally heavier, than the first pair.

She was constructed by Germaniawerft at Kiel and commissioned in August 1940. She had an active career early on, accompanying *Bismarck* when she broke out into the North Atlantic to mount Operation Rheinübung, and *Scharnhorst* and *Gneisenau* on their return to Germany from Brest during Operation Cerberus. *Prinz Eugen* was awarded to the United States as reparation and later used as a target during the Bikini Atoll atom bomb tests, being sunk in Kwajalein lagoon on 22 December 1946.

Displacement: 18,750t full load
Dimensions: 207.7m x 21.5m x 7.2m
(679ft 1in x 70ft 6in x 23ft 7in)
Machinery: three-shaft, Brown-Boveri geared turbines; 132,000hp
Armament: eight 203mm (8in); 12 105mm (4.1in), later 17 40mm (1.57in); 12 37mm (1.46in) (later deleted); eight (later 26) 20mm (0.79in); 12 533mm (21in) TT; three aircraft
Armour: 80mm (belt 3.3in); deck 50-30mm (2-1.2in); turret faces 105mm (4.1in); conning tower 150mm (5.9in)
Speed: 32.5 knots
Range: 12,600km (6800nm) at 20 knots
Complement: 1600

Kelly

Under the command of Lord Louis Mountbatten, the _Kelly_ was to become one of the most famous ships of the Royal Navy during World War II. Her career was dramatized by Noël Coward in his film _In Which We Serve._

HMS _Kelly_ was the designated leader of the eight-ship 'K' class of fleet destroyers constructed, along with the similar' 'J and 'N' classes, from 1937 onwards. Larger than the preceding 'H' class, their construction introduced the more robust longitudinal framing into British

destroyers. The hull design formed the basis of the 'L' and 'M' classes of 'war emergency' destroyers, which differed mainly in having single rather than twin gun mounts. _Kelly_ and her sisters mounted the improved 119mm (4.7in) Mk XII gun in twin gunhouses, instead of single Mk IXs, which made their centrelines much less crowded. HMS _Kelly_ was constructed by Hawthorne Leslie and was commissioned in 1939. She was sunk off Crete in May 1941.

Displacement: 1760t standard; 2330t full load

Dimensions: 108.65m x 10.85m x 4.2m (356ft 6in x 35ft 8in x 13ft 8in)

Machinery: two-shaft, Parsons geared turbines; 40,000hp

Armament: six 119mm (4.7in) guns; four 2pdr pom-poms; 10 533mm (21in) TT; DC racks

Speed: 36 knots

Range: 11,100km (6000nm) at 15 knots

Complement: 218

T-class submarine

The original British 'T'-class submarines were the pre-war 'Tritons', which superseded the 'Thames' class as the Royal Navy's long-range patrol submarines.

They were saddle-tank types, with 12mm (0.5in) pressure plating and an operating depth of 91m (300ft). Modified types were built in two groups during World War II. Improvements included greater operational depth and increased fuel

capacity, as well as alterations to the distribution of the torpedo tubes. Modifications included the two external tubes forward removed from some boats, to improve their seakeeping and depth capability; most boats had their external midships tubes altered to fire astern instead of ahead, and an additional external stern tube mounted. All survivors received a 20mm (0.79in) cannon in 1943. Some had their fuel capacity increased by simply adapting their main tanks.

Displacement: 1090t surfaced; 1575t submerged

Dimensions: 83.8m x 8.1m x 4.55m (275ft x 26ft 7in x 15ft)

Machinery: two-shaft, Vickers diesel engines, plus electric motors; 2500bhp/1450hp

Armament: 10 533mm (21in) TT (six bow, four external: 16 torpedoes); one 102mm (4in)

Speed: 15.25 knots surfaced; 9 knots submerged

Range: 14,800km (8000nm) at 10 knots surfaced

Complement: 59

T-class torpedo-boat

The designation 'torpedo-boat' as used by the Kriegsmarine in this era was somewhat misleading, for these were what other navies would call small destroyers.

The Type 35s, of which *T1*, the first, commissioned in December 1939, were built by Schichau at Elbing and Deschimag of Bremen. The yard was to construct 36 similar vessels for the Kriegsmarine. Although more capable than French and Italian ships with the same designation, and very much faster and thus more effective, the Type 35s were very expensive to construct and operate. Much

larger than the earlier Type 35s and Type 37s, the German Type 39 torpedo-boats, of which *T22* was the first, completed in 1941, were actually more akin to destroyer escorts. They were effective in the role and were also employed as minelayers – fatally for *T22* and two sister ships. They were sunk when navigational errors drove them into a minefield they had laid in the Gulf of Finland in August 1944. Wartime modifications included mounting additional light AA weaponry.

Displacement: 845t standard; 1090t full load
Dimensions: 84.3m x 8.6m x 2.35m (276ft 7in x 28ft 3in x 7ft 8in)
Machinery: two-shaft, Wagner geared turbines; 31,000hp
Armament: three 533mm (21in) TT; one 105mm (4.1in); one (later three) 37mm (1.46in); eight (later 12) 20mm (0.79in)
Speed: 35 knots
Range: 1100km (600nm) at 35 knots
Complement: 119

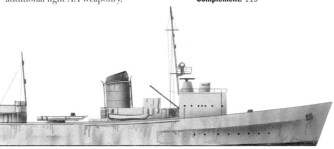

Z-class destroyer

The Third Reich built its first Zerstörers, or destroyers, in 1934. Subsequent classes were modelled on them, and all shared their shortcomings to some extent.

Although they were amongst the fastest in the world at the time, these destroyers were unstable, steered and manoeuvred poorly, and were very wet indeed. Halfway through the production of the Type 36, improvements were introduced, beginning with a new 'clipper' bow profile for the *Karl Galster*, otherwise known as *Z20*.

The type was heavily built, with innovative high-performance high-pressure steam machinery which often proved unreliable. They were well-armed ships, even from the outset, but *Karl Galster*, the only survivor of the invasion of Norway (during which all five of her sister ships were sunk) received many more AA guns. She was constructed, like all the class, by Deschimag in Bremen, and entered service in March 1939. She survived World War II and was taken as a Russian prize. Renamed *Procniy*, she served in the Baltic until about 1960.

Displacement: 1810t standard; 3415t full load
Dimensions: 125m x 11.8m x 4m (410ft 1in x 38ft 8in x 13ft 1in)
Machinery: two-shaft, Wagner geared turbines; 70,000hp
Armament: five 127mm (5in); four (later six) 37mm (1.46in); six (later 15) 20mm (0.79in); eight 533mm (21in) TT; 60 mines
Speed: 36 knots
Range: 3800km (2050nm) at 19 knots
Complement: 330
Country: Germany

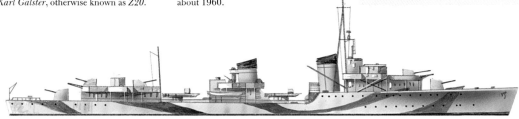

Zuikaku

The *Zuikaku* and her sister ship, the class leader *Shokaku*, were enlarged and improved versions of the fast fleet carriers *Soryu* and *Hiryu*.

Much of their additional displacement went to thicken their protective decks, although the flight deck and intermediate hangar deck remained unarmoured, as did the hangar sides – the main shortcoming in these vessels. Nonetheless, they are considered by many to have been the most successful of all the Japanese carriers, and were certainly to have the longest careers. Launched in 1939 and commissioned in 1941, they had the largest air groups of their time. Wartime modification consisted of adding light AA weapons, as usual, but in May 1944 *Zuikaku* had the air spaces around her aviation spirit bunkers filled with concrete in an effort to exclude the air and make explosion less likely. *Zuikaku* was built by Kawasaki at Kobe and entered service in late September 1941. With those of her sister ship, her aircraft sank the USS *Lexington*. *Shokaku* was sunk by the US Navy submarine *Cavalla* during the Battle of the Philippine Sea in June 1944. *Zuikaku* was badly damaged in the same battle, and was sunk by carrier aircraft at Cape Engano during the Battle of Leyte Gulf in October 1944.

Displacement: 25,675t standard; 32,105t full load

Dimensions: 844ft 10in x 95ft x 29ft 1in (257m x 29m x 8.85m)

Machinery: four-shaft, Kampon geared turbines; 160,000hp

Armament: 16 5in (127mm) DP; 42 (later 82, later 108) 25mm; 72 aircraft

Armour: belt 6.5in–1.8in (175mm–45mm); deck 5.9in–3.9in (155mm–100mm)

Speed: 34 knots

Range: 10,000nm (18,500km) at 18 knots

Complement: 1660

Audacity

Following the fall of France, Allied shipping in the Atlantic faced a new threat in the shape of ultra-long range Focke Wulf FW.200 Kondor bombers.

In an attempt to provide much-needed air cover, merchant ships were converted to become basic aircraft carriers; the first of them was HMS *Audacity*. Constructed by AG Vulcan at Vegesack, Bremen, as the 5500grt *Hannover*, she was launched on 29 March 1939 only to be captured by the Allies in the Caribbean in February 1940.

Conversion began in January 1941; she was commissioned as HMS *Audacity* in June that year. Only very rudimentary equipment was installed. There was no hangar and no need for a lift – her six aircraft were kept on deck. Tanks to hold 45,460 litres (10,000 gallons) of aviation fuel were installed. Navigation and control of air operations were carried out from a simple platform to starboard. *Audacity* escorted Gibraltar convoys for six months until torpedoed by *U-751* off Portugal on 20 December 1941.

Displacement: 12,000t full load
Dimensions: 142.4m x 18.3m x 6.6m (467ft 3in x 60ft x 21ft 7in)
Machinery: one-shaft, one 7-cylinder MAN diesel; 5200bhp
Armament: one 102mm (4in) HA; one 6pdr gun; four 2pdr pom-poms; four 20mm (0.79in) guns; six aircraft
Speed: 15 knots
Range: 22,200km (12,000nm) at 13 knots
Complement: 480

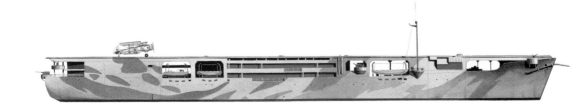

Bismarck

The Treaty of Versailles after World War I barred Germany from constructing new warships; however, the later Anglo–German Naval Treaty of 1935 permitted her to build up to 35 per cent of British naval tonnage.

Bismarck and her sister ship *Tirpitz* were the second pair of battleships built for the Kriegsmarine after the *Scharnhorst* and the *Gneisenau*. Officially, *Bismarck* was to have been a ship of 35,000t, but that was a fiction; the true figure was considerably higher – her hull armour alone weighed 17,500t. She was an outstanding sea-boat, with a shallow pitching movement and very slight roll, and required no weather helm to maintain her heading. Completed in August 1940 *Bismarck* put to sea for her first – and last – combat mission, Operation Rheinübung, in company with the cruiser *Prinz Eugen* in May 1941. After sinking the battlecruiser *Hood* in the Denmark Straits, *Bismarck* was hunted down by the full force of the Royal Navy. Damaged by aerial torpedoes, she was sunk by the battleships *King George V* and *Rodney* and the cruiser *Dorsetshire* on 27 May 1941.

Displacement: 50,900t full load

Dimensions: 248m x 36m x 10.6m (813ft 8in x 118ft 1in x 34ft 9in)

Machinery: three-shaft, Blohm & Voss geared turbines; 138,000hp

Armament: eight 380mm (15in); 12 150mm (5.9in); 16 105mm (4.1in); 16 37mm (1.46in); 12 20mm (0.79in); four aircraft

Armour: belt 318-267mm (12.5-10.5in); deck 121mm (4.75in); 51mm (2in); main turrets 362-178mm (14.25-7in); secondary turrets 102-37mm (4-1.5in); conning tower 356mm (14in)

Speed: 29 knots

Range: 15,750km (8500nm) at 19 knots

Complement: 2092

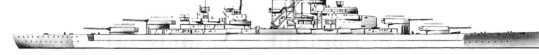

Hunt class

During World War II, Britain built just one class of escort destroyer, with a total of 86 vessels entering service. There were four sub-groups, although the last group of only two ships was markedly different in appearance.

All ships in the class were named after English hunts; the first of them, HMS *Atherstone*, was constructed by Cammell Laird at Birkenhead in 1939. Once at sea it was clear that she was dangerously unstable; the problem was corrected by the hurried removal of one of the three twin 102mm (4in) gun turrets and adding ballast. These 'Hunt'-class escort

destroyers were among the first ships of the Royal Navy to be fitted with Denny fin stabilizers. Later groups had their beam increased by 762mm (2ft 6in); this both cured the stability problem definitively and enabled them to revert to their designed armament. Somewhat surprisingly, for their mission was a dangerous one, all but 17 of the 'Hunts' survived the war. HMS *Atherstone* was broken up in 1957.

Displacement: 1000t standard; 1450t full load
Dimensions: 85.35m x 8.85m x 3.8m (280ft x 29ft x 12ft 6in)
Machinery: two-shaft, Parsons geared turbines; 19,000hp
Armament: four 102mm (4in) HA; four 2pdr pom-poms; two 20mm (0.79in) guns; 50 DC
Speed: 28 knots
Range: 11,100km (6000nm) at 18 knots
Complement: 147

Illustrious

The three 'Illustrious'-class fleet aircraft carriers constructed for the Royal Navy at the end of the 1930s were the first in the world to have fully armoured hangars.

Designed to meet the threat of attack from land-based aircraft, particularly in the Mediterranean theatre, their armour meant that the ships in the class had only one hangar deck, compared to the two built into the *Ark Royal*, and could operate only half the number of aircraft, despite being of similar size and displacement. By 1944, aircraft capacity had been increased to more than 50 by the expedient of adding a 'parking' area extension to the flight deck, on outriggers. HMS *Indomitable*, laid down as the fourth member of the class, was completed with 76mm (3in) less armour on the hangar sides and the flight deck was raised to allow an additional (shortened) hangar, to accommodate 50 per cent more aircraft on the same displacement. Her sister ship HMS *Victorious* was later modified to operate jet aircraft and remained in service into the late 1960s.

Displacement: 23,000t standard; 29,100t full load

Dimensions: 226.7m x 29.2m x 8.5m (743ft 9in x 95ft 9in x 28ft)

Machinery: three-shaft, Parsons geared turbines; 111,000hp

Armament: 16 114mm (4.5in) HA; 48 2pdr pom-poms (later 12 40mm/1.57in and 34 20mm/0.79in); 33 (later 50–54) aircraft

Speed: 30.5 knots

Range: 20,400km (11,000nm) at 14 knots

Complement: 1229 (later 1997)

Yukikaze

The 'Kagero'-class destroyers were authorized in 1937 and 1939. In November 1939, when the lead ship entered service, the Imperial Navy believed they had the best fleet destroyers in the world.

Problems with the powerplant and steering gear experienced in the preceding 'Asashios' were eliminated in the 'Kageros'. Like all Japanese destroyers of the period, their principal armament of 127mm (5in) dual-purpose guns was mounted in twin turrets, one forward and two aft; the 'X'

turret was removed from survivors from 1943, and replaced with additional light AA guns. *Hamakaze* was the first Japanese destroyer to be equipped with radar. She was sunk by US aircraft on 7 April 1945. All but one of the 'Kagero' class of 18 were lost; the sole survivor, the *Yukikaze*, was the luckiest ship in the Japanese Navy. Present at most of the major battles of the Pacific War, from the Battle of the Java Sea to Yamato's last sortie, she suffered virtually no damage. Transferred to China, then to Taiwan, she remained in service as the *Tang Yan*, being scrapped in May 1970.

Displacement: 2035t standard; c2500t full load

Dimensions: 118.5m x 10.8m x 3.75m (388ft 9in x 35ft 5in x 12ft 4in)

Machinery: two-shaft, geared turbines; 52,000hp

Armament: six (later four) 127mm (5in) guns; four (later 14) 25mm (1in) guns; eight 610mm (24in) TT; DCs

Speed: 35 knots

Range: 11,100km (6000nm) at 20 knots

Complement: 240

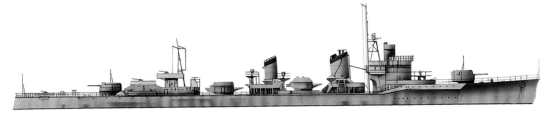

Guglielmo Marconi

A considerable force of ocean-going submarines was built by Italy before World War II, but they never achieved the success of Germany's U-boat arm.

The *Guglielmo Marconi* was the lead boat of a class of six oceangoing submarines, improved versions of the Marcellos, which entered service with the Italian navy in 1940. She was built by Cantieri Riuniti dell'Adriatico and newly delivered when Italy declared war in June 1940. Unsuitable for operations in the Mediterranean, *Guglielmo Marconi* was soon transferred to Bordeaux, to operate in the Atlantic, along with most other Italian first-class submarines. She was sunk, torpedoed in error by the German submarine *U-67*, in October 1941.

All six 'Marconi'-class submarines operated in the Atlantic out of Bordeaux; one, converted to carry cargo, was seized by the Japanese in Singapore after Italy had signed an armistice with the Allies.

Displacement: 1175t surfaced; 1465t submerged

Dimensions: 76.5m x 6.8m x 4.7m (251ft x 22ft 4in x 15ft 6in)

Machinery: two-shaft, diesel engines, plus Marelli electric motors; 3600bhp/1500hp

Armament: eight 533mm (21in) TT (four bow, four stern: 12 torpedoes); one 100mm (3.9in); four 13.2mm (0.52in) MG

Speed: 17.8 knots surfaced; 8.2 knots submerged

Range: 19,500km (10,500nm) at 8 knots surfaced

Complement: 57

Renown

The 28,000t battlecruisers *Renown* and *Repulse* were commissioned into the Royal Navy in 1916. They had six 381mm (15in) guns and were only lightly protected, but they had a maximum speed of over 30 knots.

Renown was rebuilt in 1923–26: she was bulged, a 229mm (9in) armour belt replaced the earlier 152mm (6in), thicker deck armour was fitted, and her secondary battery was renewed. Her standard displacement increased to *c*31,000t. She was reconstructed again in 1936–39: her machinery was renewed with more powerful turbines and improved boilers,

and her secondary battery was replaced again. A catapult and aircraft hangars were added, although both were later removed. During World War II, modifications consisted chiefly of additions to her light AA weaponry. *Renown* survived the war and was broken up in 1948. The only partially modernized *Repulse*, lacking effective AA defences, was sunk along with the battleship *Prince of Wales* by Japanese land-based bombers in December 1941.

Displacement: 36,100t full load
Dimensions: 242m x 31.2m x 9.8m (794ft x 102ft 4in x 32ft 3in)
Machinery: four-shaft, Parsons geared turbines; 120,000hp
Armament: six 381mm (15in) guns; 20 114mm (4.5in) guns; 24 2pdr pom-poms (later 64 20mm/0.79in); eight 533mm (21in) TT (deleted)
Armour: belt 229mm (9in); decks 102-51mm (4-2in); bulkheads 102-76mm (4-3in); secondary battery 64mm (2.5in); turret faces 280mm (11in); barbettes 152mm (6in); conning tower 254mm (10in)
Speed: 31 knots
Range: 3650nm (6760km) at 29 knots
Complement: 1200

Richelieu

The *Richelieu* was the only modern battleship France possessed during World War II, her sister ships *Jean Bart* and *Clemenceau* having been begun, but not completed.

With a top speed of 30 knots, she mounted 381mm (15in) guns in quadruple turrets, with almost 40 per cent of her entire standard displacement given over to protection. *Richelieu*, launched in January 1939, was only 95 per cent complete when France surrendered to the Germans in June 1940. She sailed for Dakar in Senegal, where she was damaged following Churchill's decision to disable the French fleet to prevent its use by the Kriegsmarine. She joined the Allies in 1942 and was sent to the United States, where she was refitted. She emerged in October 1943 with radar added, her aircraft removed and her light AA defences increased. Full load displacement rose to 46,000t. She served with the British Far Eastern Fleet for the rest of the war. Later, with some of her light AA weapons removed, she became the French flagship in Indo-China. She was paid off at Brest and hulked as an accommodation ship in 1959, and sold for demolition in 1964.

Displacement: 43,300t full load
Dimensions: 247.85m x 33m x 9.6m (813ft 2in x 108ft 3in x 31ft 3in)
Machinery: four-shaft, Parsons geared turbines; 150,000hp
Armament: eight 381mm (15in) guns; nine 152mm (6in) DP; 12 100mm (3.9in) AA; eight 37mm (1.46in) guns, later 56 40mm (1.57in); 48 20mm (0.79in); 16 13.2mm (0.52in) MG; three aircraft (later deleted)
Armour: belt 345–240mm (13.5–9.5in); bulkheads 380–240mm (15–9.5in); decks 150–50mm (6–2in); turret faces 445mm (17.5in); secondary armament 125mm (5in)
Speed: 30 knots
Range: 27,800km (15,000nm) at 15 knots
Complement: 1670

S-Boote

It was only in 1939 that the Kriegsmarine began operating S-boats (*schnellboote*) in significant numbers. A number of classes were designed, most built by Lürssen Werft at Vegesack.

The S38 group was the most numerous; their round-bilged hull form made them much more sea-kindly than equivalent British boats (such as the Fairmile Cs and Ds), and they were more effective, their highly evolved Daimler-Benz diesel powerplant providing much superior performance. From mid-1940 to 1944

(when they were known to the British as E-boats), S-boats operated in the North Sea, the Channel and even the Thames Estuary from hardened bases in the Low Countries. Light armament was progressively upgraded in the face of the threat from Allied air superiority. They also saw service in the Baltic and the Mediterranean (reached via the Rhine and Rhône rivers). A total of 249 German S-boats of all types were constructed, although fewer than 100 survived the war. The high loss rate reflected the hazardous nature of the fierce war fought by the coastal forces of both sides.

Displacement: 92t standard; 115t full load
Dimensions: 34.95m x 5.1m x 1.5m (115ft x 17ft x 5ft)
Machinery: three-shaft, Daimler-Benz diesels; 6000bhp
Armament: two 533mm (21in) TT; two 20mm (0.79in) guns
Armour: none (though the bridge on later boats was armoured against smallarms fire)
Speed: 40 knots
Range: 1600km (850nm) at 35 knots
Complement: 21

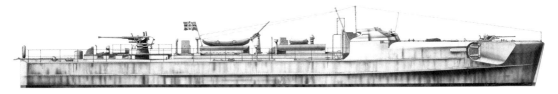

Acanthus

In 1939 the Royal Navy had an urgent need for a small escort vessel which could be constructed rapidly by non-specialist yards.

The requirement was met by modifying the design of a commercial whalecatcher, Smith's Dock's *Southern Pride*, lengthening it by 9.2m (30ft) to improve crew space, and giving it more sheer and flare forward, deeper bilge keels, and splinter protection. The 'Flower' class, as the resulting corvettes became known, was one of the most numerous in British service and ran to almost 150 ships, while Empire and other Allied navies, principally that of Canada, operated about 130 more. They were employed much more widely than first envisaged, escorting convoys as far afield as the United States and Russia. HMS *Acanthus* was one of the first of them, built by Ailsa Shipbuilding. She was transferred to Norway as the *Andenes* in 1941 and remained in service until 1957.

Displacement: 980t standard; 1245t full load

Dimensions: 62.5m x 10.1m x 4.8m (205ft x 33ft 2in x 15ft 9in)

Machinery: one-shaft, vertical triple-expansion engine; 2750hp

Armament: one 102mm (4in) guns; two 6pdr guns; four 20mm (0.79in) guns

Speed: 16.5 knots

Range: 7400km (4000nm) at 12 knots

Complement: 85–109

Howe

The 'King George V'-class battleships were built to the treaty limit of 35,000t, even though the treaty itself had expired before the first of the class was laid down.

Improvements in propulsion technology made it possible to generate 110,000hp, carry ten 356mm (14in) guns, and still have first-class protection within that limit, so the designer was hardly hampered by artificial restrictions. HMS *Howe*, the third of the class, was commissioned in August 1942, by which time one of her sister ships, the *Prince of Wales*, had already been sunk by Japanese aircraft. The upper

strake of her protective belt ran for over half the total length of the ship, between the forward and the after 356mm (14in) magazines, covering the machinery located between them. The 356mm (14in) guns were in mountings, which allowed elevation to 40 degrees, and were arranged with quadruples forward and aft, and a superfiring pair forward. HMS *Howe* survived the war, was placed in reserve in 1951 and was scrapped in 1957.

Displacement: 42,075t full load

Dimensions: 227.05m x 31.4m x 9.95m (745ft x 103ft x 32ft 7in)

Machinery: four-shaft, Parsons geared turbines; 110,000hp

Armament: 10 356mm (14in) guns; 16 135mm (5.25in) AA; eight (later 22) 40mm (1.57in) guns; 32 (later 88) 2pdr pom-poms; up to 64 20mm (0.79in); two aircraft

Armour: belt 380–356mm (15–13in); bulkheads 305–102mm (12–4in); barbettes 356mm (13in); turret faces 356mm (13in); conning tower 114mm (4.5in)

Speed: 28 knots

Range: 27,800km (15,000nm) at 10 knots

Complement: 1422

Wasp

The *Wasp* was a compromise, forced on the US Navy by the Washington Treaty, but she nonetheless proved invaluable in the relief of Malta.

Although she was not laid down until after the Washington Treaty had lapsed, USS *Wasp* was built in accordance with its provisions, to use up the 15,000t displacement left over after the completion of the *Yorktown* and *Enterprise*. Unfortunately, her designers were forced to try to incorporate as many of the features of those ships as possible into one which was only 75 per cent of their displacement. The compromise was most obvious in the powerplant and in the lack of protection – there was provision made to add an armour belt in time of war, but it was never fitted. *Wasp* was commissioned in April 1940 and joined the Atlantic Fleet, contributing significantly to Malta's survival by delivering a total of about 100 Spitfire fighters to the island. In June 1942, she transferred to the Pacific and on 15 September was torpedoed by *I19* off Guadalcanal and set ablaze. She was subsequently abandoned and sunk.

Displacement: 14,700t standard; 18,450t full load

Dimensions: 225.9m x 28.35m x 7.45m (741ft 3in x 93ft x 24ft 6in)

Machinery: two-shaft, Parsons geared turbines; 70,000hp

Armament: eight 127mm (5in) DP, later four 40mm (1.57in); 16 28mm (1.1in) MG; 16 12.7mm (0.5in) MG, later deleted; 20 20mm (0.79in) guns

Armour: deck 37mm (1.5in)

Speed: 29.5 knots

Range: 23,150km (12,500nm) at 15 knots

Complement: 1889 (later 2167)

North Carolina

The USS *North Carolina* and her sister ship the *Washington* were the first new battleships constructed for the US Navy since the *West Virginia* was completed in December 1923.

The new class broke with the American tradition of emphasizing protection and firepower at the expense of speed. Initially, the new ships were to have mounted nine 356mm (14in) guns and speed of 30 knots, but these were intended to be replaceable by 406mm (16in) triples at a cost of two knots. This forethought was rewarded when the Japanese refused to accept the treaty clause limiting battleships to 356mm

(14in) guns; as a result, the North Carolinas were completed with nine 16in (406mm) guns. USS *North Carolina* was constructed at the New York Navy Yard and completed in April 1941. Fully worked up by early 1942, she took part in most of the major actions until the war's end. She was seriously damaged only once, by a submarine torpedo, just after Guadalcanal. The *North Carolina* was decommissioned in June 1960 and, the following year, presented to the state whose name she bears, to be preserved as a memorial at Wilmington.

Displacement: 44,380t full load
Dimensions: 222.1m x 33m x 10m
(728ft 9in x 108ft 4in x 33ft)
Machinery: four-shaft, General Electric
geared turbines; 121,000hp
Armament: nine 406mm (16in) guns;
20 127mm (5in) (later 60 40mm/1.57in);
16 28mm (1.1in) (later deleted), later
83 20mm (0.79in); 12 12.7mm (0.5in) MG
(later deleted); three aircraft
Armour: belt 305mm (12in); deck 140mm
(5.5in); bulkheads 280mm (11in); barbettes
406-373mm (16-14.7in); turret faces 406mm
(16in); conning tower 406mm (16in)
Speed: 28 knots
Range: 27,800km (15,000nm) at 15 knots
Complement: 1793

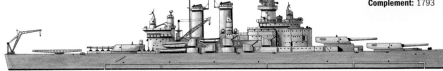

Ognevoi

The design for what was known to the Red Navy as Project 30 was finalized in 1937, as part of Stalin's planned massive expansion of the Soviet navy.

At least 24 of these destroyers were ordered, but construction was much delayed, and only two, *Ognevoi* and *Vnushitelnyi*, were completed before the end of World War II. Equipment, including a turret, were taken from the partially complete *Ognevoi* in 1941 to be used on the destroyer leader *Tashkent*, which was being rebuilt after bomb

damage. Post-war, 12 more Project 30 vessels were completed to a modified design known as Project 30K.

The *Ognevoi* was constructed at the 61 Kommunar Yard at Nikolayev on the Black Sea. Little is known about her service history, but she is believed to have remained in commission until the 1960s. The Ognevois were the best destroyers the Soviet Union built during World War II. They formed the basis for the post-war 'Skory' class which was to serve the Soviet navy in large numbers throughout the 1960s and 1970s.

Displacement: 2240t standard; 2950t full load

Dimensions: 117m x 11m x 4.2m (383ft 10in x 36ft 1in x 13ft 9in)

Machinery: two-shaft, geared turbines; 54,000hp

Armament: four 130mm (5.1in) guns; two 76mm (3in) guns; three 37mm (1.46in) guns; four 12.7mm (0.5in) MG; six 533mm (21in) TT; 96 mines

Speed: 37 knots

Range: 7400km (4000nm) at 20 knots

Complement: 250

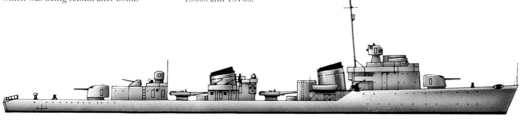

PC class

As with most other navies, that of the United States had paid little attention to anti-submarine operations and convoy escort in the inter-war years. That changed rapidly in the build-up to war.

The 'PCs' were conceived as multi-purpose ships, to serve as submarine chasers, anti-submarine pickets and coastal convoy escorts, and some were later completed as minesweepers, though they were not entirely successful in the role. Simple and cheap to build, they were constructed in huge numbers between

1940 and 1944 by small yards all over the United States. The choice of low-powered diesel engines gave them good endurance, and they were frequently operated with much greater payloads than they were designed to carry. Although intended for coastal operations, the shortage of escort vessels across two oceans meant that 'PC'-class vessels were also pressed into service for transatlantic operations.

Displacement: 414t standard; 463t full load
Dimensions: 52.95m x 7.05m x 2.35m (173ft 8in x 23ft 2in x 7ft 9in)
Machinery: two-shaft, diesel; 2880bhp
Armament: two (later one) 76mm (3in) guns, later one (or two) 40mm (1.57in); two Mousetrap AS mortars; DC throwers; DC racks
Speed: 19 knots
Range: 8900km (4800nm) at 12 knots
Complement: 59

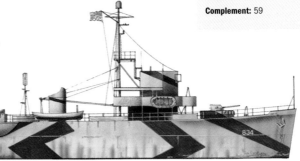

U-106

The German Type IX submarines were true oceangoing boats of over 1000t. They were developed from the clandestinely designed Type IA.

The Type IA was an improved version of the Spanish E1 designed in Holland by the German-run IvS bureau, which had been set up to get around the provisions of the Treaty of Versailles which forbade German design, development or building of submarines. The Type IX was constructed as a combat boat and later, in small numbers, as a cargo-carrier. They were double-hulled and divided into five watertight compartments; maximum operating depth was 330ft (100m), and crush depth was double that. *U-106* was a Type IXB, constructed by Deschimag in Bremen. She was commissioned on 24 September 1940 and, during a combat career which spanned 35 months, she was credited with having sunk a total of 20 ships. She was herself sunk by depth charges dropped from Sunderland flying boats of the RAF and RAAF, northwest of Cape Ortegal, on 2 August 1943.

Displacement: 1034t surfaced; 1405t submerged

Dimensions: 76.5m x 6.8m x 4.7m (251ft x 22ft 4in x 15ft 5in)

Machinery: two-shaft, diesel engines, plus electric motors; 4400bhp/1000hp

Armament: six 533mm (21in) TT (four bow, two stern: 22 torpedoes, or 44 Type TMA or 66 Type TMB mines); one 105mm (4.1in) gun; one 37mm (1.46in); one 20mm (0.79in)

Speed: 18.2 knots surfaced; 7.3 knots submerged

Range: 22,200km (12,000nm) at 10 knots surfaced

Complement: 48

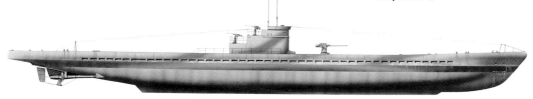

Walker

During World War II, the Royal Navy made very good use of the late World War I destroyers it still had in service. These were 'V'- and 'W'-class ships, constructed from 1917–19.

Many were converted to one of three new configurations: as AA ships; as short-range escorts, with a reduced weapons suite and fuel load, to boost performance; and as long-range escorts, with the forward boiler room converted to a fuel bunker to increase their range and the now-redundant fore funnel removed. HMS *Walker* was one of the latter and was completed originally as a minelayer and commissioned on

12 February 1918. On conversion to a long-range escort in 1943 she lost a triple bank of torpedo tubes and the aftermost 102mm (4in) gun in order to ship a Hedgehog AS mortar, depth-charge throwers and depth-charge racks – and she gained some 20mm (0.79in) guns. However, *Walker* had already made her name under the command of Donald McIntyre, when she sank two of Germany's top U-boats on 17 March 1941: Kretschmer's *U-99* and Schepke's *U-100*.

Displacement: 1100t (later 1200t) standard; 1490t (later 1690t) full load

Dimensions: 95.1m x 9m x 3.2m (312ft x 29ft 6in x 10ft 6in)

Machinery: two-shaft, Brown-Curtis geared turbines; 27,000hp (later 15,000hp)

Armament: four (later three) 102mm (4in) guns; one 76mm (3in) AA, later five 20mm (0.79in); six (later three) 533mm (21in) TT, later Hedgehog; DC throwers; DC racks

Speed: 34 (later 25) knots

Range: 6500km (3500nm) – later 8350km (4500 nm) – at 15 knots

Complement: 127

Yamato

The battleships *Yamato* and *Musashi* were the ultimate of the type: the biggest, best-protected and best-armed warships of all time.

Construction of the *Yamato* began at Kure Navy Yard on 4 November 1937. She was followed, in March 1938, by *Musashi* at Nagasaki. Commissioned nine days after Pearl Harbor, *Yamato* became Admiral Yamamoto's flagship on 12 February 1942. *Yamato* was hit by a single torpedo from the US submarine *Skate* off Truk on Christmas Day 1943, and took on 3000t of water. After repair she rejoined

the fleet on 1 May 1944. On 25 October (the day after the *Musashi* was sunk, by 17 bombs and perhaps as many torpedoes), *Yamato* finally fired her guns, 104 rounds in all, in anger. In the action off Samar, part of the Battle of Leyte Gulf, she sank an escort carrier and a destroyer. She was herself sunk off Okinawa, on what was effectively the most involved kamikaze mission of the war, on 7 April 1945. Hit by six bombs and perhaps 10 torpedoes, she went down at 14:23hrs, with the loss of all but 280 officers and men aboard.

Displacement: 63,000t (later 65,000t) standard; 71,660t (later 72,810t) full load

Dimensions: 862ft 9in x 121ft 1in x 34ft 1in (263m x 36.9m x 10.4m)

Machinery: four-shaft, Kampon geared turbines; 150,000hp

Armament: nine 460mm (18.1in) guns; 12 (later six) 155mm (6.1in) guns; 12 (later 24) 127mm (5in) DP; 24 (later 150) 25mm (1in) guns; six or seven aircraft

Armour: belt 410mm (16.1in); deck 230–200mm (9.1–7.9in); turret 650mm (25.6in); tower 500mm (19.7in)

Speed: 27 knots

Range: 13,320km (7200nm) at 16 knots

Complement: 2500

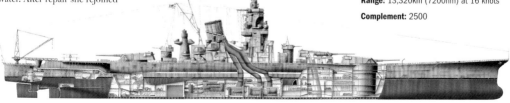

Onslaught

Britain's destroyer programme was a constant struggle between building fewer, more capable vessels or a larger number of simpler, cheaper designs.

The Royal Navy's 'L'- and 'M'-class destroyers were enlarged versions of the 'J' class. They were fitted with higher power machinery and new, much more powerful 120mm (4.7in) guns. However, they were expensive, so the 'O' and 'P' class were utility versions of the 'J's, with the same machinery on a new, smaller hull and with single 120mm guns on manual high-angle mounts and two quad pom-poms. In the early years of World War II, British destroyers were being completed with all possible speed. However, not all of them, *Onslaught* included, received the weapons suite they were designed to carry. Commissioned in June 1942, *Onslaught* got older guns in 40-degree mounts, and exchanged a bank of torpedo tubes for a single 102mm (4in) high-angle gun. She was built by Fairfield and was originally to have been HMS *Pathfinder*. She was transferred to Pakistan in 1951, remaining in service as the *Tughril* until 1971.

Displacement: 1550t standard; 2270t full load

Dimensions: 105.15m x 10.65m x 4.1m (345ft x 35ft x 13ft 6in)

Machinery: two-shaft, Parsons geared turbines; 40,000hp

Armament: four 120mm (4.7in) guns; one 102mm (4in) HA; eight 2pdr pom-poms (later eight 20mm/0.79in); four 533mm (21in) TT; DC throwers

Speed: 37 knots

Range: 7130km (3850nm) at 20 knots

Complement: 176

Akitsuki

The Imperial Japanese Navy's last class of destroyers, the 'Akitsukis', was authorized in 1939. Innovative ships, they were somewhat ahead of the general run of destroyer development.

Intended originally to act as fast escorts for carrier task forces, they were armed with a newly developed dual-purpose 100mm (3.9in) gun; before the design was finalized it was amended to include anti-submarine weaponry and four 619mm (24in) tubes for long-range torpedoes.

The Akitsukis proved to be very successful and were certainly superior to the American destroyers of the period, even if, on paper at least, they seemed to have inferior principal armament. Six of the 12 units completed actually survived the war (a rare occurrence in a navy which was almost entirely destroyed), but *Akitsuki* was not one of them. Constructed at Maizuru Navy Yard, and launched on 2 July 1941, she was sunk on 25 October 1944 by American carrier-borne aircraft, during the epic Battle of Leyte Gulf.

Displacement: 2700t standard; 3700t full load

Dimensions: 134.2m x 11.6m x 4.15m (440ft 3in x 38ft 1in x 13ft 7in)

Machinery: two-shaft, geared turbines; 52,000hp

Armament: eight 100mm (3.9in) guns; four (later up to 5) 25mm (1in) guns; four 610mm (24in) TT; DC racks; DC throwers

Speed: 33 knots

Range: 14,800km (8000nm) at 20 knots

Complement: 300

Gato

The 'Gatos', together with the similar 'Balao' and 'Tench' classes, were the standard American fleet submarines of World War II.

They were a successful design, with 10 torpedo tubes and a total of 24 torpedoes or 40 mines, a fairly powerful gun armament and a range sufficient to allow them to span the Pacific Ocean. The most significant difference between them and earlier fleet submarines was a lengthening of the hull, to allow an increase in the size of ballast tanks and to improve habitability and stability. Originally, operating depth was 91.5m (300ft), but later boats could dive to 122m (400ft) or more. Many remained in service after the war's end, and most went through the GUPPY (Greater Underwater Propulsive Power) programme. Stripped of their guns, with faired-in hulls and a new streamlined fin replacing the conning tower, the converted boats could make 16 knots underwater for short periods. USS *Gato*, the lead boat of the class and also the first to be constructed, by the Electric Boat Co at Groton, Connecticut, entered service in 1942, and survived the war. She was decommissioned and placed in reserve in 1946, and was not refurbished or modernized; she was stricken from the Navy List in 1960.

Displacement: 1525t surfaced; 2410t submerged
Dimensions: 95m x 8.3m x 4.65m (311ft 9in x 27ft 3in x 15ft 3in)
Machinery: two-shaft, diesel engines, plus electric motors; 6400bhp/2740hp
Armament: 10 533mm (21in) TT (six bow, four stern; 24 torpedoes); one 76mm (3in) gun, later 127mm (5in); two 12.7mm (0.5in) MG; two 7.62mm (0.3in) MG (later one 40mm/1.57in and one 20mm/0.79in)
Speed: 20.25 knots surfaced; 8.75 knots submerged
Range: 20,350km (11,000nm) at 10 knots surfaced
Complement: 60-80

RO-100

Japan had a large submarine force in World War II, but in spite of some individual successes it did not achieve anything like the effect of the German or US submarine arms.

The Imperial Navy thought of its submarines as scouts, the role of which was mostly to locate, shadow and attack Allied naval task forces. However, it had little thought for using submarines against commerce, or for defence, and its smaller boats were not operated with any kind of aggression. The 'KS'-class coastal submarines were built in two groups of nine boats each, between 1941 and 1943 – a further group was planned, but was cancelled. They were small, second-class boats, suited to operating in relatively shallow waters, and had only limited endurance. They were similar in character to the British 'U'-class submarines, but had inferior underwater performance. All 18 were lost in combat – many of them around the Philippines – including five to a single US destroyer escort, the *England*, in an eight-day period in the last week of May 1944. *RO-100* was the class leader, constructed at Kure Navy Yard.

Displacement: 525t surfaced; 780t submerged
Dimensions: 60.9m x 6m x 3.5m (199ft 10in x 19ft 8in x 11ft 6in)
Machinery: two-shaft, diesel engines, plus electric motors; 1100bhp/760hp
Armament: four 533mm (21in) TT; one 76mm (3in) AA
Speed: 14 knots surfaced; 8 knots submerged
Range: 6500km (3500nm) at 12 knots surfaced
Complement: 38

Indiana

The 'South Dakotas' were the penultimate class of battleships constructed for the US Navy, and were the last to be constrained by inter-war naval treaties.

They were smaller than the preceding 'North Carolinas', but had roughly the same displacement, having somewhat heavier armour, which was designed to protect them against 406mm (16in) shells. Design work began in 1936, and *Indiana* was built by Newport News Shipbuilding. Begun in late November 1939, she was completed less than 30 months later, a considerable feat even by American

standards. By the time she joined the fleet, the nature of war at sea had changed. Her wartime career was typical of the US Navy's capital ships, consisting largely of protecting carriers and bombarding shore installations; the worst damage she sustained was caused when she collided with USS *Washington* in February 1944, while manoeuvring to refuel destroyers at night. *Indiana* was placed in reserve in 1946, decommissioned in 1947 and stricken in 1962.

Displacement: 44,520t full load

Dimensions: 207.25m x 32.95m x 10.7m (680ft x 108ft 2in x 35ft)

Machinery: four-shaft, General Electric geared turbines; 130,000hp

Armament: nine 406mm (16in) guns; 20 127mm (5in) guns, later 48 40mm (1.57in); 12 28mm (1.1in) (later deleted), later 56 20mm (0.79in); 12 12.7mm (0.5in) MG (later deleted); three aircraft

Armour: belt 310mm (12.2in); deck 152mm (6in); bulkheads 280mm (11in); barbettes 440-287mm (17.3-11.3in); turret faces 457mm (18in); conning tower 406mm (16in)

Speed: 27.5 knots

Range: 27,800km (15,000nm) at 15 knots

Complement: 1793

Baltimore

The 'Baltimores' were heavy cruiser equivalents of the 'Clevelands', armed with three triple 203mm (8in) guns in place of the 'Clevelands' four triple 152mm (6in) mountings.

The 'Baltimores' extra displacement went into strengthening the hull and mounting extra weapons. In all, the class contained 14 identical ships and four which were somewhat modified. USS *Baltimore* was completed on 15 April 1943. She remained in service until February 1971, but, unlike some of her sister ships, was not extensively modernized. Four of the

class were modified to fire Regulus, the US Navy's first-generation cruise missile. Two more replaced their aft 127mm (5in) and 203mm (8in) turrets with two for Terrier surface-to-air missiles, becoming the US Navy's first guided-missile cruisers. Three more of the 'Baltimores' were even more extensively modified as missile ships, losing all their 127mm and 203mm turrets to mount both Talos and Tartar SAMs, ASROC anti-submarine missiles and six 324mm (12.75in) torpedo tubes.

Displacement: 14,470t standard; 17,030t full load

Dimensions: 205.25m x 21.6m x 7.3m (673ft 5in x 70ft 10in x 24ft)

Machinery: four-shaft, General Electric geared turbines; 120,000hp

Armament: nine 203mm (8in) guns; 12 127mm (5in) guns; 48 40mm; 24 20mm (0.79in) guns; four aircraft

Armour: belt 152-102mm (6-4in); deck 63mm (2.5in); turret face 203mm (8in)

Speed: 33 knots

Range: 18,500km (10,000nm) at 15 knots

Complement: 2039

Bogue

The US Navy began converting C3-type merchantmen as escort carriers in 1941, along the lines of the prototype *Long Island*. A total of 21 ships were converted, with one more new-built from the keel up.

The underpowered 'Long Islands' proved too slow in service. Surprisingly, this shortcoming was not remedied in the 'Bogues', which had the same installed power. When the better 'Casablanca' class became available, 10 of the 'Bogues' were transferred to the Royal Navy on Lend-Lease, and entered service as the 'Attacker' class. The 'Bogues' were fitted with two 6.5t lifts close to the ends of the wooden flight deck, and a single catapult capable of launching a 3t aircraft. USS *Bogue* started life as the *Steel Advocate*. She was built by Seattle-Tacoma Shipbuilders and converted there for the US Navy before commissioning on 26 September. Her war service was principally in the Atlantic, on transportation and anti-submarine duties. She was placed in reserve in 1946. In 1955, she was redesignated as a helicopter carrier and scrapped in 1960.

Displacement: 10,200t standard; 14,400t full load
Dimensions: 151.2m x 25m x 7.9m (496ft x 82ft x 26ft)
Machinery: one-shaft, one Allis-Chalmers geared turbine; 8500hp
Armament: two 127mm (5in) guns; four 40mm (1.57in); one 20mm (0.79in); 28 aircraft
Speed: 16.5 knots
Range: 48,150km (26,000nm) at 15 knots
Complement: 890

Lexington

Following the 'Yorktowns', the US Navy began planning a new design which would set the standard for fleet aircraft carriers for World War II – the 'Essex' class.

The new design was 30 per cent bigger than the 'Yorktowns'. Advances in steam machinery since the *Yorktown* was built meant they could make considerable weight savings in that area, while actually increasing the installed power by 25 per cent. USS *Lexington* was the second 'Essex' to be laid down (as USS *Cabot*; her name was changed after the original 'Lady Lex' was scuttled following the Battle of the Coral Sea in May 1942). She entered service just 73 weeks later on 17 February 1943. She served as the flagship of Task Force 58 during the war in the Pacific, and was present at every major engagement from Tarawa to Tokyo. In September 1953 she was rebuilt with an angled deck and recommissioned in August 1955. She succeeded *Antietam* as the US Navy's training carrier in 1963, finally being retired in 1991 after nearly half a century of service.

Displacement: 27,200t standard; 34,880t full load

Dimensions: 265.8m x 29.25m x 8.4m (872ft x 96ft x 27ft 6in)

Machinery: four-shaft, Westinghouse geared turbines; 150,000hp

Armament: 12 127mm (5in) guns; 32 (later 68) 40mm (1.57in) guns; 46 (later 60) 20mm (0.79in) guns (later 20 12.7mm/0.5in MG); 91 aircraft

Armour: belt 102–62mm (4–2.5in); hangar deck 62mm (2.5in); deck 37mm (1.5in)

Speed: 32.5 knots

Range: 27,800km (15,000nm) at 15 knots

Complement: 2682

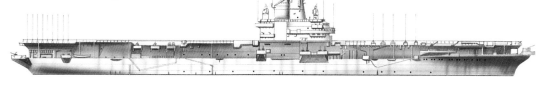

Fletcher

USS *Fletcher* was the lead ship of the largest class of destroyers – which totalled 179 in all – constructed for the US Navy during World War II.

The *Fletcher* design was the first to break entirely with the designs which had evolved during the 1930s. The standard displacement of the 'Fletchers' was 25 per cent up on that of the previous class. This allowed them to be much more heavily armed and easier to modify subsequently (although in fact lack of deck space would become a restricting factor). Flush-decked,

they were considerably more robust than earlier ships. USS *Fletcher* was built by Federal Shipbuilding at Kearny, New Jersey, and entered service in mid-1942. She saw very extensive service during World War II, and was awarded 15 battle stars. Placed in reserve from August 1946 until October 1949, she was reactivated for the Korean War (winning five more battle stars). She remained in service until 1962, when she returned to the reserve. *Fletcher* was stricken in 1967.

Displacement: 2325t standard; 2925t full load

Dimensions: 114.75m x 12.05m x 4.2m (376ft 5in x 39ft 7in x 13ft 9in)

Machinery: two-shaft, General Electric geared turbines; 60,000hp

Armament: five 127mm (5in) guns (later 10 40mm/1.57in); four 28mm (1.1in) guns (later deleted); four (later seven) 20mm (0.79in) guns; 10 533mm (21in) TT

Speed: 38 knots

Range: 12,000km (6500nm) at 15 knots

Complement: 273

Independence

As an emergency measure when the building programme for the 'Essex'-class fleet carriers seemed to be slipping in 1942, President Roosevelt ordered that nine 'Cleveland'-class large light cruisers then building at New York Shipbuilders in Camden, New Jersey, be completed as light aircraft carriers.

The resulting ships were cramped, but proved a useful addition to the wartime fleet. The conversion process was simple and based on the method evolved for adapting merchant ships as escort carriers: the hulls were bulged, which necessitated modifications to the armour belt (*Independence* and *Princeton*, the first and second units delivered, actually had no belts), and the hangar was built up from the (armoured) upper deck level and topped with a wooden flight deck. There was a small island to starboard, ahead of four offset funnels supported by outriggers. USS *Independence* originally mounted 127mm (5in) guns, which were removed after her trials. She survived the war and was sunk as a target in 1951.

Displacement: 10,660t standard; 14,750t full load

Dimensions: 189.75m x 33.25m x 7.4m (622ft 6in x 109ft 2in x 24ft 3in)

Machinery: four-shaft, General Electric geared turbines; 100,000hp

Armament: 24 (later 28) 40mm (1.57in) guns; 22 (later 4) 20mm (0.79in guns); 30 aircraft

Armour: belt 140mm (5.5in); bulkheads 127mm (5in); deck 51mm (2in)

Speed: 31 knots

Range: 24,000km (13,000nm) at 15 knots

Complement: 1569

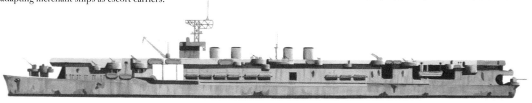

Iowa

The 'Iowa'-class battleships were the largest and fastest gun-armed capital ships ever constructed for the US Navy – and they were also the last.

They had the same basic 406mm (16in) armament as the 'South Dakotas', but with the barrels lengthened by 5 calibres, which increased the range of their 1225kg (2700lb) shells by around 5030m (5500yd), to a maximum of more than 39km (21nm). USS *Iowa* was constructed at New York Navy Yard and entered service on 22 February 1943. She deployed to the Pacific a year later, where she was engaged for the rest of the war. *Iowa* was reactivated twice, in 1951–58 and 1983–90. In her later incarnation, she carried two types of surface-to-surface guided weapons: the Tomahawk cruise missile and the Harpoon anti-ship missile. In 1990, she was again laid up. *Iowa* was stricken from the Navy List, along with her three sister ships, on 13 January 1995, but was reinstated in January 1999 and is now berthed in inactive reserve at San Francisco.

Displacement: 57,540t full load
Dimensions: 270.45m x 32.95m x 11m (887ft 3in x 108ft 2in x 36ft 2in)
Machinery: four-shaft, General Electric geared turbines; 212,000hp
Armament: nine 406mm (16in) guns; 20 127mm (5in) HA; 76 40mm (1.57in) guns; 52 20mm (0.79in) guns; three aircraft
Armour: belt 310mm (12.2in); deck 152mm (6in); bulkheads 280mm (11in); barbettes 440–287mm (17.3–11.3in); turret faces 500mm (19.7in); conning tower 440mm (17.3in)
Speed: 33 knots
Range: 27,800km (15,000nm) at 15 knots
Complement: 1921

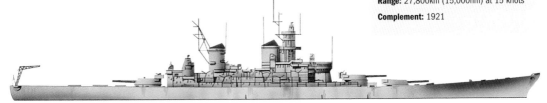

Seraph

The Royal Navy's 'S'-class submarines were constructed in two large groups between 1941 and the end of World War II, after which many of them remained in service.

They were intended for coastal operations around the British Isles, but also proved to be very satisfactory in the Mediterranean. Members of the 'S' class were reckoned to be among the handiest of all World War II boats: they could crash-dive in half the time it took a German Type VII U-boat. The boats of the first group could operate to 91.5m (300ft), but the second group

had welded pressure hulls and could dive 15m (50ft) deeper. HMS *Seraph* was one of the first group, built in Barrow-in-Furness by Vickers-Armstrong. She was taken in hand in 1944 and extensively modified: with higher capacity batteries, uprated powerplant and bigger propellers (from the 'T'-class boats), and her hull and casing cleaned up, Seraph reached 12.5 knots at periscope depth and 16.75 knots on the surface. She was the longest-serving member of the group, not being broken up until 1965.

Displacement: 715t surfaced; 990t submerged

Dimensions: 66.15m x 7.25m x 4.3m (217ft x 23ft 9in x 14ft)

Machinery: two-shaft, Vickers diesel engines, plus electric motors; 1900bhp/1300hp

Armament: seven 21in (533mm) TT (six bow, one external: 13 torpedoes); one 76mm (3in) gun

Speed: 14.75 knots surfaced; 9 knots submerged

Range: 11,100km (6000nm) at 10 knots surfaced

Complement: 48

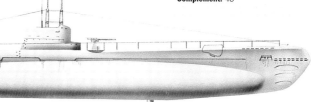

Saumarez

**The British 'S'- to 'W'-class fleet
destroyers were some of the best of
their type operated by the Royal Navy
during World War II.**

Repeats of the earlier 'Q' and 'R' classes,
they had the extended bow first seen on
the 'Tribals', which made them
considerably drier. The 119mm (4.7in)
guns were in an improved mounting,
allowing an elevation to 55 degrees, and
the quadruple 2pdr pom-poms of the
earlier class were replaced in most ships
by twin 40mm (1.57in) Bofors.
Commissioned in July 1943,

HMS *Saumarez* was constructed in with
accommodation for a captain (D) and his
small staff. Under Captain Manly Power,
she led the destroyer squadron which sank
the Japanese heavy cruiser *Haguro* at the
end of the war. Along with a sister ship,
HMS *Volage*, she was mined by Albanian
pirates in the Corfu Channel in October
1946. *Saumarez* was laid up thereafter, and
scrapped four years later. Many of the 'S'
and 'W' class were retained and converted
to frigates.

Displacement: 1810t standard;
2545t full load
Dimensions: 110.55m x 10.9m x 4.25m
(362ft 9in x 35ft 8in x 14ft in)
Machinery: two-shaft, Parsons geared
turbines; 40,000hp
Armament: four 119mm (4.7in) guns; two
(later 10) 40mm (1.57in) guns; (later eight
20mm/0.79in), later deleted); eight (later
four) 533mm (21in) TT; DC throwers
Speed: 37 knots
Range: 8330km (4500nm) at 20 knots
Complement: 180 (later 225)

Ashland

USS *Ashland* was the first landing-ship, dock. She was designed and built in the United States to a British amphibious warfare specification.

The landing-ship, dock (LSD) was essentially a self-propelled drydock. It could be flooded down at the stern by pumping seawater into ballast tanks so that the landing craft it carried in the well deck – for example, three US-pattern LCTs, each with five medium tanks aboard – could be floated out through stern gates. USS *Ashland* was the first of the type. Laid down

on 22 June 1942, at Moore Drydock Co, Oakland, California, she was launched on 21 December 1942 and commissioned as *LSD-1* on 5 June 1943. In March, 1946 she was laid up in the Pacific Reserve Fleet, San Diego Group, after earning six battle stars during World War II. She was back in commission between December 1950 and September 1957. *Ashland* was recommissioned on 29 November 1961, serving until 22 November 1969. Struck off a week later, she was sold for scrapping on 15 May 1970.

Displacement: 4030t standard; 7930t full load

Dimensions: 139.5m x 22m x 4.8m (457ft 9in x 72ft 2in x 15ft 10in)

Machinery: two-shaft, Skinner Uniflow vertical triple-expansion reciprocating engines; 7400hp

Armament: one 127mm (5in) gun; 12 40mm (1.57in) guns; 16 20mm (0.79in) guns

Speed: 15.5 knots

Range: 15,000km (8000nm) at 15 knots

Complement: 254

Artemis

World War II saw a massive expansion in amphibious warfare capabilities. Many specialized landing craft and ships were designed. One of the most important types, numerically, was the oceangoing attack cargo ship.

The original attack cargo ships were converted merchantmen. Although these ships performed an essential function, they were not optimized for the task, and it became clear that purpose-built ships were needed. Commissioned in 1944, *Artemis* was the first of a class which in the end ran to 32 vessels. The 'Artemis'-class attack cargo ships were based on the standard S4 merchantman, a war-built emergency design which was to serve in many guises during World War II. *Artemis* carried a mix of specialist landing craft on deck, disembarking them empty using her own derricks, then loading them alongside from the 900t of cargo and the 850 or so troops which she carried.

Displacement: 6740t full load
Dimensions: 129.85m x 17.7m x 4.7m (426ft x 58ft x 15ft 6in)
Machinery: two-shaft, Westinghouse geared turbines; 6000hp
Armament: 12 20mm (0.79in) guns
Speed: 18 knots
Range: 14,800km (8000nm) at 16 knots
Complement: 303

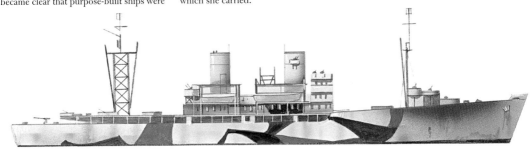

Allen M Sumner

USS *Allen M Sumner* was the lead ship of a large class of destroyers, an improvement on the 'Fletcher' class vessels, with the construction of which theirs was interleaved.

The 'Sumners' carried three twin rather than five single 127mm (5in) guns. The introduction of the new twin mounting solved the problem of crowding on the centreline of the 'Fletchers'. The extra space thus released was almost immediately filled by extra AA guns. This was the undoing of the 'Sumners': the addition of 12 40mm (1.57in) Bofors and

11 20mm (0.79in) Oerlikon cannon made them overweight and both slowed them down and cut their range. USS *Allen M Sumner* was commissioned at the New York Navy Yard on 26 January 1944, after construction by Federal Shipbuilding at Kearny, New Jersey. Having seen service during World War II in the Pacific, USS *Allen M Sumner* also took part in both the Korean and Vietnam wars, winning a total of five battle stars before she was finally stricken in August 1973.

Displacement: 2610t standard; 3220t full load

Dimensions: 114.75m x 12.45m x 4.3m (376ft 6in x 40ft 10in x 14ft 2in)

Machinery: two-shaft, General Electric geared turbines; 60,000hp

Armament: six 127mm (5in); 12 40mm (1.57in); 11 20mm (0.79in); 10 533mm (21in) TT; six DC throwers; two DC racks

Speed: 36.5 knots

Range: 6100km (3300nm) at 20 knots

Complement: 336

Taiho

The *Taiho* was the largest purpose-built Japanese carrier and, on paper, the best of them all. However, she was destroyed in her first combat action by a single torpedo.

She was similar in overall size to the 'Essex' class, with two-storey hangar decks. These were topped by an armoured flight deck, the first to be used by a Japanese carrier. She was developed from the *Shokaku*, but incorporated a number of features not found in that ship, notably the sponsonned-out island of the 'Hiyos', with its trunked-in, angled-out funnel. She had

a 'hurricane' bow, plated up to the level of the flight deck, something which the 'Essex' class would not have until well after the war was over. For all her sophistication and extensive protection, the *Taiho* had a very brief career; she completed on 7 March 1944, and after her shakedown cruise she was committed to the Battle of the Philippine Sea. On 19 June she was hit by just one torpedo from the US submarine *Albacore*; some hours later, the *Taiho* suffered a devastating explosion when petrol vapour ignited, probably as a result of either negligence or poor damage-control procedures.

Displacement: 29,300t standard; 37,720t full load
Dimensions: 260m x 30m x 9.6m (855ft x 98ft 6in x 31ft 6in)
Machinery: four-shaft, Kampon geared turbines, 160,000hp
Armament: 12 100mm (3.9in) AA; 51 25mm (1in) guns; 53 aircraft
Armour: belt 150–55mm (5.9-2.2in); hangar deck 125mm (4.9in); flight deck 80mm (3.1in)
Speed: 33.3 knots
Range: 14,800km (8000nm) at 18 knots
Complement: 1751

Esso Manchester

Merchant shipping was essential to the successful prosecution of World War II by the Allies. In 1939, however, the world's shipping fleets were relatively small.

To fill the need for shipping, a massive building programme was undertaken, particularly in the United States and Canada, and ships were mass-produced using assembly-line techniques. The *Esso Manchester* was one of the very successful 'T2-SE-A1' tankers, a standard design evolved in the United States in 1942,

a total of 481 of which were produced in four yards in just three years. The T2s were widely held to have been one of the most successful merchant ship designs of the period, and many were to stay in service long after the war was over, often with new midsections and renewed powerplants, in a wide variety of different roles, including that of floating power station. Some have been in service for more than 50 years. Built in 1944, the *Esso Manchester* had a long career, yet remained substantially unmodified when she was scrapped in Scotland in 1963.

Tonnage: 10,448grt

Dimensions: 159.6m x 20.75m x 9.15m (523ft 6in x 68ft x 30ft 1in)

Machinery: one-shaft, turbo-electric; 6000hp

Service speed: 14.5 knots

Role: tanker

Route: not applicable

Capacity: not known

Constructor: Sun Shipbuilding & Drydock Co, Chester, Pa

Material: steel

Built for: Maritime Service Commission

Comet

The 32 ships of the 'C' class were the last fleet destroyers constructed for the Royal Navy during World War II. The class was into four subclasses: the CA, CH, CO and CR groups.

HMS *Comet* was one of this large group of general-purpose fleet destroyers, constructed during the last three years of World War II. The first batch of eight, the 'CA' class, was similar to the earlier 'Z' class, and incorporated many of the improvements introduced in earlier classes, such as the transom stern of the 'Q's and the flared bow of the 'Tribals'. The 'CH' class introduced improved fire control. These vessels also mounted new 114mm (4.5in) guns in place of the 120mm (4.7in) guns carried by earlier destroyers. The new gun mounts were heavier, and the 'C' class lost one bank of torpedo tubes to compensate for the additional weight. Although the 'C's were too small to mount adequate radar and anti-aircraft armament, many served into the 1960s. Launched in 1944, *Comet* was built by Yarrow on the Clyde; she survived the war, to be broken up in 1962.

Displacement: 1730t standard; 2510t full load

Dimensions: 110.55m x 10.85m x 4.4m (362ft 9in x 35ft 8in x 14ft 5in)

Machinery: two-shaft, Parsons geared turbines; 40,000hp

Armament: four 114mm (4.5in); two (later 4) 40mm (1.57in); four 533mm (21in) TT

Speed: 36.5 knots

Range: 11,100km (6000nm) at 16 knots

Complement: 186–222

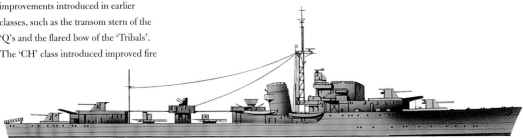

Colossus class

Designed as cheap, easy-to-build light fleet carriers, most of the vessels of the 'Colossus' class were completed too late to see action in World War II.

The 'Colossus' class was designed early in 1942, in response to the realization that the war had become global, that the large fleet carriers then in design, the 'Eagles', would not be ready until 1945 at the very earliest, and that escort carriers – the first of which, *Audacity* and *Archer*, had just completed – would clearly be incapable of providing air cover during fleet actions. The solution was to specify ships which

could be built quickly (and relatively cheaply) by non-specialist divisions of the leading yards. Hence, a design emerged with a single-storey hangar, on a large cruiser's displacement, and with a destroyer's machinery for a maximum of 25 knots. The basic principle was sound, and was later proven when 10 more such ships, in two classes and to somewhat modified designs so that they could operate bigger, heavier aircraft, were constructed. Four vessels were sold to other navies after the war. Two, the

Pioneer and the *Perseus*, were completed in February and October 1945 as maintenance support vessels.

Displacement: 13,200t standard;
18.050t full load
Dimensions: 211.5m x 24.4m x 7.1m
(694ft x 80ft x 23ft 3in)
Machinery: two-shaft, Parsons geared
turbines; 40,000hp
Armament: 24 2pdr pom-poms; 32 20mm
(0.79in) guns; 48 aircraft
Speed: 25 knots
Range: 22,200km (12,000nm) at 14 knots
Complement: 1300

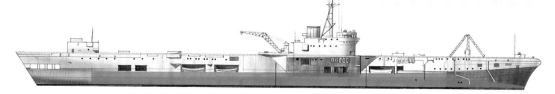

Duncan

The 'Gearing' class was equipped with the same weapons as the 'Sumner' class it followed, but was stretched and had enhanced performance.

One of the prime responsibilities of the US Navy's destroyers was to protect the fleet aircraft carriers and, to a lesser extent, the battleships which, by the end of the war, were being used exclusively for shore bombardment. This requirement meant the destroyers had to be fast, achieved by installing very powerful machinery; the last three classes of the period all developed 44,740kw (60,000hp) to give them top speeds in excess of 33 knots, even at a full load displacement of around 3500t. In all, some 93 Gearings were launched between October 1944 and July 1946. USS *Duncan* was one of the very earliest. She was one of 12 ships converted to become a radar picket in January 1945, before she had seen action. *Duncan* served for many years after 1945, finally being stricken from the Navy List in September 1973.

Displacement: 2615t standard; 3460t full load

Dimensions: 119m x 12.45m x 4.35m (390ft 6in x 40ft 10in x 14ft 4in)

Machinery: two-shaft, General Electric geared turbines; 60,000hp

Armament: six 127mm (5in) guns; 12 40mm (1.57in) guns; 11 20mm (0.79in) guns; 10 533mm (21in) TT

Speed: 36.5 knots

Range: 8350km (4500nm) at 20 knots

Complement: 336

Shinano

The Imperial Japanese Navy's *Shinano* was by far the biggest aircraft carrier of her day, a record she was to hold until the USS *Enterprise* was launched in 1960.

The *Shinano* was originally laid down as the third 'Yamato'-class battleship. In December 1941 construction on the vessel was suspended, and after the Battle of Midway it was decided that she should be completed as a carrier. She was intended as a reserve/support ship for carrier task forces. At 65,000t, *Shinano* was the biggest aircraft carrier in the world by some considerable margin, yet still capable of 27 knots. As in the British 'Illustrious' class, the weight of armour she carried precluded her from having more than one hangar deck. Nonetheless, she could still accommodate at least 70 aircraft in comfort, plus vast quantities of aviation spirit and ordnance. On 29 November 1944, as the *Shinano* was being moved from Yokosuka to Kure Navy Yard for final fitting out, USS *Archerfish* torpedoed her four times. Pumps and watertight doors had not yet been mounted, and she slowly filled and sank.

Displacement: 64,800t standard; 71,900t full load

Dimensions: 266m x 36.3m x 10.3m (872ft 8in x 119ft 1in x 33ft 10in)

Machinery: four-shaft, Kampon geared turbines; 150,000hp

Armament: 16 127mm (5in) DP; 145 25mm (1in) guns; 12 28-barrelled R/L; 70 aircraft

Armour: belt 205mm (8.1in); hangar deck 190mm (7.5in); flight deck 80mm (3.1in)

Speed: 27 knots

Range: not available

Complement: 2400

U-2326

Germany's Type XXIII U-boats, together with the larger Type XXIs, represented the culmination of submarine development in Germany up to and during World War II.

The Type XXIII was a small coastal boat of 230t standard displacement. Divided into three watertight compartments, the pressure hull was a 'figure-eight' amidships and cylindrical towards the bow and stern, with tanks for ballast and fuel below, and an outer fairing casing covering all to reduce drag to a minimum. The conning tower was small and streamlined. The XXIII had very large-capacity batteries, creeping motors

and snorkels incorporated into the conning tower casing; underwater performance and handling were better than on the surface. Maximum dive depth was 80m (260ft) and crush depth was twice that. *U-2326* was commissioned in August 1944. She was surrendered to the British at Loch Foyle on 14 May 1945, and was taken into the Royal Navy as HMS *Meteorite*. Transferred to France the following year, she was lost in an accident off Toulon, with all hands, on 6 December 1946.

Displacement: 230t surfaced; 270t submerged

Dimensions: 34.7m x 3m x 3.7m (113ft 10in x 9ft 10in x 12ft 2in)

Machinery: one-shaft, MWM diesel engine, plus AEG electric motor, plus creeping motor; 630bhp/580hp/35hp

Armament: two 533mm (21in) TT (bow: two torpedoes)

Speed: 10 knots surfaced; 12.5 knots submerged

Range: 4800km (2600nm) at 8 knots surfaced

Complement: 14

U-2501

By a very clear margin, the German Type XXI submarines were the best oceangoing boats produced anywhere during World War II.

With their streamlined form, integral snorkel, and high-capacity batteries, they were the first true submarines. The powerplant was entirely conventional, with the exception of its secondary single-commutator electric motors, designed for silent running. The battery compartment, on the other hand, had three times the capacity of the batteries of the Type IX. A total of 740 was ordered: only 121 were completed and just two made operational sorties. *U-2501* was the first constructed, by Blohm & Voss in Hamburg; she was commissioned on 28 June 1944, but never saw service. She was scuttled by her crew on 3 May 1945 in Hamburg; the wreck was later broken up. A total of six boats survived the war intact. One was salvaged (and is now preserved at Bremerhaven), and as many as 30 more were later completed by the Russians.

Displacement: 1595t surfaced; 2060t submerged

Dimensions: 76.7m x 6.6m x 6.3m (251ft 8in x 21ft 8in x 20ft 8in)

Machinery: two-shaft, MAN supercharged diesel engines, plus electric motors, plus creeping motors; 4000bhp/4200hp/226hp

Armament: six 533mm (21in) TT (bow: 23 torpedoes or 14 torpedoes plus 12 Type TMC mines); four 20mm (0.79in) guns

Speed: 15.5 knots surfaced; 17.2 knots submerged

Range: 27,800km (15,000nm) at 10 knots surfaced

Complement: 57

Midway

The largest American carriers of the World War II era, the 'Midway'-class vessels were upgraded several times over their long careers, and could operate all but the very largest of modern jet-powered carrier aircraft.

The 'Midways' originally featured heavy anti-aircraft armament and deck armour. In the early 1950s they were the only US carriers capable of carrying nuclear bombers. *Midway* entered service in September 1945. She served with the Pacific Fleet, homeported at Yokosuka and remained in frontline service until after the Gulf War in 1991. She is now a museum ship at San Diego. The USS *Coral Sea* was commissioned in October 1947 and spent most of her operational life with the US Sixth Fleet, making many North Atlantic and Mediterranean cruises. By the end of her service life, her air wing of 65 aircraft included four squadrons of McDonnell Douglas F/A-18 Hornets. Intended for retirement from the 1970s onwards, the demand for big-deck carriers kept the *Coral Sea* and the *Midway* in service. The USS *Coral Sea* was finally withdrawn in October 1989, and was formally decommissioned in April 1991. The third of the class, the *Franklin D Roosevelt*, was struck off in 1977.

Displacement: 65,200t full load
Dimensions: 307.5m x 72m x 10.7m (1003ft x 236ft x 35ft)
Machinery: four-shaft, steam turbines, 12 boilers; 212,000hp
Armament: three Mk 15 Phalanx 20mm (0.79in) CIWS (final configuration); 65 aircraft
Sensors: not available
Speed: 33 knots
Range: not available
Complement: approximately 4104

Daring

The British Admiralty decreed that HMS *Daring* and her sister ships should be classed as 'Daring-type ships' and treated as light cruisers, despite their being built as destroyers and being unremarkable in size.

Eight were built, starting with HMS *Daring* (D 05); she was laid down in September 1945, launched in August 1949 and completed in March 1952. *Daring* was armed with three twin 114mm (4.5in) gun turrets but, in 1963, trials were conducted on one of the other ships to replace the aft turret with a Seacat SAM launcher. This did not prove a success and, although some changes were made to the configuration of her 40mm (1.57in) guns, *Daring* remained essentially unchanged. While several of her sister ships were sold abroad, HMS *Daring* was retired and broken up in 1971. The first ship in the Royal Navy's forthcoming class of Type 45 frigates will be named HMS *Daring*.

Displacement: 2830t standard; 3580t full load

Dimensions: 118.8m x 13.1m x 4.1m (390ft x 43ft x 13ft)

Machinery: two-shaft, double reduction-geared turbines, two boilers; 54,000hp

Armament: six Mk 6 114mm (4.5in) guns; two/six 40mm (1.57in); one Squid ASW mortar

Sensors: tracking radar; air-search radar; hull-mounted sonar

Speed: 34.75 knots

Range: 11,112km (6000nm) at 16 knots

Complement: 297–330

Eagle

HMS *Eagle*'s career was always in the shadow of her contemporary, the *Ark Royal*, but the *Eagle* was a much more reliable ship with a far more impressive operational record.

On her completion in October 1951, *Eagle* became the most modern aircraft carrier in the Royal Navy. Although notionally a sister ship to HMS *Ark Royal*, *Eagle* was quite a different ship. *Eagle* would prove to be the sounder of the two, her design following traditional British lines, trading internal space for thorough armour protection. During 1954–55, *Eagle* was refitted with a 5-degree angled deck

(increased to 8 degrees by 1964) and the latest mirror landing-aid system. Unlike *Ark Royal*, HMS *Eagle* had a very active operational career and was involved in most of the Royal Navy's major actions during the 1950s and 1960s. The most important of these was the Suez crisis of 1956. Later, she was involved in the confrontation with Indonesia, the unrest in Aden and the 'Beira Patrol' blockade of Rhodesia. *Eagle* was withdrawn from service following the 1966 defence cuts, leaving *Ark Royal* to soldier on in failing health.

Displacement: 53,390t full load
Dimensions: 247.4m x 52.1m x 11m
(811ft 9in x 171ft x 36ft)
Machinery: four-shaft, geared steam turbines, eight three-drum boilers; 152,000hp
Armament: 16 (later 8) 114mm (4.5in) guns, 48 40mm (1.57in) AA (reduced to 9, later 6 and finally 4); all AA replaced by six GWS22 Seacat SAM in 1960s; 60 aircraft (1952), 45 aircraft (1964)
Sensors: not available
Speed: 31 knots
Range: 9260km (5000nm) at 24 knots
Complement: 2750, including air group

Neustrashimyy

The *Neustrashimyy* was the first post-war Soviet destroyer design, and introduced features including dual-purpose guns, high-pressure steam plant and new weapons.

The class was designed to survive in a nuclear environment; however, only the lead ship was built, and the class was cancelled before trials were complete. The *Neustrashimyy* was completed on 31 January 1955, but proved slower than expected. Judged to be too large, unwieldy and impractical, the *Neustrashimyy* was replaced by the smaller but similarly equipped 'Kotlin' class (Project 56).

The plans were then sold to China, which then built the 'Luda' class. The ship's pressure-fired KV-41 boilers formed the basis of the steam plant used in subsequent Soviet surface combatants. The *Neustrashimyy* was modernized in 1959, with four four-gun SM-20 ZiF turrets replacing the original four SM-16s, and with new propellers, radar and communications antennae. Thereafter, the vessel (known to NATO as the 'Tallinn' class) was used as a Baltic Fleet staff ship and as a training ship for construction workers, before being broken up in 1975.

Displacement: 3100t standard; 3830t full load

Dimensions: 133.8m x 13.6m x 4.4m (439ft 1in x 44ft 6in x 14ft 6in)

Machinery: two-shaft, geared turbines, four boilers; 66,000hp

Armament: four 130mm (5.1in) guns, eight 45mm (1.77in) guns; two unidentified ASW rocket launchers; 10 533mm (21in) ASW TT; depth charges; mines

Sensors: air-search radar; surface-search radar; sonar

Speed: 36 knots

Range: not available

Complement: 305

United States

The first attempt by the US Navy to build what would now be called a supercarrier, designed to carry nuclear bombers, was to fall foul of inter-service rivalry.

After several years of planning, on 29 July 1948 President Truman approved construction of a 'supercarrier', for which funds had been provided in the Naval Appropriations Act 1949. This first post-war carrier was laid down in April 1949. The flush-deck 65,000t CVA 58 *United States* was designed to launch and recover the 50t aircraft required to carry early nuclear weapons, which weighed as much as five tons. The ship was to be more than 300m (1000ft) long, without an island, and of a radical new design. The US Air Force viewed the *United States* as a Navy challenge to the Air Force monopoly of strategic nuclear weapons delivery. Responding to opposition from the Army and Air Force, on 23 April 1949 Defense Secretary Louis Johnson announced the cancellation of construction of the *United States*, without even consulting the Chief of Naval Operations. The *United States* was intended to be the first of a class of four carriers, which would eventually emerge as the four-ship 'Forrestal' class which entered service from 1955 onwards.

Displacement: 75,900t standard; 83,249t full load
Dimensions: 320m x 76.7m x 11.4m (1090ft x 190ft x 37ft 5in)
Machinery: four-shaft, geared turbines, eight boilers; 280,000hp
Armament: 8 x 127mm (5in)/54; 6 x 76mm (3in)/37; 57 aircraft including 12 AJ Savage nuclear bombers
Sensors: not known
Speed: 33 knots
Range: not known
Complement: 3019, plus 2480 air wing

Albacore

Although she could be described as 'just' an experimental vessel, the USS *Albacore* (AGSS 569) holds a key place in submarine history.

She was the first US submarine designed to operate entirely underwater and pioneered the bullet-shaped streamlined design of modern submarines. The smooth new lines allowed her to maintain an exceptional underwater speed without using excessive power. *Albacore* was laid down on 15 March 1952 and launched on 1 August 1953. Thanks to her large

onboard battery pack, she was capable of astonishing 'dash' speeds of 27 knots. By the end of her operational career new developments in high-capacity silver-zinc batteries had boosted that speed to 33 knots. Coupled with the advent of the first onboard nuclear powerplants, the *Albacore*-type hull form introduced greatly increased endurance, speed and manoeuvrability for all the submarines that were to follow the *Albacore*.

Displacement: 1500t surfaced; 1850t submerged
Dimensions: 64.2m x 8.3m x 5.6m (210ft 6in x 27ft 4in x 18ft 6i)
Machinery: one-shaft, two diesels and one electric motor; 1500hp/15,000hp
Armament: none
Speed: maximum 33 knots submerged
Range: varied, depending on powerplant configuration
Complement: 52

Trieste

Built for oceanographic research, the *Trieste* was the first manned craft to dive to the bottom of the world's deepest ocean trench.

The bathyscaphe *Trieste* was designed by Auguste Piccard. Built in two parts, the upper was a tank containing 106 cubic metres (3745 cubic feet) of gasoline. Being of lower specific gravity than water, this provided enough buoyancy to return the craft to the surface when water ballast held in two small tanks at the extremities was blown out by compressed air. The permanent ballast – first 9t, then later 16t, of iron pellets – was also contained in this portion. The lower section was an alloy sphere, big enough for two, with walls 10cm (4in) thick. Piccard made his first dive in August 1953, and five years later the *Trieste* was sold to the US Navy. She was fitted with a stronger passenger sphere, and in January 1960 Piccard's son Jacques and Lieutenant Don Walsh USN descended to 10,912m (35,800ft) in the Challenger Deep, southwest of Guam, which was then believed to be the deepest point in the world's oceans.

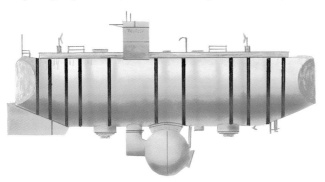

Displacement: 50t
Dimensions: 18.1m x 3.5m
(59ft 6in x 11ft 6in)
Machinery: two-shaft, electric; 2hp
Service speed: 1 knot
Role: exploration vessel
Constructor: Navalmeccanica, Naples
Material: steel/steel alloy
Built for: Auguste Piccard
Owner: US Navy

Forrestal

The development of the US Navy supercarrier was driven by the advent of heavier jet combat aircraft which required longer catapults and larger flight decks.

The first US carriers to be built with an angled deck, and the first to have the flight deck as an integral part of the ship's structure, the Forrestals were made as large as they were so that they could operate the Navy's new A3D Skywarrior. There were significant differences in the four members of the class as design changes were incorporated in successive vessels. The USS *Forrestal* (CVA 59, later CV 59) was commissioned in October 1955. Joining the fleet in 1956, *Forrestal* deployed to the Mediterranean in response to the Suez crisis. In August 1967 her only combat deployment to Vietnam was cut short when she suffered a disastrous accidental explosion and fire on board. Once repaired, *Forrestal* rejoined the Atlantic Fleet. She underwent an 18-month service life extension programme in 1983–85 and, in 1992, replaced the USS *Lexington* as the US Navy's designated training carrier (AVT 59). Following post–Cold War cutbacks, the *Forrestal* was decommissioned in September 1993.

Displacement: 78,509t full load

Dimensions: 316.7m x 76.2m x 10.3m (1039ft x 250ft x 33ft 10in)

Machinery: four-shaft, geared turbines, eight boilers; 260,000hp

Armament: three Mk 29 Sea Sparrow octuple launchers; three Mk 15 Phalanx 20mm (0.79in) CIWS

Sensors: air-search radar; surface-search radar; navigation radar; fire-control radar

Speed: 33 knots

Range: 22,224km (12,000nm) at 20 knots

Complement: 2764 crew, plus 1912 air wing

Endurance

HMS *Endurance* was constructed in Germany in 1956 by Krögerwerft of Rendsburg, for the Danish company J Lauritzen Lines of Copenhagen. In commercial service it was originally known as the *Anita Dan*.

She was acquired by the Royal Navy in February 1967, renamed after Ernest Shackleton's ship and modified by Harland & Wolff. She was equipped with helicopter facilities, workshops and laboratories to allow her to carry out her secondary duties as a hydrographic and meteorological research ship, and was armed with two 20mm (0.79in) cannon for her primary role as regional guardship in the South Atlantic. The decision (later reversed) to withdraw *Endurance* from service in 1981 encouraged the Argentine seizure of the Falkland Islands, which led to the Falklands War. She was replaced in 1991 by a Norwegian-built icebreaker.

Tonnage: 2641grt

Dimensions: 302ft x 46ft x 18ft (93m x 14m x 5.5m)

Machinery: one-shaft, diesel; 3220hp

Service speed: 14 knots

Role: guardship; research vessel

Route: South Atlantic

Constructor: Krögerwerft, Rendsburg

Material: steel

Built for: J Lauritzen Lines

Owner: Royal Navy

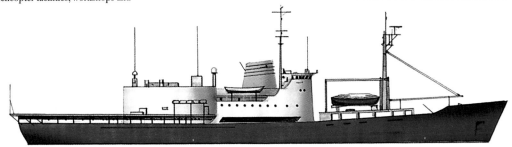

November class

The 'November' class (Project 627 Kit) submarines were Russia's first nuclear-powered attack boats. The first example of 14 built, *K-3*, was delivered in March 1959.

Originally conceived as a strategic anti-ship submarine firing a single 40km (25-mile) range nuclear torpedo, the design was refined into an attack submarine with eight torpedo tubes in the bow, capable of firing 24 conventional torpedoes. Early problems with reactor cooling often limited the performance of the 'November'-class submarines, but when working properly the vessels were extremely fast, as one demonstrated in February 1968 when chasing the US aircraft carrier *Enterprise*. Her good performance became a factor in the US Navy's acquisition of its new 'Los Angeles'-class attack submarines. Attempts to produce versions of the 'November' class armed with Ilyushin P-20 cruise missiles did not progress beyond a single prototype stage. The operational career of the 'Novembers' was overshadowed by a series of accidents and incidents, two being lost to fires following steam-generator faults and two more suffering severe reactor accidents.

Displacement: 4500t surfaced; 5300t submerged

Dimensions: 110.9m x 9m x 7.1m (363ft 11in x 29ft 6in x 23ft 5in)

Machinery: two-shaft, nuclear, one nuclear reactor; 30,000hp

Armament: eight 533mm (21in) TT (24 torpedoes)

Sensors: surface-search radar; attack sonar

Speed: 30 knots submerged

Range: limited only by reactor fuel state

Complement: 80

Hermes

HMS *Hermes* is best known for her vital role, alongside HMS *Invincible*, in the Falklands conflict of 1982. During that time she carried 20 Sea Harriers and 10 Sea Kings.

The Royal Navy intended to acquire six 'Centaur'-class aircraft carriers, but the final vessel was cancelled. The intended name for that ship, HMS *Hermes*, was applied to the fifth and last Centaur, which had been laid down (in 1944) as HMS *Elephant*. After the war the design was modified with an angled flight deck, steam catapults and long-range radar. HMS *Hermes* (R 12) was launched in February 1953 and completed in November 1959. In 1959, her air group consisted of just 20 Sea Vixens, Scimitars and Buccaneers, plus eight Gannets. With the advent of the Phantom, *Hermes* was given a new role as an ASW helicopter carrier because she could not accommodate the larger jets. When the Sea Harrier was introduced, *Hermes* returned to jet status, with a new ski jump, and went to war in the Falklands as the Task Force flagship. She was finally paid off in 1984 and transferred to India in 1987, as the *Viraat*.

Displacement: 23,900t standard; 28,700t full load

Dimensions: 226.9m x 48.8m x 8.8m (744ft 4in x 160ft x 29ft)

Machinery: two-shaft, geared steam turbines, four boilers; 76,000hp

Armament: 10 40mm (1.57in) guns (replaced by two Seacat SAM); 28 aircraft (as completed)

Sensors: long-range air-search radar; height-finding radar; tracking radar; navigation radar

Speed: 28 knots

Range: 11,112km (6000nm) at 13 knots

Complement: 1830, plus 270 air group

Farragut

Although they were the first missile-armed ships of their type to enter service with the US Navy, the 'Farragut'-class fleet escorts had not been designed as such.

Their design armament of quick-firing 127mm (5in) guns and a limited ASW weapons fit was meant for the 'Farraguts' intended role in the screening of US fast carrier battle groups. However, as the US Navy accelerated plans for the transition to an 'all-missile' fleet, and as the Soviet submarine threat was becoming increasingly serious, more emphasis was placed on the Farraguts' ASW capabilities. The USS *Farragut* (CLG 6, later DDG 6) was completed in December 1960 and, being in the right place at the right time, benefited from the transition to the new weapons fit. Thus, *Farragut* and her sister ships carried Terrier SAMs and were among the first to be armed with the ASROC system, which launched rocket-boosted anti-submarine torpedoes and could be fitted with a nuclear warhead.

Displacement: 5648t full load

Dimensions: 156.3m x 15.9m x 5.3m (512ft 6in x 52ft 4in x 17ft 9in)

Machinery: two-shaft, geared turbines, four boilers; 85,000hp

Armament: one Terrier (later Standard) SAM system (40 missiles); one 127mm (5in) gun; one ASROC rocket-boosted ASW torpedo launcher; six 324mm (12.75in) TT (Mk 32 torpedoes)

Sensors: air-search radar; fire-control radar; hull-mounted sonar

Speed: 32 knots

Range: 9260km (5000nm) at 20 knots

Complement: 360

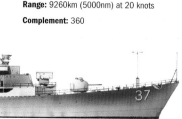

Skipjack

The teardrop-hulled 'Skipjack' class proved efficient and popular attack submarines, and their design influenced all nuclear-powered boats which followed.

Until the advent of the one-off experimental boat USS *Albacore*, submarines were designed for making headway on the surface, as well as underwater. *Albacore* adopted a teardrop hull optimized purely for underwater operation, and led directly to the diesel-electric 'Barbel' class and the nuclear-

powered Skipjacks. USS *Skipjack* (SSN 585) herself was launched in May 1958 and completed in April 1959. Equipped with six torpedo tubes in the bow, the 'Skipjack' class was too small to carry the latest sonar systems and SUBROC missiles. However, the boats were fast and manoeuvrable, and they remained in frontline use until the late 1980s. *Skipjack* was the last of the class to decommission, on 19 April 1990. One of the class, the *Scorpion*, sank with all hands some 640km (400 miles) southwest of the Azores on 22 May 1968.

Displacement: 3070t surfaced; 3500t submerged
Dimensions: 76.7m x 9.6m x 7.7m (251ft 9in x 31ft 8in x 25ft 3in)
Machinery: one-shaft, nuclear, one reactor; 15,000hp
Armament: six 533mm (21in) TT (24 torpedoes)
Sensors: surface-search radar; active/passive sonar
Speed: 30 knots submerged
Range: limited only by reactor fuel state
Complement: 85

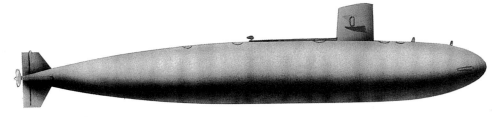

Savannah

Launched in 1959, the *Savannah* was built as an experiment to test the feasibility, both technical and economic, of fitting merchant ships with nuclear powerplants.

As such, the first two years of her operational life were taken up with demonstration voyages. She then went into (heavily subsidized) service between the United States and Mediterranean ports, first with a small number of paying passengers, latterly with cargo only. Although she was the world's first nuclear-powered freighter,

she was not the first nuclear-powered merchant ship; that honour went to the Soviet ice-breaker *Lenin*, which made her maiden voyage two months after the *Savannah* was launched. A second nuclear-powered freighter, the *Otto Hahn*, an ore carrier, was launched in Kiel in June 1964. The success of the *Savannah* experiment can perhaps be judged by the fact that she was laid up with the reserve fleet in 1972, by which time it had become clear that while technically practical, in real world terms she was uneconomical to operate commercially.

Tonnage: 13,599grt (later 15,585grt)

Dimensions: 181.5m x 23.8m (595ft x 78ft 2in)

Machinery: one-shaft, geared turbine; 22,000hp

Service speed: 21 knots

Role: passenger/cargo carrier

Route: USA–Mediterranean

Capacity: 60 sc

Constructor: New York Shipbuilders, Camden, New Jersey

Material: steel

Built for: US Department of Commerce/ States Marine Lines

Komar

The Soviet Project 183R fast attack craft were the first missile-armed vessels of their type to enter service.

Known as the 'Komar' class, they were armed with the P-15 anti-ship missile, which had a range of 29km (18 miles) and carried a 500kg (1100lb) conventional warhead. The development of the P-15 (NATO designation SS-N-2 Styx) began in 1954, with the first launch in October 1957 from a Komar fast attack craft prototype. Entering service in the late 1950s, the Komar burst onto the world stage in October 1967, when an Egyptian Komar used its Styx missiles to sink the Israeli destroyer *Eilat*. This combat success inspired a massive proliferation of missile-armed fast attack craft: cheap and relatively simple to operate, they allowed even the smallest navies to enter the missile age and there was an explosion in fast attack craft sales. The Project 183R boats were followed by the larger Project 205, known as the 'Osa' class. They were sold worldwide to the navies of the Warsaw Pact and to many Soviet client states.

'Osa' class Displacement: 172t standard; 209t full load

Dimensions: 37.5m x 7.6m x 3.8m (123ft x 24ft 11in x 12ft 6in)

Machinery: three-shaft, diesels; 12,500hp

Armament: four SS-N-2 SSM; SA-N-5 SAM (some *Osa II*s); four 30mm (1.18in) cannon

Sensors: surface-search radar; fire-control radar

Speed: 35 knots (*Osa I*); 37 knots (*Osa II*)

Range: 741km (400nm) at 34 knots (*Osa I*); 926km (500nm) at 35 knots (*Osa II*)

Complement: 26

Foxtrot

The Soviet Union's 'Foxtrot'-class attack submarines (Project 641) were an enlarged version of the 'Romeo' class and designed to operate with a snorkel.

The prototype 'Foxtrot' was launched in 1957, and from then on 62 examples were built. The majority went to the Soviet Fleet, but many more to export customers, including Cuba, India, Libya and Poland. The 'Foxtrots' could dive deeper and had greater range than the 'Zulu' class that preceded them. Both a passive and an active sonar array were concealed within the bow fairings of 'Foxtrot' class submarines. They were an important part of the Brezhnev-era planned expansion of the Soviet navy. There were more than 70 members of the class, and planned service life was 27 years. Some boats class were still in service during the late 1980s, but most had been retired by then, and none is currently active.

Displacement: 1957t surfaced; 2484t submerged
Dimensions: 91.3m x 7.5m x 6m (299ft 6in x 24ft 7in x 19ft 8in)
Machinery: three-shaft, three diesels, rated at 6000hp, plus four 112-cell batteries and three electric motors
Armament: 10 533mm (21in) TT (six bow; four stern)
Sensors: search radar; active sonar, passive array
Speed: 15.9 knots submerged
Range: not available
Complement: 75

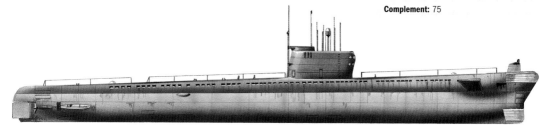

George Washington

The first US fleet ballistic missile submarines, the 'George Washington' class, were based on the 'Skipjack'-class attack submarines.

Armed with the Polaris A-1 missile, the 'George Washington' class would provide an important interim capability before the purpose-built 'Ethan Allen'-class SSBNs entered service. Five 'Skipjack' submarines under construction were modified by the insertion of a large 39.62m (130ft) centre-section 'plug' containing 16 launch tubes for the UGM-27 Polaris A-1 SLBM. The A-1 was the first submarine-launched

ballistic missile (SLBM) to be developed and fielded. The USS *George Washington* (SSBN 598) was launched its first test Polaris in July 1960. It undertook its first 64-day operational cruise just four months later. Initially attached to the Atlantic fleet, all were transferred to Pacific Fleet Ballistic Missile Force. When the class began decommissioning in 1981, the *George Washington* had its missile tubes deactivated and was redesignated as an attack submarine (SSN). She was also used as a clandestine transport for US Navy SEALS. The *George Washington* was finally decommissioned in 1985.

Displacement: 5989t surfaced; 6709t submerged
Dimensions: 116.33m x 10.06m x 8.13m (381ft 8in x 33ft x 26ft 8in)
Machinery: one-shaft, nuclear, one S5W reactor; 15,000hp
Armament: 16 UGM-27 Polaris A-1 (later A-3) SLBM; six 533mm (21in) TT
Sensors: sonar
Speed: 20 knots submerged
Range: limited only by reactor fuel state
Complement: 140

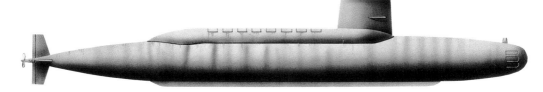

Long Beach

Apart from carriers, the nuclear-powered fleet escort missile cruiser USS *Long Beach* (CGN 9) was the largest warship built by the US Navy in the post-war years.

Along with the carrier USS *Enterprise*, she was the only US naval vessel to be fitted with the flat-panel fixed-arrays for the SPS-32/33 long-range air-search radar. Completed in September 1961, she carried a heavy air defence weapons fit with two Terrier SAM launchers and a single long-range Talos system.

In Southeast Asia in 1968, *Long Beach* shot down two North Vietnamese MiG fighters in the first successful naval SAM engagement. In the 1980s, *Long Beach* was modernized: the troublesome SPS-32/33 radar was removed, Phalanx CIWS were added and Harpoon anti-ship missiles replaced the Talos launcher. She was retired in 1994 before a further modernization programme began.

Displacement: 16,602t full load
Dimensions: 721ft 3in x 73ft 4in x 23ft 9in (219.8m x 22.3m x 7.2m)
Machinery: two-shaft, nuclear, two reactors, two geared turbines; 80,000hp
Armament: one Talos SAM system (replaced by eight Harpoon SSM); two Terrier SAM systems; two 127mm (5in) guns; two 20mm (0.79in) Phalanx CIWS (later); one ASROC launcher; six 324mm (12.75in) TT
Sensors: air-search, surface-search, fire-control navigation radars; hull sonar
Speed: 30-plus knots
Range: limited only by reactor fuel state
Complement: 1107

Oberon

The Royal Navy's HMS *Oberon* (S 09) was the first in a class of 14 diesel-electric patrol submarines derived from the successful eight-boat 'Porpoise' class.

Externally similar to the 'Porpoises' but with detail improvements, the Oberons had a maximum dive depth in excess of 305m (1000ft). Completed between 1961 and 1967, *Oberon*, *Onslaught*, *Ocelot* and *Onyx* were built at Chatham (*Onyx* going straight to the Royal Canadian Navy); *Odin*, *Oracle*, *Opossum* and a replacement *Onyx* by Cammell-Laird; *Orpheus*, *Olympus* and *Osiris* by Vickers-Armstrong; and *Otter*, *Otus* and

Opportune by Scotts. Exceptionally quiet, the 'Oberons' were renowned as being deadly hunter-killers, and three were bought by the Royal Canadian Navy. Extensively modified and modernized in the 1980s, most 'Oberons' received a new sonar, EW and combat systems, and a clip-on towed array. Intended to remain in service until fully replaced by new 'Upholder'-class submarines, the 'Oberons' were retired early as part of the 1991 defence cuts.

Displacement: 2030t surfaced; 2410t submerged
Dimensions: 88.5m x 8.1m x 5.6m (290ft 3in x 26ft 6in x 18ft 3in)
Machinery: two-shaft, diesel-electric, two diesels plus two electric motors; 3680hp/6000hp
Armament: eight 533mm (21in) TT (30 Mk 24 torpedoes)
Sensors: search radar; navigation radar; sonar
Speed: 12 knots surfaced; 17 knots submerged
Range: 16,668km (9000nm) at 12 knots
Complement: 64

Devonshire

The 'County'-class guided-missile destroyers were the first Royal Navy vessels capable of embarking a medium helicopter and the first to be armed with operational anti-ship missiles, the Exocet.

They were also first to be fitted with COSAG (COmbined Steam And Gas) machinery. HMS *Devonshire* (D 02) was the lead ship in the class. She was launched in June 1960 and completed in November 1962, mounting Mk 6 gun turrets and the (then) new Seaslug SAM system. The beam-riding Seaslug was

a first-generation surface-to-air missile. It was fired from a complicated lattice-frame launcher mounted aft. On later ships, Seaslug was supplemented by the short-range Seacat. *Devonshire* was never fitted with the Exocets that replaced the 'B' turret on some of class. The 'Countys' were due to be withdrawn after the 1981 defence cuts, but the Falklands conflict prolonged their service lives. While four ships were later sold to Chile and one to Pakistan, HMS *Devonshire* was expended as a target in July 1984.

Displacement: 6200t standard; 6800t full load

Dimensions: 158.3m x 16.4m x 6.2m (521ft 6in x 54ft x 20ft 6in)

Machinery: two-shaft COSAG, geared steam turbines, two Babcock & Wilcox boilers, plus four gas turbines; 30,000hp/30,000hp

Armament: one launcher for Seaslug SAM; four 114mm (4.5in) gun; two 20mm (0.79in) cannon; one helicopter

Sensors: air-surveillance radar; air/surface-search radar; height-finding radar; fire-control radar; hull-mounted sonar

Speed: 30 knots

Range: 6482km (3500nm) at 28 knots

Complement: 440–471

Valiant

Although there were only five submarines in the class, the Valiants gave valuable service in the Royal Navy, not least in the Falklands conflict, when *Conqueror* torpedoed the cruiser *General Belgrano*.

The first British nuclear submarine was the one-off *Dreadnought*, which was in many respects a British copy of the US 'Skipjack' class. The first British production nuclear submarines, the 'Valiant' class, were essentially productionized copies of the Dreadnought, enlarged to accommodate the bulkier British reactors. *Valiant*

(S 102), the first of the class, was launched in December 1963 and completed in July 1966. The 'Valiants' were equipped with six tubes for Mk 24 Tigerfish torpedoes, although they could also use the older Mk 8s and wire-guided Mk 23s. In the early 1980s the 'Valiants' were modified to carry the Sub-Harpoon anti-ship missile. By the end of the 1980s, the age of the 'Valiant' class reactors was causing concern, and the five submarines were withdrawn from service from 1990.

Displacement: 4000t surfaced; 4900t submerged
Dimensions: 86.7m x 10.1m x 8.2m (285ft x 33ft 3in x 27ft)
Machinery: one-shaft, nuclear, one PWR1 reactor with geared steam turbine plus diesel-electric auxiliary; 15,000hp
Armament: six 533mm (21in) TT (Mk 23 Tigerfish torpedoes and Sub-Harpoon SSM)
Sensors: search and navigation radar; active/passive sonar and towed array
Speed: 32 knots submerged
Range: limited only by reactor fuel state
Complement: 52

Enterprise

As the world's first nuclear-powered aircraft carrier, the USS *Enterprise* (CVN 65, formerly CVAN 65) was an epoch-making ship.

She owed much of her great size to a bulky first-generation nuclear powerplant, but this allowed her to use space once reserved for ship's fuel for aviation fuel instead. *Enterprise*, or 'Big E' as she became known to her crews, was built with SPS-32/SPS-33 electronically scanned phased-array radar mounted in flat panels around her main island. However, the radar were not as successful as had been hoped, proved difficult to maintain and were replaced with more conventional antennae in 1980. The USS *Enterprise* was laid down in February 1958, launched in September 1960 and completed in November 1961. *Enterprise* joined the Atlantic fleet in 1961 and participated in the blockade of Cuba in 1962. In May 1963 she made a round-the-world cruise to join the Pacific Fleet and, in 1964, began the first of her eight combat deployments during the Vietnam War. *Enterprise* was badly damaged in a fire during 1973, but she bounced back to become the first carrier to operate Grumman F-14 Tomcat fighters in 1974.

Displacement: 71,277t standard; 89,084t full load

Dimensions: 342.4 x 77.7m x 11.3m (1123ft 2in x 255ft x 37ft 1in)

Machinery: four-shaft, nuclear, eight A2W reactors, four geared turbines; 280,000hp

Armament: three Mk 29 Sea Sparrow octuple launchers; 90 aircraft

Sensors: air-search radar; surface-search radar; navigation radar; fire-control radar

Speed: 32 knots

Range: limited only by reactor fuel state

Complement: 3325, plus 1891 air wing

Iwo Jima

Development of the large helicopter assault ship for the US Marine Corps was driven by new Cold War concepts of conducting landings opposed by nuclear weapons.

Concentrations of landing craft were felt to be vulnerable to nuclear attack. Helicopters provided greater stand-off range and concentrated delivery, offered higher speeds and allowed the assault fleet to remain dispersed. The 'Iwo Jima'-class LPHs were developed with an all-new hull design and a large flight deck. *Iwo Jima* could carry 2000 troops and had space on deck for seven CH-46s or four CH-53s,

with hangar space below for another 19 and 11, respectively. *Iwo Jima* (LPH 2) was the lead ship in a class of seven and was launched in September 1960. In 1963, she made the first of several deployments to Vietnam and later joined the Atlantic Fleet. *Iwo Jima*'s original 76mm (3in) guns were replaced by Sea Sparrow SAMs and Phalanx CIWS (close-in weapon systems). After three decades of service, she was decommissioned in 1993.

Displacement: 10,717t standard; 18,004t full load

Dimensions: 103.6m x 25.7m x 8m (602ft 4in x 84ft 2in x 26ft 1in)

Machinery: one-shaft, geared turbine, two boilers; 22,000hp

Armament: two Sea Sparrow SAM; two Mk 15 Phalanx 20mm (0.79in) CIWS (later 25mm/ 1in Bushmaster); up to 30 helicopters

Sensors: air-search radar; surface-search radar

Speed: 23.5 knots

Range: 11,112km (6000nm) at 18 knots

Complement: 667, plus 2057 marines

John F Kennedy

Although nominally one of the four 'Kitty Hawk'-class carriers, the USS *John F Kennedy* (CV 67) has substantial design differences that almost set her in a class apart.

The *Kennedy* incorporated an all-new underwater protection system, designed for the nuclear-powered carriers, but entered service with no defensive weapons (Sea Sparrows were added later). The *Kennedy* was launched in May 1967 and completed in September 1968. *Kennedy* spent most of her operational life in the North Atlantic and Mediterranean. She was the first carrier to deploy the S-3 Viking, and during the 1980s she saw action off Lebanon and Libya. During Operation Desert Storm the *Kennedy* was the last carrier to deploy with A-7 Corsairs, and her air wing flew a total of 11,000 combat sorties. Today, the *Kennedy* is one of only two non-nuclear carriers remaining in US Navy service. Although she is officially classed as a Naval Reserve vessel, she spends almost her entire time in the regular fleet.

Displacement: 60,005t standard; 80,945t full load

Dimensions: 320m x 76.7m x 11.4m (1052ft x 251ft 8in x 36ft)

Machinery: four-shaft, geared turbines, eight boilers; 280,000hp

Armament: three Sea Sparrow octuple launchers; three Mk 15 Phalanx 20mm (0.79in) CIWS

Sensors: air-search radars; surface-search radar; navigation radars; fire-control radars; fitted for hull-mounted sonar

Speed: 33.6 knots

Range: 22,224km (12,000nm) at 20 knots

Complement: 3306, plus 1379 air wing

Boykiy

When they appeared in the late 1950s, the Project 57Bis, or 'Krupny'-class missile destroyers, were the first missile-armed warships in the Soviet fleet. They were designed to carry the primitive SS-N-1 'Scrubber' anti-ship missile.

Boykiy, a 'Krupny'-class missile destroyer, was launched in December 1960 and completed in June 1961 – the seventh of eight ships constructed. The 'Krupny' class was charged with surface attack and shore bombardment, using the SS-N-1 missile; however, lacking sufficient self-defence armament, these vessels were transferred to ASW tasks. *Boykiy* received a new bow sonar, torpedo tubes, an anti-submarine mortar, an aft helicopter pad to accommodate a Kamov Ka-25 helicopter, sonobuoys, the SA-N-1 SAM system and new 23mm (0.91in) guns. Her machinery had to be uprated to cope with the increased weight. This conversion proved to be both difficult and expensive, and was never again attempted with any other similar class of Soviet ship.

Displacement: 3850t standard; 4192t full load

Dimensions: 138.9m x 14.84m x 4.2m (455ft 9in x 48ft 8in x 13ft 9in)

Machinery: two-shaft, geared turbines, four boilers; 72,000hp

Armament (as built): two SSM launchers with 12 missiles; 16 57mm (2.24in) guns; two ASW RL; six 533mm (21in) TT

Sensors: air-search; missile-control and navigation radar; hull-mounted sonar

Speed: 34.5 knots

Range: 5556km (3000nm) at 18 knots

Complement: 310

Canberra

The *Canberra* was one of the last purpose-built passenger liners, but the changing economic climate soon saw her converted to cruising.

Canberra, instantly recognizable then by her futuristic lines, was constructed in 1960 as a passenger liner to operate in the newly merged P&O-Orient Line's UK–Australia service alongside the *Oriana*. However, within 10 years, the widespread use of jet liners meant that air fares had reached a level with which passenger liners could not compete. In 1973 she was switched to the rapidly growing cruise trade, and began year-round cruises. Canberra had just completed one such cruise in April 1982 when she was requisitioned by the British government to carry troops to the Falkland Islands. Rapidly converted for military operations, she was known as the 'Great White Whale'. Despite operating close inshore, she was undamaged and later returned to the cruise trade.

Tonnage: 45,270grt

Dimensions: 250m x 31m x 9.9m (818ft x 102ft x 32ft)

Machinery: two-shaft, turbo-electric; 88,000hp

Service speed: 27.5 knots

Role: passenger liner; cruise ship; troopship

Route: Southampton–Australia

Capacity: 556 1st, 1716 tr; 1737 tr

Constructor: Harland & Wolff, Belfast

Material: steel & aluminium

Built for: P&O Steam Navigation Co

Owner: P&O Line

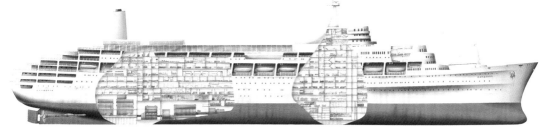

France

The Compagnie Générale Transatlantique was France's major transatlantic passenger line, and its vessels vied with the great Cunard liners for speed and luxury.

The third passenger liner to be named *France* was, by design, the longest passenger ship in the world overall when she was laid down. Launched in 1961, she was also the last of the true North Atlantic express liners, the later *Queen Elizabeth 2* having been designed with cruising in mind (although the *France*, too, was later given over to cruising). Her maiden circumnavigation in 1972 took her round Cape Horn, for as with most of the last generation of superliners she was marginally too broad in the beam to be able to transit the locks in the Panama Canal. She was sold in 1979 to the Norwegian Caribbean Line and, renamed *Norway*, was refitted as a cruise ship. The refit which transformed the *France* into the *Norway* cost $80 million; two of her turbine sets were removed in the course of it, making her slower, but much more economical to run.

Tonnage: 66,348 grt

Dimensions: 315.5m x 33.8m x 11.2m (1035ft 2in x 110ft 11in x 34ft)

Machinery: four-shaft (later two-shaft), double-reduction turbines

Service speed: 30 (later 16) knots

Role: passenger liner; cruise ship

Route: Le Havre–New York

Capacity: 500 1st, 1550 tr; 2181 tr

Constructor: Chantiers de l'Atlantique

Material: steel

Built for: Compagnie Générale Transatlantique

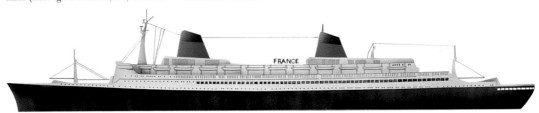

Dido

The Royal Navy's 'Leander'-class frigates were of an innovative design that allowed smaller ships to again become multipurpose escorts, instead of being single-role vessels.

Excellent sea boats, the 'Leanders' are generally considered to have been among the best of their type ever built, and they proved to be immensely popular in service. The design incorporated improvements built into the 'Tribal' class vessels, as well as work done for the Royal New Zealand Navy's Type 12 frigates. HMS *Dido* (F 104), was the third vessel of the 16 frigates in the class; she was launched in

December 1961 and completed in September 1963. *Dido* was one of eight of the class to have their 114mm (4.5in) turrets replaced by Ikara ASW missile systems. The other 'Leanders' were modified to carry the Exocet anti-ship missile. HMS *Dido* was recommissioned in her new form in October 1978. She remained in Royal Navy service until 1983, when she was sold to New Zealand, becoming HMNZS *Southland*.

Displacement: 2860t full load

Dimensions: 113.4m x 12.5m x 5.5m (372ft x 41ft x 18ft)

Machinery: two-shaft, geared steam turbines, two boilers; 30,000hp

Armament: one launcher for Seaslug SAM; one GWS22 Seacat SAM system; two 114mm (4.5in) guns; two 40mm (1.57in) AA guns (deleted); one GWS40 Ikara ASW missile system (added); one helicopter

Sensors: air-surveillance radar; air/surface-search radar; navigation radar; fire-control radar; hull-mounted sonar

Speed: 28 knots

Range: 7408km (4000nm) at 15 knots

Complement: 251-263

Galileo Galilei

Built for the Lloyd Triestino Line's Italy–Australia service, *Galileo Galilei* was another of the last generation of regular passenger liners built in the 1960s to fall victim to the inexorable rise of low-cost air travel.

Launched in 1963 the *Galileo Galilei* was withdrawn from service in 1977 and laid up for two years. As with other liners, she then became a cruise ship. Sold in 1983, she was refitted and her name was shortened, becoming simply the *Galileo*. She was extensively rebuilt in 1989–90, increasing her gross tonnage from 28,000 to 30,500, to re-enter service as the *Meridian*, cruising in the Caribbean. She was sold in 1996 to a Singapore-based cruise line, Sun Cruises, and once again was renamed, becoming the *Sun Vista*.

On the afternoon of 20 May 1999, while passing the Straits of Malacca on a voyage between Phuket Island and Singapore, a fire in the main engine room switchboard caused a complete power loss and a blackout. Inexplicably, the ship took on a heavy list and, at 01:22 the next morning, sank. Fortunately, all 1104 passengers and crew aboard were saved.

Tonnage: 27,907grt (later 30,440grt)
Dimensions: 213.65m x 28.6m x 8.65m (700ft 11in x 93ft 10in x 28ft 4in)
Machinery: two-shaft, geared turbines; 44,000hp
Service speed: 24 knots
Role: passenger liner; cruise ship
Route: Italy–Australia; Caribbean; Far East
Capacity: 156 1st, 1594 tr; 1440 sc
Constructor: Cantieri Riuniti dell'Adriatico, Monfalcone
Material: steel
Built for: Lloyd Triestino Line

Ognevoy

Although designed as an air defence and ASW destroyer, *Ognevoy* and her sister ships of the 'Kashin' class soon found that the air defence role came to dominate their operations.

The Soviet Project 61 design was an air defence/ASW patrol ship to replace the 'Kotlin' and 'Riga' classes. Launched in 1963, *Ognevoy* was the third of 20 Project 61 guided missile destroyers (known to NATO as the 'Kashin' class). Six ships, including the *Ognevoy*, were modified in the mid-1970s with the addition of improved electronics and four rear-firing SS-N-2c Styx missiles. Its armament

includes 10 torpedoes, 32–36 SA-N-3 missiles and 4 SS-N-2C missiles. The hull was lengthened by approximately 2m (6ft), and a stern-mounted variable depth sonar and an improved hull-mounted sonar were also fitted. She was one of the last in the class to be retired, and was broken up in 1990. Two or three examples may remain in reserve. Five additional 'Kashins' were built for India almost 10 years after the last was completed for the Soviet navy, entering service from 1980.

Displacement: 4390t full load

Dimensions: 144m x 15.8m x 4.6m (472ft 5in x 51ft 10in x 15ft 1in)

Machinery: two-shaft, CODAG, four gas turbines; 72,000hp

Armament: two SA-N-1 SSM launchers; four 76mm (3in) guns; two RBU-6000 and two RBU-1000 ASW RL (replaced by 30mm/ 1.18in AK-630 CIWS); five 533mm (21in) TT (original fit)

Sensors: air-search radar; navigation radar; fire-control radar; hull-mounted sonar

Speed: 18 knots

Range: 6482km (3500nm) at 18 knots

Complement: 266

Voronezhskiy Komsomolets

The Project 1171 large landing ships (Bol'shoy Desantnyy Korabl', or BDK) were better known to NATO as the 'Alligator' class.

The Soviet Navy built 16 'Alligator' class BDKs at Kaliningrad, in four slightly differing classes, between 1964 and 1967. The first vessel, *Voronezhskiy Komsomolets* (BDK-10), was completed in 1966. All the 'Alligators' were built to a beachable, general-purpose LST-type (landing ship tank) design and had large bow and stern ramps. Each could carry between 25 and 30 APCs, or 1500t of cargo. Early production ships had three deck cranes, while later examples had just one. These later ships also had an enclosed bridge, plus gun and rocket armament. Many have been retired, and remaining units may be in reserve, given the Russian navy's decreased emphasis on amphibious operations. One example was transferred to the Ukraine.

Displacement: 3400t standard; 4700t full load

Dimensions: 370ft 6in x 50ft 2in x 14ft 5in (112.8m x 15.3m x 4.4m)

Machinery: two diesels; 8000hp

Armament: two or three SA-N-5 SAM launchers (some examples); two 37mm (1.46in) guns; four 25mm (1in) guns; one 122mm (4.8in) RL (fit varies from ship to ship)

Speed: 18 knots

Range: 25,910km (14,000nm) at 10 knots

Complement: 75, plus 300 troops

Moskva

The two Project 1123 Kondor ships were developed to hunt down Polaris submarines in the open ocean, then call on an accompanying battle group to destroy them.

These were the first Soviet aviation ships, and their design was something of a hybrid, with features of a missile cruiser forward and a flight deck aft of the superstructure. The design was heavily influenced by the French helicopter carrier *Jeanne D'Arc* and the Italian helicopter carrier *Vittorio Veneto*. *Moskva* was laid down in December 1962, launched in

January 1964 and commissioned in December 1967. *Moskva* and *Leningrad*, the second ship, operated in the Mediterranean, the Atlantic and the Indian Ocean. Despite their graceful appearance, the Moskvas had a tendency to ride down in the bow, and ultimately they proved ineffective and unreliable. *Moskva* was retired to the reserve in 1983 and scrapped in 1997. *Leningrad* was scrapped even earlier, in 1991.

Displacement: 17,500t full load
Dimensions: 189m x 26m x 13m
(620ft 1in x 85ft 4in x 42ft 8in)
Machinery: two-shaft, steam turbines; oil-fired steam boilers; 90,000–100,000hp
Armament: two twin SA-N-3 SAM launchers (44 missiles); one twin SUW-N-1 missile launcher; two twin 57mm (2.24in) AA; 10 533mm (21in) TT (later removed); 14 Ka-25 'Hormone' helicopters
Sensors: air/surface-search radar; fire-control radar; hull-mounted sonar
Speed: 31 knots
Range: 25,002km (13,500nm)
Complement: 850 (including air group)

Fearless

The landing platform docks *Fearless* and *Intrepid* gave the Royal Navy a versatile, flexible platform to launch and control amphibious operations all over the world.

The two 'Fearless'-class assault ships were ordered for the Royal Navy in 1962. *Fearless* was commissioned in 1965, with *Intrepid* following two years later. They could accommodate up to 700 Royal Marines, although 400 was normal load, plus 15 tanks and 27 vehicles. *Intrepid* was rotated in and out of the reserve following the 1976 defence cuts, but was recalled into service for the Falklands conflict in 1982, and along with *Fearless* provided the British task force with an essential amphibious capability. *Intrepid* was withdrawn in 2001 after years in mothballs. *Fearless* retired on 18 March 2002, with her replacement *Albion* coming into service the following year. At the time, she was the oldest ship still in in service with the Royal Navy.

Displacement: 11,060t standard; 12,120t full load

Dimensions: 158.5m x 24.4m x 6.3m (520ft x 80ft x 20ft 6in)

Machinery: two-shaft, geared steam turbines, two boilers; 2000hp

Armament: four Seacat SAM; four 30mm (1.18in) guns; two 20mm (0.79in) guns; up to four helicopters

Sensors: surface-search radar; navigation radar

Speed: 21 knots

Range: 5000nm (9260km) at 20 knots

Complement: 580, plus 400–700 troops

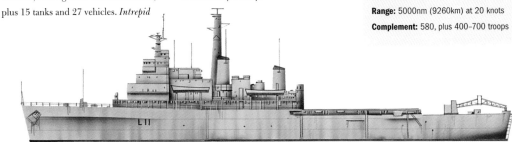

Queen Elizabeth 2

The last Cunard built for the transatlantic passenger service, the passenger liner *Queen Elizabeth 2* was an anachronism even before her launch on 20 November 1967.

From the outset she was plagued by mechanical problems – Cunard refused to accept her at first, and her maiden voyage was delayed by five months. She was twice the subject of threats of terrorism. In 1972, the Royal Air Force delivered four bomb disposal experts to her in mid-Atlantic in response to a hoax. In 1973 she was targeted by Libya's President Gaddafi,

who wanted her torpedoed. The following year she was adrift off Bermuda after an engine failure; in 1975, she hit a reef off the Bahamas; and in 1976, she was partially crippled by an engine-room fire. In 1982, she redeemed herself in many eyes by her successful performance as a troopship during the Falklands War and later, appropriately refitted and re-engined, she had an active career as a cruise ship. In 2005, she was still operating as a pleasure cruiser in the Mediterranean Sea and Atlantic, Pacific and Indian oceans.

Tonnage: 65,836grt (later 67,107grt)

Dimensions: 293.5m x 32.1m x 9.75m (963ft x 105ft x 32ft)

Machinery: two-shaft, geared turbines (later diesel-electric); initial power figures not known (later 118,000 hp)

Service speed: 29 knots

Role: passenger liner; cruise ship; troopship

Route: Southampton–New York

Capacity: 564 1st, 1441 tr; 1820 sc

Constructor: John Brown & Co, Glasgow

Built for: Cunard Line

Grayling

Until the introduction of the 'Los Angeles' class, the 'Sturgeon' class was the backbone of the US Navy's attack submarine fleet.

The 'Sturgeons' were larger than the earlier 'Permit'-class boats and were fitted with a more advanced sonar. They were dedicated hunter-killer submarines, designed to seek out and destroy the Soviet submarine fleet. They could carry a wide range of ASW weapons, including the Mk 45 ASTOR nuclear torpedo, before it was retired from the US inventory in the late 1970s, but the total onboard weapons capacity was relatively low. This made the 'Sturgeon' class less effective than it might otherwise have been and hastened the introduction of the multipurpose Mk 48 torpedo. Most of the 35 boats in the class were retired in the 1990s. The USS *Grayling* (SSN 646) was the seventh 'Sturgeon'-class submarine to be built. She was launched in June 1967 and completed in October 1969. The USS *Grayling* was a 'full-spec' 'Sturgeon'-class vessel, although some of her early sister ships were hybrid 'overlaps' between the 'Sturgeons' and the 'Permits'. She was decommissioned and struck from the Navy List in July 1997.

Displacement: 4246t surfaced; 4777t submerged

Dimensions: 89.1m x 9.7m x 7.8m (292ft 3in x 31ft 8in x 25ft 6in)

Machinery: one-shaft, one nuclear reactor; 15,000hp

Armament: four 533mm (21in) TT firing ASW torpedoes, SUBROC, Sub-Harpoon or Tomahawk cruise missiles

Sensors: long-range sonar

Speed: surfaced speed unknown; 26 knots submerged

Range: limited only by reactor fuel state

Complement: 99

Kronstadt

The 'Kresta' class (Project 1134) ships were designed for ASW and surface warfare, and to provide additional air defence for Soviet task forces.

There were two variants in the class. The Project 1134 Berkut (NATO designation 'Kresta I') ships were surface warfare cruisers. Responding to an urgent ASW requirement, the SS-N-14 anti-submarine system was fitted to the much more capable Project 1134A Berkut-A ('Kresta II') ships. This replaced the SS-N-3 anti-ship missiles of the 'Kresta I'. The 'Kresta II' could carry a Ka-25 'Hormone A' helicopter, which could deliver nuclear depth bombs. The 'Kresta II' was also equipped with 76mm (3in) guns, replacing the 57mm (2.24in) mounts on 'Kresta Is'. Four 'Kresta I' class cruisers became operational during 1967–69, and 10 'Kresta II' cruisers entered service during 1969–78. Launched in October 1968 and commissioned in December 1969, *Kronstadt* was the lead 'Kresta II'. All 'Kresta'-class ships had been stricken by 1994 and, as of early 2000, most had been sold to foreign shipbreakers.

Displacement: 7535t full load

Dimensions: 158.9m x 16.7m x 5.3m (521ft 6in x 54ft 10in x 17ft 5in)

Machinery: two-shaft, two steam turbines, four boilers; 100,000hp

Armament: two quad SS-N-14 launchers; two twin SA-N-3 SAM launchers; two twin 57mm (2.24in) guns; four 30mm (1.18in) AK-630 CIWS; two 533mm (21in) TT; two RBU-1000 ASW RL; one Ka-25 helicopter

Sensors: air/surface-search radar; navigation radar; fire-control radar; hull-mounted sonar

Speed: 34 knots

Range: 19,446km (10,500nm) at 14 knots

Complement: 380

Resolution

HMS *Resolution* was the first of four ballistic missile submarines based on the US Navy's 'Lafayette' class which were built for the Royal Navy.

The four submarines (a fifth was cancelled) used US Polaris missiles, missile tubes, and fire control systems, plus British engines and other equipment. These submarines allowed the Royal Navy to take over responsibility for Great Britain's strategic nuclear deterrent from the RAF's Blue Steel–armed V-bombers. Launched in September 1966, HMS *Resolution* was completed in October 1967, and went on her first patrol in 1968 as planned. To improve the ability of the Polaris missile to penetrate Moscow's fabled ABM defences, Great Britain embarked on an expensive and ambitious upgrade programme code-named Chevaline, adding decoys to the Polaris warhead. The 'Resolution'-class submarines were replaced by the new Trident-armed 'Vanguard' class. HMS *Revenge* was withdrawn in 1992, and *Resolution* followed in 1994. The remaining two submarines in the class were withdrawn during 1995–96.

Displacement: 7500t surfaced; 8500t submerged
Dimensions: 129.5m x 10m x 9.1m (425ft x 33ft x 30ft)
Machinery: one-shaft, nuclear, PWR1 reactor with two geared steam turbines plus auxiliary diesel engine; 15,000hp/4000hp
Armament: 16 UGM-27C Polaris A-3 SLBM; six 533mm (21in) TT
Sensors: general-purpose radar; active/passive multi-function sonar
Speed: 20 knots surfaced; 25 knots dived
Range: limited only by reactor fuel state
Complement: 143

U-12

In the early 1960s, Germany began building her first submarines since World War II, launching the tiny Type 201 boats.

After just three examples, Germany's Type 201 coastal submarines had to be rebuilt as Type 205s, when it was discovered that their non-magnetic steel hulls corroded easily. *U-4* to *U-8* were modified with a tin covering; however, *U-9* to *U-12* were built with a new corrosion-resistant steel. This was then used to rehull the original *U-1* and *U-2*. *U-12* was launched in September 1968 and was one of the last Type 205s to remain operational, serving as a sonar trials platform into the twenty-first century.

The later Type 206 coastal submarine introduced sonar in a swollen, rounded bow, and also had wire-guided torpedoes, improved manoeuvrability and lower noise characteristics. The first of the class (*U-13*) was launched in 1971; the last (*U-30*) in 1974.

Displacement: 419t surfaced; 455t submerged
Dimensions: 45.7m x 4.6m x 4.2m (150ft x 15ft x 13ft 9in)
Machinery: one-shaft, electric drive, two diesels with one electric motor; 1200hp/1500hp
Armament: eight 533mm (21in) TT
Sensors: surface-search radar; active/passive sonar
Speed: 10 knots surfaced; 17.5 knots submerged
Range: 7038km (3800nm) at 10 knots
Complement: 21

Yankee class

Apparently designed with the help of stolen American Polaris missile submarine plans, the 'Yankee' class formed the most important part of the Soviet SSBN fleet in the 1970s.

The Project 667A SSBNs, known to NATO as the 'Yankee' class, were the first Soviet submarines designed to fire their missiles from underwater and the first with SLBM launch tubes inside the pressure hull. The first boat of the 34 in this class was launched in August 1966, and the remainder were completed between 1967 and 1974. The class was armed with 16 SS-N-6 missiles, although one boat was converted to 'Yankee II' specification and carried 12 solid-fuelled SS-NX-17 missiles. The 'Yankees' were withdrawn gradually from 1980 onwards to comply with SALT treaty limitations. Those boats withdrawn had their missile sections cut away, although some were later converted for other roles. The 'Yankee'-class submarines ceased patrols of the US coast in 1987. The number of these submarines in strategic service dwindled: 12 in 1991, six in 1992, and none by the end of 1993. The last non-strategic 'Yankee' was withdrawn in 1994.

Displacement: 7700t surfaced; 9300t submerged

Dimensions: 130m x 11.6m x 8m (426ft 6in x 38ft 1in x 26ft 4in)

Machinery: two-shaft nuclear, two pressurised water reactors; 40,000hp

Armament: 16 SS-N-6 SLBM; six 533mm (21in) TT

Speed: 20 knots surfaced; 27 knots submerged

Range: limited only by reactor fuel state

Complement: 130

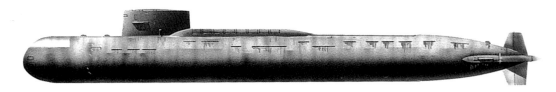

Gus class

Developed in the 1960s from the 50-seat 'Skate'-class passenger ferry, the 'Gus'-class logistic support air cushion vehicle was deployed by all four Soviet fleets – Northern, Baltic, Black Sea and Pacific.

The Soviet Union developed a number of types of air cushion craft in the 1960s and 1970s, pushing hovercraft technology much further than other nations. The Project 1205 Skat transport hovercraft, known to NATO as the 'Gus' class, were the smallest to enter service. The 'Gus'-class ACV could carry either a naval infantry platoon or several tons of supplies. It was used for river patrolling, special forces, beach reconnaissance, amphibious assault and logistics missions. The 'Ivan Rogov'-class large assault ship could carry three 'Gus' class hovercraft in place of two of the larger 'Lebed' class and one 'Ondatra' class conventional landing craft which were usually embarked. Several 'Gus' craft were later modified to serve as hovercraft trainers. About 30 were built between 1969 and 1974, and, while the status of the current fleet is uncertain, given the relatively short operating life of ACVs, it is likely that few are still active. The 'Skat' class was an assault modification of the 'Gus', with the turret of a PT-76 tank mounted forward of the bridge.

Displacement: 27t standard

Dimensions: 21.4m x 7.3m x 0.5m (70ft 3in x 23ft 11in x 1ft 8in)

Machinery: two propellers, two gas turbines; 1800hp

Armament: two 23mm (0.91in) guns

Sensors: not available

Speed: 60 knots

Range: 426km (230nm) at 43 knots

Complement: 4, plus 25 troops

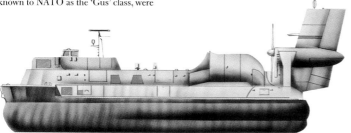

Vittorio Veneto

The helicopter carrier *Vittorio Veneto* (C 550), officially classed as a guided missile helicopter cruiser, was built instead of a planned third 'Andrea Doria'-class vessel.

The larger hull of the new ship allowed a larger flight deck, with the hangar located below instead of in front of it. This allowed the ship to embark six SH-3 Sea Kings or up to nine AB212s, compared to the four AB212s embarked aboard the 'Andrea Doria'-class ships. The ship was laid down in June 1965, and the design was recast several times before launch on 5 February 1967; sea trials began on 30 April 1969. The ship proved extremely efficient, with its two sets of stabilizers proving particularly effective. Originally armed with ASROC and Terrier ASW and anti-aircraft missiles, the *Vittorio Veneto* later received Standard SAMs. The ship also had six torpedo tubes and eight 76mm (3in) gun turrets. The *Vittorio Veneto* served as the Italian fleet flagship until replaced by the new carrier *Giuseppe Garibaldi* in the late 1980s, at which point she was relegated to training duties.

Displacement: 7500t standard; 8850t full load

Dimensions: 179.6m x 19.4m x 6m (589ft 3in x 63ft 7in x 19ft 9in)

Machinery: two-shaft, geared steam turbines, four boilers; 73,000hp

Armament: one Mk 26 combined Standard/ASROC launcher; eight 76mm (3in) guns; six 324mm (12.75in) TT; nine helicopters

Sensors: long-range air/surface-search radar; fire-control radar; hull-mounted sonar

Speed: 30.5 knots

Range: 9260km (5000nm) at 17 knots

Complement: 550

Han class

**The 'Han'-class attack submarines
were the first nuclear-powered vessels
to be built in Communist China –
although the Chinese needed
considerable German help.**

The People's Liberation Army Navy
acquired four 'Han'-class submarines, the
first of which (401) was launched in 1970.
These submarines use a teardrop hull
shape, as pioneered by the US Navy
submarine *Albacore* in the early 1950s.
Much of the design expertise for the
nuclear propulsion system came from
Germany. A total of five 'Han'-class boats

were built over the next 20 years, so
overall progress can best be described as
leisurely. Once in service, the 'Han' class
suffered from build-quality and reliability
problems, but the three lmost recently
built vessels are understood to have been
armed with the Chinese-developed YJ-1
anti-ship missile. According to some
reports, as of 2000 only two of China's
'Han'-class SSNs remained operational,
despite the extended refits that all of them
underwent.

Displacement: 5000t submerged
Dimensions: (401) 100m x 11m x 8.5m
(328ft x 36ft x 28ft)
Machinery: one-shaft, one nuclear reactor,
turbo-electric drive; 15,000hp
Armament: six 533mm (21in) TT; Ying Ji
(Eagle Strike) SSM
Sensors: navigation radar; sonar
Speed: 30 knots surfaced; 25 knots
submerged
Range: limited only by reactor fuel state
Complement: 75

Knox class

With the 'Knox' class, the US Navy sought to develop an oceangoing frigate that could be manned by a crew fewer in number than in earlier vessels of this type.

The ships were designed around a new type of pressure-fired boiler, which promised better cruise performance in terms of range. The 'Knox' class had a primary anti-submarine role, but the ships were surprisingly lightly armed, with just one 127mm (5in) gun and an ASROC launcher as their primary offensive weapons. USS *Knox* (DE 1052) was launched in November 1966 and completed in April 1969. Over the next seven years a total of 45 'Knox'-class vessels were launched. With the end of the Cold War, they were among the first US Navy vessels to be retired under the new financial climate – a reflection of their small size and lack of overall capability. Many were sold abroad. USS *Knox* herself was decommissioned in 1992 and transferred to Taiwan a few years later.

Displacement: 4066t full load

Dimensions: 133.5m x 14.3m x 7.6m (438ft x 47ft x 25ft)

Machinery: one-shaft, geared turbines, two boilers; 35,000hp

Armament: one Sea Sparrow SAM launcher; one ASROC launcher; one 127mm (5in) gun; two 533mm (21in) and four 324mm (12.75in) TT; one SH-2 Seasprite (LAMPS I) helicopter

Sensors: air/surface-search radar; navigation radar; fire-control radar; hull-mounted sonar

Speed: 27 knots

Range: 8334km (4500nm) at 20 knots

Complement: 224

California

Two nuclear-powered 'California'-class cruisers were built for the US Navy after plans for a pair of earlier guided missile destroyers fell through.

They proved to be very different from the ships they notionally succeeded, as they incorporated a host of new systems – most importantly their nuclear powerplants. The 'Californias' were redesignated as nuclear-powered cruisers (CGNs) in 1975. Standard SAMs replaced the earlier Tartars, and the 'Californias' had a much-improved reactor design. A helicopter deck was fitted, but no hangar. The USS *California* (CGN 36, formerly DLGN 36) was launched in

September 1971 and completed in February 1974. She was built with an ASROC system located behind the forward 127mm (5in) gun, under the bridge (it was removed in 1993). In 1992–93 the nuclear refuelling process was carried out in both the *California* and her sister ship, the USS *South Carolina*, thereby extending their service lives to the end of the 1990s, when they were finally decommissioned.

Displacement: 10,150t full load

Dimensions: 181.7m x 18.6m x 6.3m (596ft x 61ft x 20ft 6in)

Machinery: two-shaft nuclear, two D2G reactors, two geared turbines; 60,000hp

Armament: two twin Standard SAM launchers (40 missiles each); two 127mm (5in) guns; four 20mm (0.79in) cannon; one ASROC rocket-boosted ASW torpedo launcher (deleted); four 324mm (12.75in) TT (Mk 32 ASW torpedoes)

Sensors: navigation radar; air/surface-search radar; fire-control radar

Speed: 30-plus knots

Range: limited only by reactor fuel state

Complement: 533

Le Redoutable

When France left NATO's command structure, the country had to develop its nuclear submarines from scratch, without US assistance.

To build the 'Redoubtable'-class SSBNs therefore, France had to design all-new reactors, new missiles and their associated guidance systems, and the submarines themselves. *Le Redoubtable* (S 611) was the first of six submarines in its class. She was launched in March 1967 and completed in December 1971. The first two submarines were armed with the M-1 SLBM, broadly equivalent to the US Poseidon. The next three had the 3000km (1864-mile) range M-2 missile. The M-20, with a 1MT thermonuclear warhead and improved re-entry vehicle, replaced these early weapons. The sixth vessel (*L'Inflexible*) had M-4 missiles with six 150kT MIRVs and a range of 4000km (2486 miles), together with new sonar and improved systems. *Le Redoubtable* was decommissioned in 1991. The remainder have been withdrawn as the new 'Le Triomphant'-class submarines have been commissioned, leaving France with a four-boat deterrent force.

Displacement: 8045t surfaced; 8940t submerged
Dimensions: 128.6m x 10.7m x 10m (422ft x 35ft x 33ft)
Machinery: one-shaft, nuclear, one PWR, two turbines with two turbo-alternators, one electric motor plus one auxiliary diesel engine; 15,000hp/2670hp
Armament: 16 Aerospatiale SLBM; four 550mm (21.66in) TT (18 torpedoes)
Sensors: general-purpose radar; active/passive multi-function sonar
Speed: 20 knots surfaced; 25 knots submerged
Range: limited only by reactor fuel state
Complement: 111

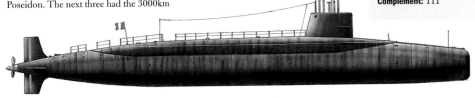

Active

The Royal Navy acquired eight Type 21 'Amazon'-class frigates between 1974 and 1978, of which HMS *Active* (F 171) was the third.

She was laid down at the Vosper Thornycroft yard on 23 July 1971, and completed on 17 June 1977. From *Active* onwards, the Type 21s were fitted with a quad launcher for MM38 Exocet anti-ship missiles, in the 'B' position (behind the main gun). The 'Amazon'-class vessels were well liked by those who served on them because they were comfortable and handled well. However, they had very limited growth potential and were not big enough to accommodate the new weapons and sensors that were required during their service lifetime. At war during the Falkland Islands campaign of 1982, the lightweight aluminium construction of the Type 21s proved unable to withstand rigours imposed by heavy seas and combat. HMS *Active* survived the Falklands conflict, however, unlike two of her sister ships, and was later sold to Pakistan.

Displacement: full load 3600t

Dimensions: 117m x 12.7m x 5.9m (384ft x 41ft 7in x 19ft 5in)

Machinery: two-shaft CODOG, two gas turbines; 56,000hp

Armament: four MM38 Exocet SSM; one Seacat SAM system; one 114mm (4.5in) gun; two 20mm (0.79in) cannon; six 324mm (12.75in) TT

Sensors: search radar; fire-control radar; hull-mounted sonar

Speed: 30 knots

Range: 7408km (4000nm) at 17 knots

Complement: 175–192

F172

Kiev

The Soviet Union's large and heavily armed Project 1143 Krechyet 'aircraft carriers' (designated 'Kiev'-class by NATO) marked a dramatic step forward in Soviet naval capabilities.

In Soviet service they were classified as heavy aircraft-carrying cruisers and were capable of engaging in surface, anti-submarine and anti-air warfare. The Kievs could carry more than 20 fixed-wing Yak-38 'Forger' VTOL aircraft and a further 15 helicopters. The ships' Bazalt anti-ship missile system had eight (or 12) missile launchers, while the Krechyet air defence system consisted of 24 reinforced vertical launchers and 192 SAMs. Each of the

Project 1143 warships had significant differences from the others, and some of the later vessels were almost one-off designs. *Kiev* was completed in December 1975. Three more ships were built in the class: *Minsk*, *Baku* (later renamed *Admiral Gorshkov*) and *Novorossiysk*. A fifth Project 1143 was approved in 1979, but not built. *Kiev* remained in service with the Northern Fleet until 1993, when she was retired from the fleet and held pending her scrapping. The *Admiral Gorshkov* has been sold to India, and after major modification is planned to enter service in 2009.

Displacement: 43,500t full load

Dimensions: 275m x 47.2m x 8.2m (902ft x 154ft 10in x 26ft 11in)

Machinery: four-shaft, four steam turbines, eight turbo-pressurised boilers; 200,000hp

Armament: eight SS-N-12 SSM; two twin SA-N-3 and SA-N-4 SAM launchers; two twin 76mm (3in) guns; eight 30mm (1.18in) AK-630 CIWS; 10 533mm (21in) TT; 12–13 Yak-38 'Forger'; 14–17 Ka-25 Ka-27/-29 'Helix' helicopters

Sensors: air/surface-search radar; navigation radar; fire-control radar; hull-mounted sonar

Speed: 32 knots

Range: 25,002km (13,500nm) at 18 knots

Complement: 1200–1600, incl. air group

Nanuchka class

Known as small missile ships, all 'Nanuchka I's served with Soviet forces. The 'Nanuchka II' was built for India and the 'Nanuchka III' for the Soviet Union, Algeria and Libya.

The heavily armed Project 1234 'Nanuchka I'-class guided missile corvettes had a heavier armament than previous Soviet missile ships. Primary armament was six P-50/4K85 Malachit (SS-N-9 'Siren') anti-ship missiles, which could deliver a 500kg (1,102lb) HE or a 200kt nuclear warhead at a range of 110km (68 miles). The remarkable amount of firepower and combat electronics mounted on such a small platform was apparently purchased at the price of poor seakeeping characteristics. Seventeen units were built from 1969, along with three 'Nanuchka IIs' for India. Nineteen 'Nanuchka IIIs' were built between 1977 and 1986. All the 'Nanuchka I's are being scrapped, while the three Indian 'Nanuchka IIs' were decommissioned between 1999 and 2002.

Displacement: 560t standard; 660t full load

Dimensions: 59.3m x 12.6m x 2.4m (194ft 7in x 41ft 4in x 7ft 11in)

Machinery: three paired diesel engines; 30,000hp

Armament: six SS-N-9 SSM; one SA-N-4 SAM launcher (20 missiles); one 76mm (3in) guns or two 57mm (2.24in)

Sensors: search radar; navigation radar; fire-control radar; hull-mounted sonar

Speed: 32 knots

Range: 4630km (2500nm) at 12 knots

Complement: 60

Tango class

The 'Tango'-class submarines were built as the Soviet Navy's interim successor to the 'Foxtrot' class, and they were intended for service in the Northern and Black Sea fleets.

Project 641 BUKI (NATO code name Tango) submarines were a derivative of the earlier Project 641 (Foxtrot), with more automated systems, a sonar complex linked to a combat information control system, and an autopilot. The class carried 20 per cent more torpedoes and had improved silencing and crew accommodation. The first example was launched in 1972 and 18 BUKIs, in two slightly differing variants,

were used to provide a defensive screen for the Northern Fleet. The later boats were several metres longer than the original 'Tangos', in order to accommodate the fire control systems necessary to operate with the tube-launched SS-N-15, the Soviet equivalent of the American SUBROC ASW missile. Most units of this class were retired starting in 1995. As of early 2000 perhaps four units were thought to remain in the Northern Fleet, although largely inoperable, with another six units believed to be in reserve, but unlikely to return to service.

Displacement: 3100t surfaced; 3900t submerged

Dimensions: 91.5m x 9m x 7m (300ft 3in x 29ft 6in x 23ft)

Machinery: three-shaft, diesel engines; 6000hp

Armament: six 533mm (21in) TT

Sensors: active/passive sonar fit

Speed: 20 knots surfaced; 16 knots submerged

Range: not available

Complement: 72

Type 42 class

The Type 42 destroyer was designed to provide area air defence to a Royal Navy task force, and was the smallest platform able to carry Sea Dart SAMs.

The original design was much larger than the vessels which were actually built, as a result of Treasury pressure to minimize costs. The ships, which entered service in two batches between 1975 and 1982, lacked close-range weapons systems, had reduced endurance at full power, and their short forecastles made them very wet in any kind of sea. The loss of two vessels in the Falklands conflict of 1982 underlined the shortcomings of the Type 42s, but the Royal Navy had already moved to change the design with a revised Batch 3 Type 42, commissioned between 1982 and 1985. They are nearly 42.67m (140ft) longer at the waterline than their Batch 1/2 sister ships, and about 1000t heavier. For close-in defence the Batch 3 vessels can be fitted with both individual 20mm (0.79in) cannon and the Phalanx CIWS. Ten Batch 1/2 vessels were built, along with two for Argentina, and four Batch 3s.

Displacement: 4350t full load

Dimensions: 410ft x 46ft x 19ft (124.99m x 14m x 5.8m)

Machinery: two-shaft, CODOG, four gas turbines; 50,000hp/8000hp

Armament: one GWS30 Sea Dart SAM launcher (22 missiles); one 114mm (4.5in) gun; four 20mm (0.79in) cannon; six 324mm (12.75in) TT; one Lynx helicopter

Sensors: air/surface-search radar; navigation radar; fire-control radar; hull-mounted sonar

Speed: 30 knots

Range: 11,112km (6000nm) at 16 knots

Complement: 312

Charlie class

'Charlie'-class missile-armed attack submarines were intended to mount surprise pop-up missile attacks on high-value targets such as the US Navy's carrier battle groups.

The Soviet Union's Project 670M 'Skat-M' cruise missile submarines were given the NATO code name 'Charlie-II' when they first appeared in 1973. Six Charlie-IIs are believed to have followed on from 12 'Charlie-Is', which were smaller, shorter submarines with a different missile armament. The 'Charlie-IIs' were armed with the SS-N-9 'Siren' anti-ship missile,

which could be fitted with a nuclear warhead for use against US carrier battle groups. The 'Charlie-II' class was, in effect, the finished version of what the 'Charlie-I' design had tried to be – after the latter was rushed into production to cover problems with the 'Papa'-class attack submarines. Throughout its service life the 'Charlie' class was hampered by its single reactor powerplant, which did not provide enough speed to keep up with US carrier battle groups. The fleet remained in Russian service until the late 1990s.

Displacement: 4300t surfaced; 5100t submerged
Dimensions: 103.6m x 10m x 8m (340ft x 32ft 10in x 26ft 3in)
Machinery: one-shaft, nuclear, one reactor; 15,000hp
Armament: eight SS-N-9 SLCM; four 533mm (21in) TT, four 406mm (16in) TT
Speed: 24 knots surfaced
Range: limited only by reactor fuel state
Complement: 98

Sparviero

The 'Sparviero'-class hydrofoils were the product of a collaboration between the Italian Government, the commercial hydrofoil manufacturer Carlo Rodriguez and Boeing.

The craft used Boeing's jetfoil system, with a single forward foil, and two aft. The boats were powered by a Proteus gas turbine driving a waterjet when 'foilborne', while using a diesel when waterborne. This gave the boats a maximum speed of around 50 knots. *Sparviero* (P420) was launched in May 1973, and a production series of six were completed during 1980–83. The 'Sparviero' class was always limited by the lack of onboard accommodation for the crew, restricting the radius of action. *Sparviero* was the first of the class to be stricken, in September 1991, while another was paid off in 1996. The remainder had been withdrawn from service by the end of 2002. The 'Sparviero' class formed the basis of the Japanese 'PG 1' class of fast attack hydrofoils built by Sumitomo.

Displacement: 62.5t full load
Dimensions: (hull) 24.5m x 7m x 1.9m (80ft 7in x 23ft x 6ft 2in)
Machinery: one gas turbine with waterjet; (hull-borne) one-shaft, one diesel; 4500hp/180hp
Armament: two Otomat SSM; one 76mm (3in) gun
Sensors: surface-search radar
Speed: 50 knots
Range: 2222km (1200nm) at 18 knots
Complement: 10

Daphne

A successful design, the 'Daphne' class was used by the French Navy, 11 being delivered from 1964, and 10 were sold for export. They were succeeded by 'Agosta' class in the 1980s, six of which design were also exported or built under licence.

The 'Daphne' class was slower than its contemporaries, performance being sacrificed to allow for deeper diving and a heavier armament fit. A Pakistani 'Daphne' made the first submarine attack since World War II, sinking an Indian frigate in the 1971 war. Four of the much more advanced 'Agosta'-class oceangoing attack submarines supplemented the 'Daphnes' from the 1970s, with a double-hulled construction and conventional motors. An emergency boost allowed 20.5 knots to be reached for five minutes of evasive action, and a small 'creep' motor provided a capability for extended silent operations at just 3.5 knots.

Displacement: 869t surfaced; 1043t submerged
Dimensions: 57.8m x 6.8m x 4.6m (189 ft 7in x 22ft 4 in x 15ft 1in)
Machinery: two-shaft, two diesels and two electric motors; 2448hp
Armament: 12 550mm (21.6in) TT; 12 torpedoes or 24 mines
Speed: 13.5 knots surfaced; 16 knots submerged
Range: 15,742km (8500nm) at 9 knots
Complement: 45

Los Angeles

The 'Los Angeles' class is the mainstay of the US Navy's attack submarine fleet, and its boats are among the largest vessels of their kind in service.

USS *Los Angeles* (SSN 688) was launched in April 1974 and completed in November 1976. A total of 62 examples have been built, making this class by far the most important type in the US submarine fleet. Over the life of the design many important changes have been made to the 688s. From 1984 onwards, with the launch of the USS *Providence* (SSN 619), all the 'Los Angeles' class have been fitted with vertical launch tubes for the Tomahawk land-attack cruise missile. From the USS *San Juan* (SSN-751) onwards, the 'Improved 688' class were fitted with the new BSY-1 submarine combat system. A more obvious change was the replacement of the sail-mounted diving planes, with bow planes – for better under-ice operations. Although they were designed as classic hunter/killer submarines, the role of the 'Los Angeles' class has been greatly expanded in the modern US Navy by their stand-off land attack capability.

Displacement: 6000t surfaced; 6900t submerged

Dimensions: 109.7m x 10m x 9.8m (360ft x 33ft x 32ft 4in)

Machinery: one-shaft, nuclear, one reactor; 30,000hp

Armament: four 533mm (21in) TT (maximum of 26 Mk 48 torpedoes, up to eight Tomahawk cruise missiles); 20 vertical launch Tomahawks (SSN 719 onwards)

Sensors: general-purpose radar; active/passive multi-function sonar

Speed: 31 knots submerged

Range: limited only by reactor fuel state

Complement: 127

Tachikaze

Designed to enhance the Japanese Maritime Self Defence Force's anti-aircraft defences, the guided missile destroyer *Tachikaze* and her two sister ships are armed with Standard SM-1 MR area defence missiles.

Tachikaze (DDG-168) was the first of three graceful destroyers built for the Japanese Maritime Self Defence Force between 1973 and 1979. In order to save on costs, the class used the same propulsion plant and machinery as was being built in the contemporary 'Haruna' class of helicopter-carrying ASW destroyers. The preceding 'Takatsuki' class carried the American ASW DASH drone-helicopter anti-submarine system, but the 'Tachikazes' carried only ASROC missiles and lightweight torpedoes for self-defence. They introduced a considerable improvement in air defence capability over their predecessors. Each ship in the class had a progressively more advanced combat data system, and all have been upgraded since being commissioned. *Tachikaze* gained Harpoon SSM and Phalanx CIWS in 1983, and the other ships in the class followed in 1987.

Displacement: 3850t standard; 4800t full load
Dimensions: 143m x 14.3m x 4.6m (469ft 2in x 46ft 10in x 15ft 1in)
Machinery: two-shaft, geared turbines, two boilers; 70,000hp
Armament: eight Harpoon SSM; one Mk 13 Standard SAM launcher; one ASROC launcher; two 127mm (5in) guns; two 20mm (0.79in) Phalanx CIWS; six 324mm (12.75in) TT; one SH-60J helicopter
Sensors: air/surface-search radar; fire-control radar; hull-mounted sonar
Speed: 32 knots
Complement: 277

Nimitz

Far and away the largest, most powerful and most versatile warships ever built, the nine carriers of the 'Nimitz' class are the backbone of the United States' ability to project power.

The design of the 'Nimitz'-class supercarriers drew heavily on the experience gained from the USS *Enterprise*, the first nuclear carrier. However, the USS *Nimitz* was commissioned in 1975. Being 12 years younger than the 'Big E' it is considerably more efficiently laid out. One big advance was the introduction of a new form of compact two-reactor powerplant, which freed up more internal space for aviation fuel and armaments. A 'Nimitz'-class carrier can carry 90 per cent more aviation fuel and 50 per cent more aviation ordnance for its air wing than a 'Forrestal'-class carrier; it can absorb three times the most severe damage suffered by 'Essex'-class carriers in World War II. The first three 'Nimitz' carriers can be distinguished from later versions by the single bridle-catching 'broom' at the end of the starboard bow catapult. The tenth and last 'Nimitz' will enter service in 2009.

Displacement: 73,973t standard; 91,440t full load

Dimensions: 331.7m x 78.5m x 11.2m (1088ft x 257ft 6in x 36ft 8in)

Machinery: four-shaft nuclear, two A4W reactors, four geared turbines; 260,000hp

Armament: three Mk 29 Sea Sparrow octuple launchers; four Mk 15 Phalanx 20mm (0.79in) CIWS; 90 aircraft

Sensors: air-search radar; surface-search radar; navigation radar; fire-control radar

Speed: 30-plus knots

Range: limited only by reactor fuel state

Complement: 5621 ship, plus air wing

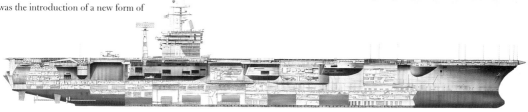

Spruance

'Spruance'-class destroyers have been among the US Navy's busiest and most useful warships since the Cold War. The type has been a regular delivery platform for Tomahawk TLAMs fired at Iraqi targets.

USS *Spruance* (DD 963) was the lead ship in a class of 30 destroyers ordered in June 1970. Completed in September 1975, *Spruance* was a large destroyer, its size dictated by the requirement for a 30-knot speed and by a common hull for planned ASW and anti-aircraft versions. The 30 'Spruance'-class destroyers entered service between 1975 and 1980, and the class has been subject to a succession of modifications and upgrades. Nine ships were fitted with pairs of armoured launcher boxes for Tomahawk cruise missiles from 1984, but since then Mk 41 vertical launchers for 45 TLAMs and 16 ASROCs have been fitted in place of the original Mk 26 launchers which contained Standard SAMs and/or ASROC. The class is also receiving improved ASW and sonar equipment. Four anti-aircraft variants were ordered by pre-Revolution Iran, and these were purchased for the US Navy as the 'Kidd' class.

Displacement: 7800t full load

Dimensions: 171.70m x 16.76m x 6.25m (563ft 4in x 55ft x 20ft 6in)

Machinery: two-shaft, four gas turbines; 80,000hp

Armament: one Sea Sparrow SAM launcher (24 missiles); one ASROC launcher; two 127mm (5in) guns; six 324mm (12.75in) TT; one SH-2 Seasprite (LAMPS I) helicopter

Sensors: air/surface-search radar; navigation radar; fire-control radar; hull-mounted sonar

Speed: 30 knots

Range: 11,112km (6000nm) at 20 knots

Complement: 296

Broadsword

The Royal Navy's Type 22 frigates were developed to counter the Soviet Union's new fast, deep-diving attack submarines which began to appear during the 1970s.

They had to be capable of finding and destroying these submarines, while coping with the latest submarine-launched anti-ship missiles that were also being introduced. For this, they fielded the Sea Wolf SAM, which was designed to defeat high-speed, close-in targets. HMS *Broadsword* (F 88) and her three sister ships were all big, could maintain high

speed in high seas and had plenty of room for future modernization – the latter a primary design consideration. Completed in May 1979, *Broadsword* went to war in the Falklands in 1982. In 1988–89 she was refitted, gaining new funnels and expanded crew quarters to handle training details. Britain ordered four enlarged Batch 3 frigates, otherwise known as the 'Cornwall' class, to make up for losses suffered during the Falklands conflict.

Displacement: 4000t standard; 4400t full load

Dimensions: 131.2m x 14.8m x 6.1m (430ft x 48ft 6in x 19ft 10in)

Machinery: two-shaft, COGOG, four gas turbines; 54,600hp plus/9700hp

Armament: four MM38 Exocet SSM; two six-round launchers for SAM system; two 40mm (1.57in) (or two 30mm/1.18in); six 324mm (12.75in) TT; two helicopters

Sensors: air/surface-search radar; navigation radar; fire-control radar; hull-mounted sonar

Speed: 30 knots

Range: 8334km (4500nm) at 18 knots

Complement: 407

Delta class

The Soviet-era Project 667B ballistic missile submarines (NATO code name 'Delta' class) are still a vital element of the Russian navy's strategic fleet.

The type's origins lie in the 'Yankee'-class submarines of the mid-1960s, which were steadily improved into the today's 'Deltas'. Four subtypes of the 'Delta' class have been identified, each with new systems and improved main missile armament. The 'Delta-I' carried 12 SS-N-8 'Sawfly' SLBMs, while the larger 'Delta-II' carried 16 missiles. The first 'Delta-III' (K-441) was launched and completed in 1976, and a total of 13 followed by 1982 – when the further improved 'Delta-IV' came on stream. All the 'Delta' missile submarines have a distinctive hump behind the main sail, housing their bulky SLBM payload. The 'Delta-III' boats operate at a depth of 366m (1200ft) and are thought to have test dived to 366m (1900ft). The improved 'Delta-IV' boats are fitted with a housing for a towed-sonar and towed decoy system.

Displacement: 10,500t surfaced; 13,250t submerged
Dimensions: 140m x 12m x 8.7m (459ft 4in x 39ft 4in x 28ft 7in)
Machinery: two-shaft, nuclear, one reactor, rated at approximately 500,000hp
Armament: 16 SS-N-18 SLBMs, four 533mm (21in) TT; two 406mm (16in) TT
Sensors: sonar suite, ECM, navigation radar
Speed: 25 knots submerged
Range: limited only by reactor fuel state
Complement: approximately 120

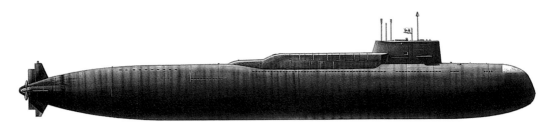

Lupo

The Italian 'Lupo'-class frigates are a modern and efficient design. The Italian Navy has acquired a fleet of eight 'Lupos', including four ordered by Iraq which were never delivered.

The lead ship in the class, *Lupo* (F 564), was launched in June 1976 and completed in September 1977. Together with the 'Sparviero'-class attack boats, the *Lupo* was the first Italian ship to introduce the Otomat SSM into service. The *Lupo* is noteworthy for adopting the US Sea Sparrow SAM. She is built around a SADOC automated combat control system, allowing her to work as part of an integrated, data-linked surface battle group. The 'Lupos' were succeeded in production by the 'Maestrale'-class frigates, which are based on the 'Lupo' design, but are about 10 per cent bigger. This increase in size means that they are slightly slower than the 'Lupos', but also more seaworthy. *Maestrale* (F 570), the first of eight ships in its class, was launched in February 1981 and completed in March 1982.

Displacement: 2500t full load

Dimensions: 112.8m x 12m x 3.6m (370ft 2in x 39ft 4in x 12ft)

Machinery: two-shaft, CODOG, two gas turbines and two diesel; 50,000hp/8490hp

Armament: eight Otomat SSM; one Sea Sparrow SAM ; one 127mm (5in); four 40mm (1.57in) cannon, two 20mm (0.79in) cannon; six 324mm (12.75in) TT; two helicopters

Sensors: air/surface-search radar; navigation radar; fire-control radar; hull-mounted sonar

Speed: 35 knots

Range: 8056km (4350nm) at 16 knots

Complement: 185

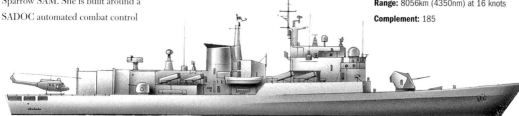

Oliver Hazard Perry

The US Navy acquired 51 'Oliver Hazard Perry'-class frigates as a direct successor to the 'Knox' class ASW vessels. They also replaced remaining WWII-era FRAM destroyers.

USS *Oliver Hazard Perry* (FFG 7) was launched on 25 September 1976. The new ships were deliberately austere, with more emphasis placed on anti-ship and anti-aircraft capability than on ASW. The 'Perry' class was optimized as AAW vessels, although the combination of towed sonar and helicopter-delivered ordnance soon provided a formidable stand-off ASW capability. From USS

Underwood (FFG 36) onwards, an enlarged flight deck and hangarage for two LAMPS helicopters were fitted, these features being retrofitted to many of the earlier vessels. Despite their lightweight construction, the 'Oliver Hazard Perry' vessels have proved to be remarkably robust. In the Persian Gulf the USS *Stark* survived two Exocet hits, while the USS *Samuel B Roberts* withstood a contact mine explosion in the same area. Both vessels were repaired and returned to service.

Displacement: 3486t full load

Dimensions: 135.6m x 14.5m x 4.4m (445ft x 47ft 6in x 14ft 5in)

Machinery: one-shaft, two LM-2500 gas turbines; 40,000hp

Armament: one Mk 13 launcher for Harpoon SSM (four) and Standard SAM (36); one 76mm (3in) gun; six 324mm (12.75in) TT; one SH-60B Seahawk (LAMPS III) helicopter

Sensors: air/surface-search radar; navigation radar; fire-control radar; hull-mounted sonar

Speed: 28.5 knots

Range: 8334km (4500nm) at 20 knots

Complement: 176

Tarawa

The 'Tarawa' class of large assault ships incorporate comprehensive command and control facilities, allowing them to fulfil a flagship role. They also have an austere 3-D radar, enabling them to perform limited fighter control functions.

The USS *Tarawa* (LHA 1) was the first of a class of five of the largest, most capable assault ships built up to that time. She was launched in December 1973 and commissioned in May 1976. The 'Tarawa'-class ships routinely embark up to six AV-8B Harrier II+ fighters in addition to a mix of helicopters, or they can operate nine CH-53 Sea Stallion or as many as 12 CH-46 Sea Knight helicopters. There have been periodic attempts to produce a full carrier conversion of the 'Tarawa' class LHA hull, for the US Navy or for export customers such as Australia. Apart from its 'Air Wing', each 'Tarawa'-class ship has a floodable well-deck for landing craft, and can carry up to 1903 troops who have access to a 464.5sq m (5000 sq ft) acclimatization/training room.

Displacement: 25,588t standard; 38,761t full load

Dimensions: 249.9m x 38.4m x 7.8m (820ft x 126ft x 25ft 9in)

Machinery: two-shaft, geared turbines, two boilers; 70,000hp

Armament: two RAM launchers; two 127mm (5in) guns; six Mk 24 25mm cannon; two 20mm (0.79in) Phalanx CIWS; one helicopter

Sensors: air/surface-search radar; navigation radar; fire-control radar

Speed: 24 knots

Range: 18,520km (10,000nm) at 20 knots

Complement: 892, plus 1903 troops

Ivan Rogov

The appearance of the *Ivan Rogov* amphibious assault ship, launched in 1976, seemed to signal the beginning of a major elevation in the Soviet Union's international power-projection capabilities.

The *Ivan Rogov* was three times the size of the preceding 'Alligator'-class large landing ships and was compared by some to a US Navy LPH. *Ivan Rogov* was completed in 1978. She could carry an entire naval infantry battalion plus 10 tanks and 30 APCs – and introduced a new class of 'Lebed' assault hovercraft to take them ashore. If no landing craft were carried, the *Ivan Rogov* could carry up to 55 tanks. A flight deck, situated aft, was large enough to accommodate four helicopters. *Ivan Rogov* also had bow doors to allow a beaching landing, if necessary. However, production of the subsequent ships progressed very slowly and, by 1989, only three had been built. *Ivan Rogov* was stricken in 1996, while the status of the two remaining vessels is

Displacement: 8260t standard; 14,080t full load
Dimensions: 158m x 24m x 8.2m (518ft 4in x 78ft 9in x 26ft 11in)
Machinery: two-shaft, geared gas turbines with thrusters; 20,000hp
Armament: two SS-N-3 SSM; two SA-N-4 SAM; one Grad-M rocket launcher; one twin 76mm (3in) gun; four 30mm (1.18in) guns
Sensors: navigation radar; air-search radar; fire-control radar; helicopter-landing control radar
Speed: 23 knots
Range: 22,224km (12,000nm) at 14 knots
Complement: 239, plus 520 troops

Kirov

Originally designed to seek and destroy ballistic missile submarines, Russia's Project 1144.2 Orlan ('Kirov' class) are the world's largest cruisers.

Their role was expanded to engage large surface and air targets. *Kirov* was completed in December 1980 and was armed with the Granit (SS-N-19 'Shipwreck') long-range anti-ship missile. Twenty missiles were installed under the upper deck, mounted at a 60-degree elevation. The S-300F Kashtan air defence missile system was also installed, with 12 launchers and 96 vertical launch SAMs. In addition, *Kirov* had two

Osa-Ma (SA-N-4) double launchers with 40 air defence missiles. The ship's propulsion system is a combined nuclear and steam turbine. In 1990, *Kirov* (renamed as the *Admiral Ushakov*) suffered a major nuclear accident. She was stricken in 1998 to provide spares for the only other active ship of the class, the *Admiral Nakhimov*. However, in January 1999 the Russian Duma (lower parliament) voted for the *Admiral Ushakov* to be repaired and restored to service.

Displacement: 25,396–26,396t full load

Dimensions: 248m x 28.5m x 7.5m (813ft 8in x 93ft 6in x 24ft 7in)

Machinery: two-shaft, two nuclear reactors, four steam turbines; 280,000hp

Armament: 20 SS-N-19 SSM; S-300F (12 launchers, 96 SAMs); two twin SA OSA-MA (40 missiles); 10 533mm (21in) TT with SS-N-14; two 100mm (3.9in) guns; eight 30mm (1.18in) CIWS; two RBU-1000 and one RBU-6000 ASW RL; three Ka-25/-27 helicopters

Sensors: air/surface-search, navigation. fire-control radars; hull-mounted sonar

Speed: 32 knots

Range: 25,002km (13,500nm) at 18 knots

Complement: 1200–1600

Invincible

Britain's trio of 'Invincible'-class carriers was born in the aftermath of the CVA-01 debacle, which in 1966 signalled the end of the Royal Navy's plans to operate large carriers.

Soon afterwards a new programme of large helicopter-carrying ships was drawn up. Redesigned to have a proper (if short) flight deck, they became known as 'through-deck cruisers'. With the advent of the Sea Harrier they became fully fledged VSTOL aircraft carriers. HMS *Invincible* was commissioned in 1980, and played a major part in Britain's Falklands campaign. *Illustrious* was completed in June 1982. Immediately afterwards, she replaced

Invincible in the Falklands. *Ark Royal* was commissioned in 1985. The Invincibles were built with a 6.5-degree ski jump for their Sea Harriers, but as each ship has been refitted the ski jump has been increased to 12 degrees. Each vessel was armed with a Sea Dart twin launcher, installed on the forecastle of the ship near the ski ramp. However, the missile system has been removed from all three carriers and the flight deck extended, to provide more aircraft capacity and to enable RAF Harrier GR.7/9 aircraft to be operated.

Displacement: 16,000t standard; 20,600t full load
Dimensions: 206.3m x 27.5m x 7.3m (677ft x 90ft x 24ft)
Machinery: two-shaft, COGOG, four gas turbines; 112,000hp
Armament: one twin Sea Dart SAM; one 30mm (1.18in) Goalkeeper CIWS; two 20mm (0.79in) guns; nine aircraft; 12 helicopters (maximum)
Sensors: air-search radar; surface-search radar; navigation radar; fire-control radar; hull-mounted sonar
Speed: 20 knots
Range: 9260km (5000nm) at 18 knots
Complement: 557, plus 318 air group

Näcken

Sweden has long maintained a sophisticated submarine design and manufacturing capability.

The three 'Näcken' class (A14) boats were laid down in 1976. The lead ship in the class, *Näcken*, was launched in April 1978 and completed in April 1980. Each of the submarines carried large three-letter pennant letters on their conning towers – in *Näcken*'s case they read 'Näk'. During 1987–88, the three Näckens were taken back into dry dock and fitted with a new closed-cycle air independent propulsion (AIP) system. These new powerplants

required the submarines' hulls to be extended by 8m (26ft 3in). Experience with these AIP engines paved the way for the latest generation of AIP-powered Swedish submarines, the Vastergötland class, which are now entering service. As a result of substantial cuts to the Swedish defence budget, only the three Vastergötlands will ultimately remain in service, so the 'Näcken' class has now been retired.

Displacement: 980t surfaced; 1150t submerged

Dimensions: 49.5m x 5.7m x 5.5m (162ft 5in x 18ft 8in x 18ft)

Machinery: one-shaft, diesel engine, electric motor; 2100hp/1150kW (later with AIP)

Armament: six 533mm (21in) and two 400mm (15.75in) TT (12 torpedoes)

Sensors: surface-search radar; active sonar

Speed: 20 knots surfaced; 25 knots submerged

Range: not available

Complement: 19

Sovremennyy

The *Sovremennyy* was the first of a class of 20 missile cruisers (actually designated as destroyers in the Soviet navy) which replaced the 'Kresta' class in production at Zhdanov.

The new vessels used basically the same hull, steam plants and broadly similar armament, with the addition of fore and aft turrets each containing a pair of rapid-fire 130mm (5.1in) guns. The primary offensive weapon was the Moskit (SS-N-22), a deadly anti-ship missile with a range of about 129km (70nm). The 'Sovremennyy'-class ships entered service as a lighter RKR which, intended to

complement the heavy 'Slava' class cruisers then being built. The *Sovremennyy* was completed on Christmas Day 1980, and since then the Zhadanov yard has completed some 19 ships in the class. At the beginning of the twenty-first century, the only large Russian Navy surface combatants active in significant numbers were 'Sovremennyy'-class vessels, together with a few 'Udaloy' class destroyers. The two remaining unfinished 'Sovremennyys' were sold to China, the first of which was delivered early in 2000.

Displacement: 7800t full load
Dimensions: 155.5m x 17.3m x 5.8m (511ft 10in x 56ft 9in x 21ft 4in)
Machinery: two-shaft, two steam turbines, four high-pressure boilers; 100,000–102,000hp
Armament: two SS-N-22 SSM, two SA-N-7 SAM, one SA-N-12 SAM launchers; two 130mm (5.1in) guns; four 30mm (1.18in) CIWS; four 533mm (21in) TT; two RBU-1000 ASW RL; 40 mines; one Ka-27 helicopter
Sensors: air/surface-search, navigation, fire-control radars; hull-mounted sonar
Speed: 35 knots
Range: 19,446km (10,500nm) at 14 knots
Complement: 380

Typhoon class

The enormous Project 941 Akula submarines, known to NATO as 'Typhoons', were the world's largest and most sinister weapons of war.

Built to allow the Soviet Union to deliver a retaliatory strike, the vast Akula submarine was designed to lie on the seabed under the ice for up to a year, surviving a nuclear exchange before emerging to unleash as many as 20 SLBMs, with 200 warheads, on the enemy's heartland. The missiles are arranged in silos in two rows in front of the sail between the main hulls. The Akula submarine's huge size includes crew accommodation that is spacious enough to allow the provision of a sauna and even an aviary! TK-208, the first of six 'Typhoons', was laid down at Severodvinsk in March 1977 and launched in 1980. A seventh 'Typhoon' was broken up on the slipway, and a further seven planned submarines in the class were cancelled. In June 2000 the Russian navy claimed that it operated 26 SSBNs. This force was said to include five 'Typhoons', but according to one report, as of 1999 only a single 'Typhoon' remained operational..

Displacement: 24,500t surfaced; 48,000t submerged
Dimensions: 171.5m x 22.9m x 12.2m (562ft 9in x 75ft x 40ft)
Machinery: two-shaft, nuclear, two pressurised-water reactors, two steam turbines; 100,000hp
Armament: 20 SS-N-20 SLBM); two 650mm (25.6in) and four 533mm (21in) TT
Sensors: general-purpose radar; active/passive multi-function sonar
Speed: 16 knots surfaced; 27 knots submerged
Range: limited only by reactor fuel state
Complement: 150

Victor III

The Project 671 Victor I attack submarine was developed for the Soviet navy to succeed the early 'November' class hunter-killers.

A second-generation nuclear-powered attack boat with a modern teardrop hull, the first 'Victor' was delivered in November 1967. Some 15 were built before production switched to the longer 'Victor II'. These seven boats carried a new ASW weapon (the SS-N-16) and were assigned to the Soviet Northern Fleet. Komsomolsk and Leningrad built 26 improved (and further lengthened) Victor IIIs, in two subvariants. The 671RTMs had a new sonar suite, silenced engines and four (instead of six) torpedo tubes. They also had a towed VLF buoy, and most had an innovative new propeller system, with two four-bladed screws turning on a common shaft but inclined 22.5 degrees apart to reduce cavitation. In the 1980s, surviving 'Victors' were updated and armed with new SS-N-21 cruise missiles. Like the earlier 'Victors', the 'Victor IIIs' began to be retired from the mid-1990s when the time came for their reactors to be recored.

Displacement: 4900t surfaced; 6000t submerged
Dimensions: 104m x 10m x 7m (341ft 2in x 32ft 10in x 23ft)
Machinery: one-shaft, nuclear, one pressurised-water reactor; 30,000hp
Armament: six 533mm (21in) TT (18 torpedoes and SS-N-15)
Sensors: surface-search radar; low-frequency active sonar
Speed: 30 knots submerged
Range: endurance 4500 power hours
Complement: 94

MEKO Frigate

Developed by Blohm & Voss in Germany, the MEKO family of corvettes and frigates have been adopted by navies around the world.

The MEKO family of warships includes frigates, corvettes and oceangoing patrol boats. The MEKO concept began in the 1970s when Blohm & Voss designed the MEKO 360 H1 for Nigeria. MEKO is a registered trademark. The German acronym stands for 'multipurpose combination'. It is a thoroughly modern naval shipbuilding concept based on modular construction of hulls, armament, electronics and other equipment, aiming at ease of maintenance and reduced cost of building. MEKO frigates and corvettes have been built for Argentina, Australia, Greece, Malaysia, New Zealand, Nigeria, Poland, Portugal, South Africa and Turkey, and MEKO characteristics have also been built into the Type 124 frigates of the German navy. A typical MEKO design is the MEKO 200 ANZAC series which were built for Australia and New Zealand, which are the most modern vessel in their respective fleets.

Displacement: 3600t full load

Dimensions: 118m x 14.4m x 4.4m (387ft 1in x 47ft 1in x 14ft 5in)

Machinery: one-shaft CODOG, gas turbine plus two diesels; 30,000hp/8840hp

Armament: one eight-cell Mk 41 VLS for Sea Sparrow SAM; one 127mm (5in) gun; two 12.7mm (0.5in) MG; six 324mm (12.75in) TT; one helicopter

Sensors: air-search radar; air/surface-search radar; navigation radar; fire-control radar; hull-mounted sonar

Speed: 31.75 knots

Range: 7593km (4100nm) at 18 knots

Complement: 163

Udaloy

The Project 1155 *Udaloy* was the first in a class of 14 large ASW vessels broadly equivalent to the US Navy's 'Spruance'-class destroyers.

Cruiser-sized but described as destroyers by their Soviet/Russian users, each embarks a pair of helicopters and is armed with SS-N-14 SSM, SA-N-9 SAMs and two 100mm (3.9in) cannon. The *Udaloy* and her sister ships succeeded the 'Kara' class and acted as ASW flotilla leaders. *Udaloy* was completed on the last day of 1980. Integration of the SA-N-9 on the

'Udaloys' was delayed, and the first two ships were originally delivered without the weapon; the fourth ship was the first with both the missiles and their associated directors. Two late vessels were ordered as Project 1155.1s, with SS-N-15s or SS-N-22 missiles as used by the 'Krivak III' class, and these were ultimately taken over by the Border Guards. *Simferopol* and *Admiral Vinogradov* were designated as Project 1155 bis cruisers.

Displacement: 7900t full load
Dimensions: 162m x 19.30m x 6.20m (531ft 6in x 63ft 4in x 20ft 4in)
Machinery: two-shaft, two gas turbines and two boost gas turbines; 120,000hp
Armament: eight SS-N-14 SSM; eight SA-N-9 SAM launchers; two 100mm (3.9in) guns; four 30mm (1.18in) AA cannon; four 30mm (1.18in) CIWS; eight 533mm (21in) TT; two RBU-6000 ASW RL; two helicopters
Sensors: air/surface-search, navigation and fire-control radars; hull-mounted sonar
Speed: 34 knots
Range: 19,446km (10,500nm) at 14 knots
Complement: 300

AP.1-88

The AP.1-88 built by the British Hovercraft Corporation was the first diesel-powered air cushion vehicle to enter widespread commercial service; it reduced the notoriously high operating costs of hovercraft, originally powered by very expensive gas-turbine engines.

By the 1980s, advances in diesel engine technology enabled this much cheaper powerplant to be substituted for the complex jet engine, a fact which went a long way towards making the small hovercraft commercially viable. In 1982 the Type AP.1-88 was the first to come to market, and it made a considerable commercial impact, both as a freight carrier and as a passenger ferry. A militarized version, armed with a Rarden 30mm (1.18in) cannon and lightweight surface-to-air missiles is also available.

Maximum operating weight: 40t

Dimensions: 24.5m x 11m (80ft 4in x 36ft)

Machinery: four diesel engines; 1800hp

Service speed: 40 knots

Role: general cargo and passenger carrier

Route: not applicable

Capacity: 101 passengers or 12t cargo

Constructor: British Hovercraft Corporation

Material: aluminium

Built for: not applicable

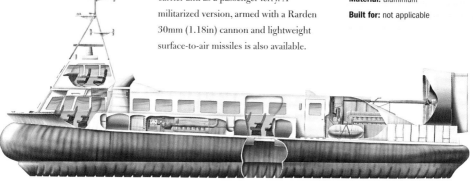

Ticonderoga

Based on the hull of the 'Spruance'-class destroyer, the 'Ticonderoga' class was originally conceived as part of a conventional/nuclear mix of missile frigates, later redesignated as cruisers.

The nuclear strike cruiser programme was subsequently cancelled. The advanced Aegis air defence system, based around the powerful SPY-1 phased array radar system, was installed in what was viewed as a minimum platform for Aegis, affordable in relatively large numbers. USS *Ticonderoga* (CG 47) led a class of 27 ships, and was launched in April 1981. She was less powerfully armed than the planned nuclear strike cruiser, with no 203mm (8in) gun, and with only two quadruple canisters of Harpoon missiles. The ship also carried Standard SAMs, ASROC, torpedoes and two 127mm (5in) guns, and two SH-60B Seahawk (LAMPS III) helicopters. Later ships in the class (CG 52 onwards) have vertical launch systems with enlarged missile storage, increased to 122 rounds, and Tomahawk cruise missiles.

Displacement: 8910t full load
Dimensions: 171.60m x 19.81m x 9.45m (563ft x 65ft x 31ft)
Machinery: two-shaft, four gas turbines; 80,000hp
Armament: eight Harpoon SSM; two Mk 26 launchers (68 Standard SAM and 20 ASROC torpedoes); two 127mm (5in) guns; six 324mm (12.75in) TT; one SH-60J helicopter
Sensors: Aegis air defence system; air/surface-search, navigation, fire-control radars; hull-mounted sonar and towed array
Speed: 30 knots
Range: 11,112km (6000nm) at 16 knots
Complement: 343

Giuseppe Garibaldi

When the *Giuseppe Garibaldi* (C 551) was laid down in 1981, the Italian navy was still restricted by a 1923 law that forbade the operation of combat aircraft from its ships.

The *Giuseppe Garibaldi* was completed in September 1985. Her original design foresaw the *Garibaldi* operating VSTOL aircraft in the Harrier class, but initially the ship embarked Agusta-built ASH-3D Sea Kings. *Garibaldi*'s below-deck hangar can accommodate up to 12 Sea Kings. Typically, the *Giuseppe Garibaldi* serves

as a flagship, but it also has a secondary amphibious assault capability with space for 600 troops on board. In 1992, the anachronistic restrictions on shipborne aircraft were finally lifted and Italy ordered 16 McDonnell Douglas (now Boeing) AV-8B Harrier II+ V/STOL attack aircraft. The Harriers made their first deployment aboard in December 1994.

Displacement: 13,850t full load

Dimensions: 180.2m x 30.4m x 8.2m (591ft 2in x 99ft 9in x 26ft 9in)

Machinery: two-shaft, two gas turbines; 80,000hp

Armament: four Teseo Mk 2 SSM; two Albatros SAMs; six 40mm (1.57in) guns; six 324mm (12.7in) TT; 16 aircraft or 18 helicopters

Sensors: air-search, air/surface-search, surface-search/target indication navigation and fire-control radars; hull-mounted sonar

Speed: 29.5 knots

Range: 12,964km (7000nm) at 20 knots

Complement: 550, plus 230 air group

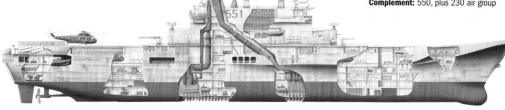

Sierra class

Designed as a follow-on to the 'Victor III', only four examples of the Project 945 'Sierra'-class attack submarine were built before production switched to the cheaper Project 971 Akula (not to be confused with the Akula ballistic missile submarine, known to NATO as 'Typhoon').

Designed by the Lazurit OKB, the Project 945 submarines used the 'Victor III' acoustics suite and a very quiet powerplant based on the Arktika reactor. The titanium-hulled vessels combined a deep-diving capability (variously quoted as 700m/ 2297ft, 800m/2625ft or 1000m/3280ft) with excellent accommodation and safety systems for the crew, including an escape pod (or two pods on the third and fourth Project 945A 'Sierra II' submarines) in the wide sail. The lead ship, *Barrakuda*, was launched in June 1983 and completed in June 1984, while *K-534*, the first Project 945A submarine, a slightly enlarged variant known as the 'Sierra II', was launched in May 1988 and completed one year later. Three Project 945 submarines were scrapped before completion in 1992.

Displacement: 5200–7200t surfaced; 6800–10,100t, submerged

Dimensions: 107m x 12m x 8.8m (351ft x 39ft 5in x 28ft 11in)

Machinery: one-shaft, one pressurised-water nuclear reactor; 47,000–50,000hp

Armament: four 533mm (21in) and four 650mm (25.6in) TT with provision for SS-N-22, SS-N-16, Shkval underwater rockets, torpedoes or 42 mines; one SA-N-5/SA-N-8

Sensors: surface-search radar; active/passive sonar suite

Speed: 18 knots surfaced; 36 knots submerged

Range: endurance 4500 power hours

Complement: 61

Slava

The Project 1164 Atlant (NATO code name 'Slava') class were surface strike cruisers, but with considerable air defence and ASW capability.

The 'Slavas' may have been intended as a cheaper complement to the massive 'Kirov' class 'battlecruisers'. Sixteen SS-N-12 anti-ship missiles are mounted in four pairs on either side of the superstructure, giving the ship a distinctive appearance. Initially designated 'Black Com1' by Western intelligence and subsequently the 'Krasina' class, the first 'Slava'-class cruiser became operational in 1983, and by 1990 three were in the fleet, with the third

beginning sea trials in August 1989. The end of the Cold War and the break-up of the Soviet Union led to the transfer of two ships to the Ukraine, with *Lobov* (originally *Komsomolets*) becoming *Poltava*, *Bohdan Khmenytsky* and finally *Vilna Ukraina*. The ship was then sold back to Russia in 1995. *Slava* itself was sent to the Ukraine and began a refit in December 1990, but this was stopped when only 40 per cent complete. Its future remains uncertain.

Displacement: 12,500t full load

Dimensions: 187m x 20.8m x 7.5m (613ft 6in x 68ft 3in x 24ft 7in)

Machinery: four-shaft, COGOG, four gas turbines; 108,800–110,000hp

Armament: 16 SS-N-12 SSM; eight SA-N-6 SAM launchers, two SA-N-4 SAM launchers; two 130mm (5.1in) guns; six 30mm AK-630 CIWS; 10 533mm (21in) TT; two RBU-6000 ASW RL; one Ka-25 'Hormone' helicopter

Sensors: air/surface-search, navigation, fire-control radars; hull-mounted sonar

Speed: 34 knots

Range: 16,668km (9000nm) at 15 knots

Complement: 529

Trafalgar

The first advanced 'Trafalgar' class submarine was launched on 1 July 1981, having been ordered by Britain's Royal Navy in 1977.

The new class followed on directly from the 'Swiftsure' attack boats, which it closely resembled. Reckoned to be the world's quietest nuclear submarines, the 'Trafalgars' are covered with conformal anechoic tiles and have retractable foreplanes and a strengthened fin for under-ice operations. They are also capable of operating at extreme depths

(below 500m/1640ft) according to some sources. Armed with up to 21 wire-guided torpedoes (fired from five bow tubes) and four UGM-84A Sub-Harpoon anti-ship missiles, the 'Trafalgar'-class submarines also have a powerful anti-ship capability. While early boats in the class had a conventional seven-bladed propeller, later boats have a shrouded propulsor instead. Colloquially known as 'T-boats' in Royal Navy service, the submarines were extensively modified during the 1990s, receiving Tomahawk cruise missile firing capability.

Displacement: 4700t surfaced; 5200t submerged
Dimensions: 85.4m x 9.8m x 9.5m (280ft 2in x 32ft 2in x 31ft 3in)
Machinery: one-shaft, nuclear PWR reactor, two steam turbines, diesel-electric auxiliary and two batteries; 15,000hp/4000hp
Armament: five 533mm (21in) TT (21 torpedoes, four Harpoon anti-ship missiles)
Sensors: general-purpose radar; active/passive multi-function sonar
Speed: 20 knots surfaced; 30 knots submerged
Range: limited only by reactor fuel state
Complement: 97

Aster

More than 30 'Tripartite' minehunters operated by France, the Netherlands and Belgium provide a significant part of Western Europe's mine countermeasure capability.

During the 1980s and early 1990s, Belgium acquired 10 minesweepers under the French-led 'Tripartite' programme, which also involved the Netherlands. *Aster* (M 915) was the lead ship in her class and was launched in June 1985. She can carry a varying crew, depending on her mission, and has provision for up to six divers

operating with a portable decompression chamber carried above deck. Three of the class served during Operation 'Desert Storm' as part of the Coalition naval effort. The *Aster* is fitted with a pair of PAP 104 remote-controlled mine locators, carried on her rear deck. She uses mechanical sweep gear to clear the mines found by either the locators or the divers.

Displacement: 511t standard; 595t full load
Dimensions: 51.5m x 8.9m x 2.5m (168ft 9in x 29ft 2in x 8ft 2in)
Machinery: one-shaft, twin active rudders and bow thruster, one diesel; 1900hp
Armament: one 20mm (0.79in) cannon; one 12.7mm (0.5in) MG (optional); two PAP 104 remote-controlled mine-locating vehicles
Sensors: navigation radar; sonar
Speed: 15 knots
Range: 4630km (2500nm) at 12 knots
Complement: 34–46

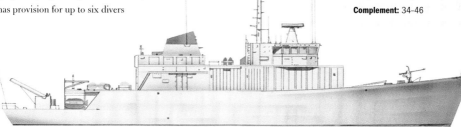

Whidbey Island

One of the key elements in the US armed forces amphibious capability, the dock landing ship force of the US Navy was rapidly aging in the 1970s and 1980s, and needed replacement.

New amphibious techniques designed to speed landing operations were being developed, most notably the use of air-cushion landing craft. Loosely based on the earlier 'Anchorage' class of dock landing ship, the USS *Whidbey Island* (LSD 41) was the lead ship in what was originally planned as a six-ship class. In the event, eight ships were funded and built, and these were designed to be able to handle LCAC air cushion landing craft as well as conventional landing craft. This necessitated a deeper well deck (which could be flooded to accommodate boats and landing craft), with a raised helicopter deck above, from which the ship could operate CH-46 Sea Knight helicopters and AV-8B Harrier vertical take-off aircraft. *Whidbey Island* was launched in June 1983, while the eighth and last ship of the class was launched in November 1989.

Displacement: 11,125t standard; 15,726t full load
Dimensions: 185.8m x 25.6m x 6m (609ft 6in x 84ft x 19ft 8in)
Machinery: two-shafts, two diesels; 41,600hp
Armament: two 20mm (0.79in) CIWS; two 20mm (0.79in) cannon; eight 12.7mm (0.5in) MG; platform for two assault helicopters
Sensors: air-search radar; surface-search radar; navigation radar
Speed: 22 knots
Range: 14,805km (8000nm) at 18 knots
Complement: 376, plus 440 marines

Xia class

China's only ballistic missile submarine of the 'Xia' (Type 92 SSBN) class resembles a scaled-down Soviet 'Yankee'-class boat.

Based on the 'Han'-class nuclear-powered attack submarine, the *Xia* is armed with up to 12 JL2 (CSS-N-3) ICBMs. The JL2 is an 8000km (4970-mile) range missile with a two-stage solid-fuel rocket motor carrying three or four 90kT MIRVs, or a single 250kT warhead. The *Xia* (406) was launched in 1981 and completed in 1987,

although it was unable to make a successful missile firing until 1988. Since then, the submarine has spent a great deal of time in refit and has made only a few operational patrols. The *Xia* is probably a one-off, although some sources do suggest that a sister submarine was built but lost in service; further units, with four more missile launch tubes, might be under construction. A Soviet-built 'Golf' submarine was used as a trials vessel for the JL2 missile and more boats of this class are believed to be in service with the

Chinese navy. It is widely believed that a longer-range SSBN, the Type 94, is under development to replace the *Xia*.

Displacement: 8000t submerged
Dimensions: 120m x 10m x 8m (394ft x 33ft x 26ft)
Machinery: one-shaft nuclear, one pressurised water reactor, turbo-electric drive
Armament: 12 SLBMs; six 533mm (21in) TT
Sensors: not available
Speed: 22 knots submerged
Range: not available
Complement: 100

Jacob van Heemskerck

The Dutch decided to develop an air defence version of their 'Kortenaer' class multi-purpose frigate, and the result was the two frigates of the 'Jacob van Heemskerck' class.

The 'Kortenaer', or 'Standard'-class, frigate design was authorized in the late 1960s as a replacement for the 12 aging ASW destroyers of the 'Holland' and 'Friesland' classes. The same basic design was used for the German navy's eight Type 122 'Bremen' class of general-purpose frigate, although the Germans replaced the two low-powered gas turbines used for cruising with more economical diesels. The conversion to the AA role for the *Jacob van Heemskerck* and her sister ship the *Witte de With* did away with the ASW systems of the 'Kortenaers'. The new vessels also lost the forward 76mm (3in) gun and carried a more advanced fit of Standard missiles (compared with the 'Kortenaer's' Sea Sparrows) fired from a Mark 13 launcher carried in place of the helicopter hangar. *Jacob van Heemskerck* (F 812) was completed in January 1986, and she is an important element of the modern Dutch fleet.

Displacement: 3750t full load

Dimensions: 130.2m x 14.4m x 6m (427ft x 47ft x 20ft)

Machinery: two-shaft, COGOG, two speed gas turbines plus two cruise gas turbines; 51,600hp/9800hp

Armament: eight Harpoon SSM; Standard SM-1MR SAM; Sea Sparrow octuple launcher; Goalkeeper 30mm (1.18in) CIWS; two 20mm (0.79in) guns; four 324mm (12.7in) TT

Sensors: surface-search, air/surface-search, fire-control radars; hull-mounted sonar

Speed: 30 knots

Range: 7408km (4000nm) at 20 knots

Complement: 197

Vastergötland

**Ordered in 1981, the *Vastergötland*
(pennant letters 'Vgd'), was the first of
four Type A17 submarines to enter
Swedish navy service. She was
completed at the end of 1987.**

With the mid-sections of the hull built by
Kockums and the bows and sterns coming
from Karlskronavarvet, the submarines
featured nine bow-mounted torpedo
tubes, external containers for mines, and

an anechoic coating on the hull. Plans to
mount four vertical launch tubes for anti-
ship missiles in the sail have been
abandoned, and Vastergötlands' armament
remains torpedoes and mines. The first
two boats have been retired, replaced by
three 'Götland'-class boats. The last two,
renamed the 'Sodermanland' class, have
been fitted with the Stirling Air
Independent Propulsion system. The
Stirling section adds 12m (39ft) to the
submarine length and is installed aft of
the boat's tower.

Displacement: 1070t surfaced;
1143t submerged
Dimensions: 49.5m x 5.7m x 5.5m
(162ft 5in x 18ft 8in x 18ft)
Machinery: one-shaft, diesel engine, electric
motor; 2100hp/1150kW
Armament: six 21in (533mm) and three
400mm (15.75in) TT (twelve 533mm and
six 400mm torpedoes)
Sensors: surface-search radar; active sonar
Speed: 20 knots surfaced; 25 knots
submerged
Range: not available
Complement: 19

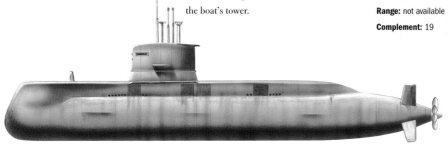

Halifax

When the plans for Canada's 'City'-class frigates (also known as the 'Halifax' class) were drawn up in 1977, it was intended to be a major programme, totalling 20 ships.

The plans to acquire such a large fleet of ships were progressively scaled back as lengthy delays arose, and the initial order, for six frigates, was not signed until 1983. A total of 12 'City'-class ships have been ordered to date – the second batch was signed for in December 1987. The first ship in the class, *Halifax* (FFH 330), was launched in May 1988 and completed

in June 1992. Canada's 'City'-class (or 'Halifax'-class) frigates are large and somewhat boxy ships, with a distinctive oversized and squared-off funnel, which is offset to port. They are equipped with a modern suite of anti-surface and air defence weapons, plus an embarked ASW helicopter. The Canadians have described these vessels as 'helicopter frigates', although their single helicopter capability is a standard feature found in most frigates in most navies.

Displacement: 4750t full load
Dimensions: 134.1m x 16.4m x 4.9m (440ft x 53ft 9in x 16ft 2in)
Machinery: two-shaft, COGOG, gas turbines and one diesel; 46,000hp/8800hp
Armament: eight Harpoon SSM; two VLS for Sea Sparrow SAM; one 57mm (2.24in) gun; one Mk 15 Phalanx 20mm (0.79in) CIWS; eight 12.7mm (0.5in) MG; four 324mm (12.75in) TT; one helicopter
Sensors: air-search, air/surface-search, navigation and fire-control radars; sonar
Speed: 28 knots
Range: 13,149km (7100nm) at 15 knots
Complement: 225

Neustrashimyy

The Project 1154 'Neustrashimyy'-class frigate was designed to meet a long-standing Soviet specification for a small ASW frigate to replace the Project 1124 'Grisha' class, and also the Project 1135 'Krivak' class.

The new ship was supposed to displace about 800 tons and develop a speed of 35 knots. Designed for low signature, the rakish-looking *Neustrashimyy* has a flat-flared hull, with superstructure levels broken up and the stacks shaped to reduce and disperse radar returns. The *Neustrashimyy* was designed to fire a version of the standard submarine ASW

missile (the SS-N-15) from catapults, leaving the rear deck free for a helicopter. Although four ships were to be built, only three were started and only the *Neustrashimyy* was completed after a long and protracted development process, entering service with the Baltic Fleet in 1993. The design was not a success, and two vessels were scrapped while still under construction. The vessels were replaced by 'Parchim'-class corvettes bought from East Germany, and by modernizing the Russian navy's 'Grisha'-class frigates.

Displacement: 3500t full load

Dimensions: 130m x 15.5m x 5.6m (426ft 6in x 50ft 11in x 18ft 5in)

Machinery: two-shaft, four gas turbines; 110,000hp

Armament: one SS-N-25 SSM launcher; one SA-N-9 SAM launcher; two CADS-N-1 gun/missile CIWS; one RBU-12000 ASW RL; six torpedo launchers; one helicopter

Sensors: air/surface-search, navigation, fire-control radars; hull-mounted and VDS/towed array sonars

Speed: 32 knots

Range: 8334km (4500nm) at 25 knots

Complement: 210

Club Med 1

The auxiliary five-masted staysail schooner *Club Med 1* was one of the first of a new generation of sailing cruise ships.

Constructed in France by Ateliers et Chantiers du Havre, she entered service in 1990 with a month-long cruise the length of the Mediterranean and back, then crossed the Atlantic. Sail-handling was motorized and under computer control, the auxiliary diesel engine being brought into operation as and when required. After 10 years of service with her original owners she was sold to Winstar Cruises, but continues to operate as before.

Tonnage: 1600dwt

Dimensions: 187m x 20m x 5m (613ft 6in x 65ft 6in x 16ft 5in)

Machinery: two-shaft, auxiliary diesel-electric

Service speed: 12 knots

Role: cruise ship

Route: Mediterranean; Caribbean

Capacity: 410

Constructor: Ateliers et Chantiers du Havre, Le Havre

Material: steel

Built for: Club Med

Arleigh Burke

The 'Arleigh Burke' class of missile destroyers augment the US Navy's larger 'Ticonderoga' cruisers in the protection of carrier battle groups.

Like the 'Ticonderogas', the 'Arleigh Burkes' are fitted with the Aegis automated air-defence system. USS *Arleigh Burke* (DDG-51) was completed in 1991. The US Navy has plans to acquire more than 30 vessels of this class. They have phenomenal striking power for their size, being armed with two Mk 41 vertical launcher systems with more than 90 cells, which can launch Tomahawk long-range land-attack cruise missiles, Harpoon anti-ship missiles and Standard SM-2MR

Block IV surface-to-air missiles. Three different 'Flights' have emerged within the class. Flight II ships incorporate improvements to the SPY radar and the Standard missile, active electronic countermeasures and communications. Flight IIA, introduced in fiscal year 1994, added a helicopter hangar with one anti-submarine helicopter and one armed attack helicopter. The US Navy considers the latest destroyers to be its most capable and survivable surface combatants.

Displacement: 8315t full load

Dimensions: 153.8m x 20.4m x 6.1m (504ft 7in x 66ft 11in x 20ft)

Machinery: four gas turbines; 100,000hp

Armament: two Mk 41 VLS for Harpoon, Tomahawk, and Standard missiles; one 127mm (5in) gun; two Mk 15 Phalanx 20mm (0.79in) CIWS; six Mk 32 324mm (12.75in) TT

Sensors: air-search/fire-control, surface-search, navigation, fire-control radars; hull-mounted and passive towed array sonar

Speed: 30 knots

Range: 8334km (4500nm) at 20 knots

Complement: 341

Floréal

Responding to a French navy requirement for a cheap, affordable, vessel for general patrol duties, the 'Floréal' class of frigates/corvettes was authorized in the late 1980s.

The first warships to be built by a private yard for the French military in more than 30 years, the work involved the use of standard mercantile construction techniques and modular assembly. *Floréal* (F 730) was launched in October 1990 and completed in May 1992. She has a modern mission systems fit and can embark a helicopter as large as a Super Puma. The 'Floréal' class of frigates/corvettes are lightly armed, and are built to commercial rather than military standards. Described as 'ocean capable patrol vessels', the 'Floréal'-class frigate is designed for low-intensity or low-threat operations. The class includes six vessels; the *Floréal* (F730), *Prairial* (F731), *Nivose* (F732), *Ventose* (F733), *Vendemiaire* (F734) and *Germinal* (F735). All were built and commissioned between 1990 and 1994.

Displacement: 2600t standard; 2950t full load
Dimensions: 93.5m x 14m x 4.3m (307ft x 46ft x 14ft)
Machinery: two-shaft, four diesels; 8800hp
Armament: two MM38 Exocet SSM; one 100mm (3.9in) gun; two 20mm (0.79in) cannon
Sensors: air/surface-search radar; navigation radar
Speed: 20 knots
Range: 16,668km (9000nm) at 15 knots
Complement: 80, plus 24 embarked troops

Kongo

Named after World War II Japanese battleships, the 'Kongo'-class destroyers of the Japanese Maritime Self Defence Force are equally important vessels to their users.

They are based on the US Navy's 'Arleigh Burke'-class missile destroyers and are fitted with the Aegis air defence radar and missile system found only on the 'Burkes' and the 'Ticonderoga' class cruisers. To date, Japan is the only foreign nation to be allowed access to this technology. The Aegis system combines the Standard SM-2 missile with the SPY-1 phased-array radar and a highly sophisticated computerized battle management and fire-control system. Ships such as the *Kongo* are hugely expensive and Japan has so far built just four, when once it planned to acquire eight. *Kongo* (DD 173) was launched in September 1991 and completed in March 1993. The ship has a flight deck aft for an SH-60J Seahawk, but no hangar. *Kongo* is armed with two Mk 41 vertical launch systems, fore and aft, that carry up to 29 and 61 SM-2MR missiles, respectively.

Displacement: 9485t full load
Dimensions: 160.9m x 20.9m x 6.2m (528ft 2in x 68ft 7in x 20ft 4in)
Machinery: two-shaft, COGAG, four gas turbines; 102,160hp
Armament: eight Harpoon; two Mk 41 VLS with Standard and ASROC; one 127mm (5in) gun; two 20mm (0.79in) Phalanx; six 324mm (12.75in) TT; one SH-60J Seahawk
Sensors: Aegis air defence system; air/ surface-search, navigation and fire-control radars; hull-mounted and towed array sonar
Speed: 30 knots
Range: 8334km (4500nm) at 20 knots
Complement: 300

Jervis Bay

Containers, together with ships and ports designed to handle them, have revolutionized cargo traffic in the second half of the twentieth century.

Named after an armed merchant cruiser destroyed while protecting a convoy from German battlecruisers in World War II, P&O-Nedlloyd's 50,000t *Jervis Bay* is a fast container ship with a capacity of more than 4000 6m (20ft) containers or equivalent units, some 240 of which can be refrigerated. While she and her six sister ships were constructed to be employed mainly in the

Europe – Far East service – the round trip from Southampton to Yokohama and back takes 63 days – their beam measurement was marginally within the maximum able to pass through the locks of the Panama Canal. Despite her huge size, the *Jervis Bay*, which was launched in 1992, has a crew of just 9 officers and 10 men. The specialized container handling equipment now standard at major cargo ports enable even such large vessels to unload and reload with astonishing speed: the *Jervis Bay* is expected to take just 24 hours to turn around at Southampton.

Tonnage: 51,000grt

Dimensions: 292.15m x 32.2m x 11.2m (958ft 6in x 105ft 6in x 36ft 9in)

Machinery: one-shaft, diesel; 46,800hp

Service speed: 23.5 knots

Role: general cargo vessel

Route: Europe–Far East

Capacity: 4038 TEU

Constructor: Ishikawajima-Harima Heavy Industries, Kure

Material: steel

Built for: P&O Containers

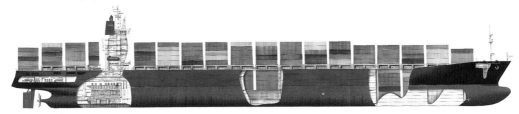

Futura

Oil is the life blood of modern industry, and the twentieth century has seen the tanker take on increasing importance as the means by which oil is transported from its source to the developed countries for which it is an essential resource.

Since the 1950s, oil tankers have been growing to mammoth proportions. The larger the tanker, the more oil it can carry, and the more economical it is to transport. But large size can also mean a large risk when accidents happen. The environmental impact of the wrecking, or even the running aground, of a supertanker is so devastating, and the public outcry so loud, that oil companies were forced to go to considerable lengths to improve the chances of an oil or petroleum-products tanker surviving such an incident without releasing its cargo into the sea. The Dutch-owned *Futura* was built with a double hull, the space between the two hulls being empty save for pumping equipment and venting pipes. Launched in Finland in 1992, the *Futura* is enormous by any standards save those of her own industry; able to carry 96,000t, she is less than a third the size of the real giants.

Tonnage: 50,907grt

Dimensions: 241m x 40m x 14.5m (790ft 8in x 131ft 3in x 47ft 6in)

Machinery: one-shaft, diesel; about 12,000hp

Service speed: 14 knots

Role: oil carrier

Route: not applicable

Capacity: 96,000t

Constructor: Wärtsilä

Material: steel

Built for: Fortum Oil & Gas

Brandenburg

The Type 123 'Brandenburg'-class destroyers were built by a consortium of three German shipyards. They were introduced to replace the German navy's 'Hamburg'-class ships which dated back to the early 1960s.

Four ships were ordered, *Brandenburg* (F 215) being the lead ship. She was completed in October 1994. The design draws on the experience of the aborted NATO 'Frigate for the Nineties' project and the more successful Type 122 multi-mission frigate, as well as incorporating the modular construction used on Blohm &

Voss MEKO designs. The primary role for the Type 123s is air defence; they are armed with medium-range Sea Sparrow SAMs and close-range Rolling Airframe Missile (RAM) systems. The Sea Sparrows are housed in a vertical launch system forward of the bridge, while two boxy Mk 49 RAM launchers are located forward and aft. *Brandenburg* is also equipped with Exocet anti-ship missiles and can embark a pair of Lynx Mk 88 helicopters, with a flight deck and hangar aft. Similar ships are in service with the navies of Portugal and Turkey.

Displacement: 4275t full load

Dimensions: 138.9m x 16.7m x 6.3m (455ft 8in x 57ft 1in x 20ft 8in)

Machinery: two-shaft, two gas turbines, plus two diesels; 25,480hp/5630hp

Armament: four MM38 Exocet SSM; one VLS for Sea Sparrow SAM; two 21-cell RAM launchers; one 76mm (3in) gun; six 324mm (12.75in) TT; two helicopters

Sensors: air-search, air/surface-search and navigation radars; two trackers (fire-control); hull-mounted sonar

Speed: 29 knots

Range: 7408km (4000nm) at 18 knots

Complement: 219

Le Triomphant

The SNLE-NG (Sous-Marins Nucleaires Lanceurs Engins-Nouvelle Generation), or 'Le Triomphant' class SSBNs, are replacing the 'Redoutable'-class SSBNs in French navy service.

Plans for six boats were initially cut back to three for budgetary reasons, but President Chirac decided that the SNLE-NG programme should include four submarines. The first of the class, *Le Triomphant* (S-616), was commissioned in March 1997. The final vessel will be commissioned in 2008. It will receive a new model missile, the M-51. Delays in the M-51 programme have forced the use of the interim M-45 on the first three boats. Strenuous efforts have been made to reduce all emitted noise and the hydrodynamic effect of water flow around the submarine. Machinery is housed in cradles to avoid any direct connection to the hull, cutting down transmitted sound. To avoid the cavitation problems caused by standard propellers, *Le Triomphant* uses a new form of ducted propeller, called a 'propeller pump' or propulsor.

Displacement: 12,640t surfaced; 14,335t submerged
Dimensions: 138m x 17m x 12.5m (453ft x 55ft 8in x 41ft)
Machinery: one-shaft, nuclear pressurised-water reactor with turbo-electric drive pump jet propulsor; two auxiliary diesels and one emergency motor; 41,500hp
Armament: 16 Aérospatiale M51 with 10–12 MRV each; four 533mm (21in) TT for torpedoes or SM 39 Exocet SSM
Sensors: radar; active/passive sonar
Speed: 20 knots surfaced; 25 knots submerged
Range: limited only by reactor fuel state
Complement: 111

Vanguard

In 1980, the British Ministry of Defence announced that the Royal Navy's Polaris missile submarines would be replaced by four new submarines armed with Trident I.

By 1982, the choice of missile had changed to the Trident II (D5). The new submarines were to be much larger than those they replaced, but had similar features and a slightly smaller complement. Lead ship HMS *Vanguard* (S 28) was completed in August 1993 and conducted missile firings in May 1994. *Vanguard* made her first operational patrol in early 1995, and the first three new Trident submarines had fully replaced the Polaris boats by the end of 1996. The end of the Cold War has led to the Trident missiles being armed with fewer than their theoretical maximum number of warheads – 16 missiles able to carry 12 MIRVs each give a possible warhead total of 192, and it is reported the 'Vanguard' submarines deploy with a maximum of only 96 warheads. There is also the option of arming the missiles with low-yield, 'sub-strategic' warheads.

Displacement: 14,000t surfaced; 15,900t submerged

Dimensions: 491ft 8in x 42ft x 39ft 4in (149.8m x 12.8m x 12m)

Machinery: one-shaft, nuclear, one PWR2 reactor with geared steam turbine plus diesel-electric auxiliary; 27,500hp

Armament: 16 Trident D5 SLBM; four 21in (533mm) TT

Sensors: search and navigation radar; active/passive sonar and towed array

Speed: 25 knots submerged

Range: limited only by reactor fuel state

Complement: approximately 150

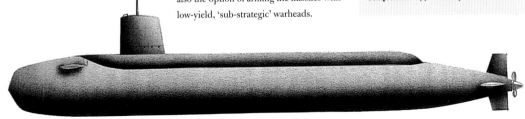

Murasame

The 'Murasame' class are third-generation general-purpose escort ships, classified by some as large frigates, of Japan's Maritime Self Defence Force.

The 'Murasame'-class ships are the latest destroyers to enter Japanese service. Designed to operate alongside the 'Kongo'-class Aegis destroyers, the 'Murasames' are essentially medium-range air defence missile carriers, armed with two large vertical launch Sea Sparrow SAM systems. The launcher boxes can also fire ASROC missiles and may yet be upgraded to carry Standard SAMs. The

first of nine destroyers of the same class, *Murasame* (DD 101), was launched in September 1994 and commissioned in 1996. Initially, it was planned to build a total of 14 units, but the tenth vessel, *Takanami* (DD 110), was built to an enlarged 'Murasame' design. *Takanami* and its successors have added surface action capability with a rapid-firing 127mm (5in) gun and will be used as the surface action escort in task groups based on the 'Kongo'-class destroyers.

Displacement: 5100t full load

Dimensions: 151m x 16.9m x 5.2m (495ft 5in x 55ft 7in x 17ft 1in)

Machinery: COGAG, four gas turbines; 84,630hp

Armament: eight Harpoon SSM; two Mk 41 VLS with 100 Standard missiles and ASROC torpedoes; one 76mm (3in) gun; two 20mm (0.79in) Phalanx CIWS; six 324mm (12.75in) TT; one SH-60J helicopter

Sensors: air/surface-search, navigation and fire-control radars; hull and towed sonars

Speed: 33 knots

Range: 8334km (4500nm) at 20 knots

Complement: 170

Chakri Naruebet

A new chapter in the history of the Royal Thai Navy, and in the story of Pacific Rim sea power, has opened with the introduction of Thailand's aircraft carrier *Chakri Naruebet*.

This ship is the only aircraft carrier – apart from Japan-based US Navy vessels – to be based in the region. *Chakri Naruebet* was built in Spain and is a smaller version of the Spanish navy's *Principe de Asturias*. She was completed in March 1997 and features a 12-degree ski jump designed to operate Harrier VSTOL jets as well as helicopters. Thailand bought up the former Spanish navy fleet of AV-8A(S)

Harriers and built an entirely new maritime air group around them. Seven AV-8A(S)s and a pair of two-seat TAV-8A(S)s were delivered in September 1997. Six S-70B Seahawks were also acquired to operate alongside them. However, the Harriers have proved to be maintenance-intensive and very expensive to operate, while funding troubles have also hit the *Chakri Naruebet* itself. As a result the Thai carrier has seen little sea time since being commissioned in August 1997.

Displacement: 11,300t full load
Dimensions: 182.5m x 30.5m x 6.15m (599ft 1in x 110ft 1in x 20ft 4in)
Machinery: two-shaft (CP propellers) CODOG, two gas turbines, plus two diesels; 44,250hp/11,780hp
Armament: two launchers for Mistral SAM; two 12.7mm (0.5in) MG; six AV-8S Harriers, four S-70B Seahawks
Sensors: surface-search radar; fire-control radar; navigation radar; aircraft-control radar; hull-mounted sonar
Speed: 26 knots
Range: 18,520km (10,000nm) at 12 knots
Complement: 455, plus 162 air crew

Oyashio

Japan depends on maritime trade for survival. A primary mission of its Maritime Self Defence Force is anti-submarine warfare, as submarines offer the major threat to that trade.

A major part of the Japanese Maritime Self Defence Force's capability is invested in a fleet of advanced, high-performance, conventionally powered submarines. The *Oyashio* (SS 590) is the lead ship in a new class of diesel-electric attack submarines built at Kobe by Kawasaki and Mitsubishi,

beginning in 1994. Named after Japan's first indigenous post-war submarine, the second *Oyashio* is an improved 'Harushio'-class submarine, with large sonar arrays on its flanks and a reduced crew compared to previous classes thanks to increased use of automated systems. The *Oyashio* has an unusual single hull/double hull compound design. It is the latest in a line of Japanese attack submarines and there are plans to acquire 10 such vessels through to 2007. Five had entered service by 2002, with three more building.

Displacement: 3600t submerged

Dimensions: 81.7m x 8.9m x 7.8m (268ft x 29ft 2in x 25ft 9in)

Machinery: one-shaft, diesel and electric motor; 7750hp

Armament: six 533mm (21in) TT (torpedoes and Harpoon SSM)

Sensors: hull/flank sonar arrays and towed array

Speed: 20 knots submerged

Range: not available

Complement: 75

Ferry Lavender

Despite the growing number of submarine tunnels, by the end of the twentieth century many fast, short-route passenger/vehicle ferries were still being built every year.

To a land of many islands, such as Japan, ferries are an accepted part of the everyday way of life. Indeed, statistics gathered in the 1990s showed that there were some 510 car ferries running on 260 routes around and between the islands. Competition on the busiest routes can be very intense, and the largest operators go to considerable lengths to outdo each other in terms of speed and passenger comfort. *Ferry Lavender*, operated by Shin Nihonkai Ferry Co in Japan and put into service in 1991, is typical of third-generation fast ferries, able to carry around 800 passengers and up to 300 light vehicles. The stern ramp gives access to the two-storey car deck, which is wide enough to allow 'U-turn' drive-through loading and unloading. This simplifies docking procedures considerably.

Tonnage: 19,905grt

Dimensions: 193m x 29.4m x 9m (632ft x 96ft 6in x 29ft 5in)

Machinery: two-shaft, diesel; 23,600hp

Service speed: 21 knots

Role: passenger/vehicle ferry

Route: inter-island, Japan

Capacity: 880 passengers; 300 vehicles

Constructor: IHI

Material: steel

Built for: Shin Nihonkai Ferry Co

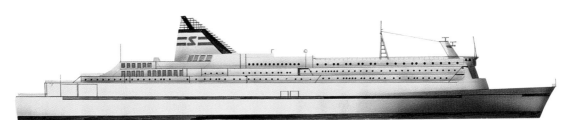

Voyager of the Seas

The first of a series of five 'Voyager' class cruise ships to be completed by 2008, Royal Caribbean Cruise's *Voyager of the Seas* was the world's biggest passenger ship when launched in 1999.

At 310.9m (1020ft) overall, she is only marginally shorter than the Cunard Queens. Designed for a different business, her performance does not come near to that of the last generation of 'ocean greyhounds'. The *Voyager of the Seas* was designed with all the facilities of a terrestrial holiday resort. She has 2221 guest and crew staterooms and enormous public spaces on a total of 14 decks, with three others given over to ship's services. The vessel was completed in just 57 weeks by a 10,000-strong workforce, embarking on her maiden cruise in November 1999. The ship herself needs a crew of 1180 to cater to the needs of her 3880 passengers, each of whom expects the voyage of a lifetime during a week spent cruising the islands of the Caribbean.

Tonnage: 137,300grt

Dimensions: 310.9m x 38.7m (1020ft x 127ft)

Machinery: three-shaft, diesel-electric; 101,340hp

Service speed: 22 knots

Role: cruise ship

Route: Caribbean

Capacity: 3880 single class passengers

Constructor: Kvaerner, Helsinki

Material: steel

Built for: Royal Caribbean Cruises

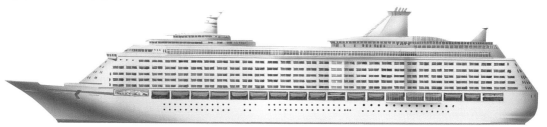

Index